Three Decades of Enterprise Culture

# Three Decades of Enterprise Culture

## Entrepreneurship, Economic Regeneration and Public Policy

By

Francis J. Greene,

Kevin F. Mole

and

David J. Storey

palgrave
macmillan

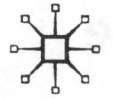

First published in 2008 by
PALGRAVE MACMILLAN
Houndmills, Basingstoke, Hampshire RG21 6XS and
175 Fifth Avenue, New York, N.Y. 10010
Companies and representatives throughout the world

PALGRAVE MACMILLAN is the global academic imprint of the Palgrave
Macmillan division of St. Martin's Press, LLC and of Palgrave Macmillan Ltd.
Macmillan® is a registered trademark in the United States, United Kingdom
and other countries. Palgrave is a registered trademark in the European
Union and other countries.

ISBN-13: 978–1–4039–4102–2 hardback
ISBN-10: 1–4039–4102–5 hardback

This book is printed on paper suitable for recycling and made from fully
managed and sustained forest sources. Logging, pulping and manufacturing
processes are expected to conform to the environmental regulations of
the country of origin.

A catalogue record for this book is available from the British Library.

A catalog record for this book is available from the Library of Congress.

10  9  8  7  6  5  4  3  2  1
17 16 15 14 13 12 11 10 09 08

Printed and bound in Great Britain by
CPI Antony Rowe, Chippenham and Eastbourne

# Contents

# List of Tables

# List of Figures

# Acknowledgements

There are a number of organisations and individuals that contributed to the development of this book. One of the most obvious of these is the Leverhulme Trust whose grant allowed the fieldwork for the research. We are particularly grateful for this support. We would also like to thank Paul Reynolds who was insistent that we included new businesses from outside of Teesside, so as to make additional and valid comparisons.

A great deal of thanks must also go to the individual entrepreneurs on whose interviews this research is based. Equally valuable were the research team involved in conducting the interviews. People of particular importance here were John Anderson, Bridget Reah and Kevin Amess. Much of the secondary research for this book was collected at the following libraries: the Bodelian Library, the British Library, Middlesbrough Central Reference Library, Teesside University Library, and Durham University Library. We are grateful for the support provided by each of these organisations.

Particular thanks must also go to Swinburne University in Melbourne Australia who provided Francis Greene space and time to allow the bulk of the book to be written. Finally, we are also extremely grateful to Macmillan and Jacky Kippenberger who saw the potential of a book that looked at the historical and spatial dimensions of entrepreneurship. As usual, any omissions or errors are down to us.

# Part I

# Entrepreneurship, Economic Regeneration and Public Policy: The Context

# 1
# A Study of Three Decades and Three Regions

## Introduction

The demand for entrepreneurs has perhaps never been greater. Entrepreneurs are seen as almost having a magical effect on economies – alchemists, whose innovatory capacity allows for water to be turned into wine, lead into gold. Equally, they appear omnipotent: able to create markets, shape markets, and, ultimately, destroy markets. En route, they provide jobs, offer new products and services, and induce productivity gains.

Little wonder that since the 1970s there have been successive attempts to increase the supply of entrepreneurs in all developed economies. The basic thinking is that economies need greater numbers of people to set up their own businesses. The more that do, the better the economic outcomes for a whole set of social and economic problems ranging from international competitiveness to improving the lacklustre performance of particular regions.

This book weighs up the value of new businesses. It asks basic questions such as what sort of people set up their own business, how do they *do* business, what sorts of funding they make use of, and what is the economic contribution of such businesses. To achieve this, the book makes use of interviews with over 900 entrepreneurs.

What, however, is distinct and unique about the book is that it charts the contribution of new businesses, primarily in an entrepreneurially moribund region. The thinking here is that if new businesses are so special, surely they will make an invaluable contribution in the worst area that can be found? One such area is Teesside, a deep pocket of economic deprivation located within the least entrepreneurial region of England. Teesside has had the lowest rate of new business start-ups in the United Kingdom since Value Added Taxation (sales tax) records began.

Using Teesside as a case study also has further advantages. First, our interviews with entrepreneurs cover three decades. The first iteration occurred in 1981 when interviews were held with 157 Teesside entrepreneurs who set up their businesses in the 1970s. A further 214 interviews were held in 1991 to examine 1980s entrepreneurs. In the last iteration, conducted in 2001, a further 320 interviews were held with entrepreneurs who set up in the 1990s. This book, then, affords a rare picture of the characteristics, behaviours and value of new businesses over three decades.

A second value in examining Teesside entrepreneurs is that it provides a case study of successive intervention experiments across the three decades. In the early 1970s, Teesside was seen as an economically vibrant area, full of potential, and able to lead the future development of the economy. Nothing then was done to support the creation of new businesses. By the 1980s, this potential was lost, replaced by endemic structural unemployment. Huge resources were devoted to initiatives to increase the entrepreneurial capacity and propensity of the area. The problems of the 1980s continued into the 1990s. So, although the nature of interventions changed, the purpose of enhancing economic and social welfare through the creation of an 'enterprise culture' remained a central policy objective.

Examining new Teesside businesses across the three decades allows for an historical evaluation of the success of particular interventions. This is important because there is a distinct tendency to recycle particular interventions even when they were not successful when they were tried previously. For instance, many of the present policies designed to support new businesses are basic facsimiles of policies developed in the 1980s, tweaked to focus on modern problems such as social exclusion rather than what once was called poverty and unemployment. This book gives a sense of the nature and range of interventions and the almost funny (if it were not so expensive) flip-flop pattern of interventions to correct perceived problems.

The final value of focusing on Teesside is that, as the weakest performing entrepreneurship area (lowest rate of new business start-ups), the book is able to compare it with an area approximating to the middle in the business start-up league (Shropshire) and an area with one of the highest rates of business start-up (Buckinghamshire). For the 1990s, besides the interviews with Teesside entrepreneurs, another 150 interviews were held with Shropshire entrepreneurs. Equally, 150 interviews were held with Buckinghamshire entrepreneurs.

The advantage of examining an area with high rates of entrepreneur-ship with that of more modest entrepreneurial means and one with hardly any means at all, is that it reflects that each nation has spatially differing rates of new business start-ups. By comparing and contrasting a 'rich' area (Buckinghamshire) with a middling area (Shropshire) and a poor area (Teesside), the book reflects not only on what 'works' but also considers what the barriers are for new businesses in more unfavoured regions.

In the rest of this introduction, the focus is on tracing the outline of the book. It begins by sketching out issues of definition and how the empirical research for this book was conducted. The chapter then moves on to introducing the three regions more fully. Finally, the chapter syn-thesizes the nine other chapters.

## Issues of definition

One of the root problems with analysing entrepreneurs is that there is no one single definition that suits. Instead, there is a vast range of dif-fering ways of describing such individuals. For instance, it used to be largely thought that entrepreneurs were special people, pre-programmed with distinctive traits that compelled them to become entrepreneurs. This is still the common sense view and more or less the view of the European Commission (2004) who point to entrepreneurs having a par-ticular 'mindset'. Repeated attempts, however, to find any traits that can be readily associated with entrepreneurs have proved fruitless (Gartner, 1988). If not traits, entrepreneurs have been seen as having a distinctive set of behaviours. Typical here is to suggest that entrepre-neurs are innovative. What innovation means does, of course, vary. One example is some form of Schumpeterian entrepreneur who is able to create, shape and break markets. The reality is rather less exciting. As is shown in this book, most new businesses start in very traditional sec-tors, providing much the same goods and services in much the same way as many other businesses. In that sense then, perhaps, a distinction may be drawn between those that start a new business and those who might be called Schumpeterian innovators. The reality is that the former dominate the latter.

So, for the more mundane amongst us, the alternative is simply a set of behaviours that lead to the creation of new businesses. This is often what is meant when entrepreneurs and entrepreneurship are mentioned in the same sentence. Hence, Reynolds et al. (1999) tend to equate it with the set of activities and behaviours needed to create a new business.

Others, meanwhile, talk of the need to look at discovery, evaluation and exploitation of business opportunities. Yet more disagreements, however, might result if the context of the entrepreneur or entrepreneurship is moved into other areas such as corporate entrepreneurship (intrapreneurship) or social entrepreneurship. Finally, there is the issue of the unit of analysis: is it right that attention should focus on the individual entrepreneur or should it be wider and focus on the enterprising nature of a society?

This book shares with MacDonald and Coffield (1991) – the classic book on Teesside entrepreneurs – a sense that such discussions of the meaning of entrepreneur, entrepreneurship and enterprise tend rapidly to dissolve. They say, and we agree:

> We are not dealing with a tightly defined, agreed and unitary concept, but with a farrago of hurrah words such as 'creativity', 'initiative', and 'leadership'. Too many of the definitions tend to be circular or consist of managerial tautologies, tricked out with the rhetoric of progressive education. (p. 29)

To address this, we have a clear focus on particular economic activities. Its principal focus is on new or *de novo* businesses. This means we do not care much about in what order people create a business. Similarly, the book is unconcerned with the 'might' or 'could be' (nascent) entrepreneurs. It also excludes corporate entrepreneurship or social entrepreneurship. Finally, what entrepreneurs want to get out of their business (e.g. community harmony, make money, or be their own boss) is something not covered in this book. Our focus is therefore on the characteristics of new businesses, the factors that influence its performance and their impact on wider society.

## The three-decade studies

Even if this book prefers a more economic to a psychological treatment of those that actually create and sustain a new business, there still remain particular issues. For instance, separating out the *new* from those that are actually *de novo* is tricky.

The first general difficulty is the absence of any complete census of new business activity in the United Kingdom. This is because new ventures are too new, too small or the available datasets are either biased or unreliable (Birley et al. 1995). To counter this, the study had for each of the three decades (1970s, 1980s and 1990s) made use of publicly available British Telecom county telephone lists. With these county telephone books – or 'White books' (as opposed to the Yellow pages) as they are called in the United Kingdom – the research followed an identical methodology.

For example, in the most recent iteration of the research, the 2000 'White telephone books' for Teesside, Shropshire and Buckinghamshire were selected (see Figure 1.1 – Stage I). These directories were then manually cross-referenced with earlier 1995 directories for each of the three counties (Stage I). If a business appeared in the 2000 directory but not in the 1995 directory, it was seen as a 'potential' new business. The entrepreneurs of these 'new' businesses were then telephoned to establish that they met our specified criteria for a *de novo* business: that they were new businesses, independent of outside control (not subsidiaries or part of larger enterprises), indigenous to the local area, non-retail, still in operation, and were not a charity or other not-for-profit organization. From this process, the total population of wholly new businesses was identified (Stage II). Subsequently, every third business was re-telephoned (Stage III) to arrange face-to-face interviews with the entrepreneurs given that very many new businesses were likely also to be small (indeed, more than a third of the entrepreneurs had no employees). Interviews were held at the normal place of work of the entrepreneur and took about an hour to complete. The entrepreneurs followed a structured interview format which was subjected to a pre-test in order to check for biased, misleading or confusing questions. Prior to this being administered, the businesses were again checked to make sure that the ventures were actually *de novo* (Stage III).

There were, of course, differences between the 1970s, 1980s and 1990s. In the 1970s, for example, the interviews were not principally focused around the attributes of the entrepreneur. This was rectified in the 1980s and 1990s iterations with attention given to attributes that had been found to be associated with either entrepreneurship (e.g. prior sectoral experience) or attributes describing alternative entrepreneurship paths (e.g. those running concurrent businesses). Equally, the 1970s interviews were rather poor at investigating how entrepreneurs do business. Indeed, a more rounded investigation of business strategy issues only really appeared for the 1990s interviews. In essence, then, to try to ensure temporal reliability and robustness, the three decade comparisons largely make use of what was available from the 1970s interviews, supplemented, where appropriate, with comparisons between the 1980s and the 1990s.

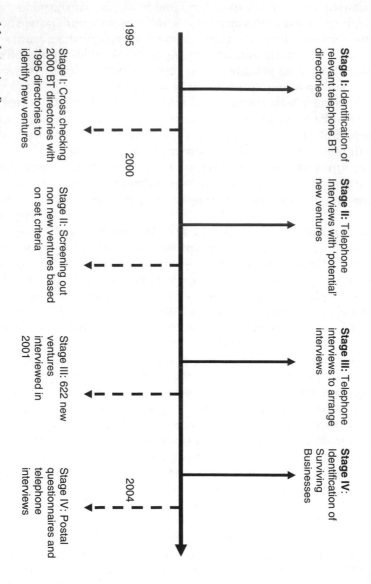

*Figure 1.1* Interview Process.

There is also one other evident difference between the interviews collected between the three decades. For the 1970s and the 1980s, no information was collected on whether the businesses subsequently survived after they were interviewed. This issue was remedied for the 1990s study which sought to identify survivors amongst the three counties (Figure 1.1, Stage IV).

Overall, therefore, the aim of each iteration of the study has been to make sure that there is a core set of issues that run through the 1970s, 1980s and 1990s. Likewise, the 1990s study was informed by a greater awareness of business strategy and the need to control for survival issues.

## The three region studies

The study conducted for Teesside new businesses in the 1990s was replicated with the same selection procedures for identifying *de novo* businesses, the same interview format, and the same follow up survival studies for the other two areas. The cardinal difference, however, was that the regional study sought to compare and contrast the low performance of Teesside with that of two other areas (counties) of England. The basis of this contrast was some clear and identifiable measure of enterprise performance between the three regions. One obvious measure was the number of new value added taxation (VAT) registered businesses in a given year. As a proxy for 'entrepreneurship', this suggested that the most enterprising county in 1998 (when we first conceived of a regional comparison) was Buckinghamshire (excluding London). The county which had middling VAT registrations of the English counties (excludes London) was Shropshire. This is not a unique event. In 1994, Buckinghamshire had the highest rate of VAT registrations per 10,000 of the population of any English county. This was also true in 2005. Equally, Teesside continued to have, along with other North East counties, the lowest rates of new VAT registrations per 10,000 of the population.

The rigidity of these differences is further evident when Figure 1.2 is examined. This shows the historical rates of VAT registration per 10,000 of the population over the period between 1980 and 2005. It clearly shows that the VAT registration rates follow a similar pattern for each of the three regions. In the 1980s, for example, there was a rapid increase in the number of registrations. This fell away in the late 1980s/early 1990s for each of the three counties as the recession of this period intensified. Since then, rates have remained fairly stable. The second evident feature of Figure 1.2 is that these movements are in parallel. The

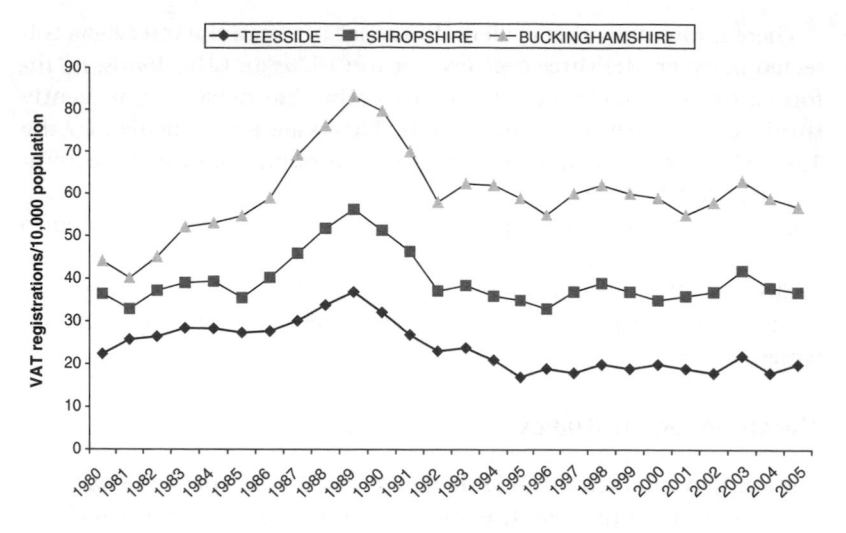

*Figure 1.2*   VAT registrations per 10,000 population, 1980–2005.

differences were fairly modest in the early 1980s but rose dramatically in the late 1980s.

There are also second order differences between the three regions. Put bluntly, Teesside is relatively geographically isolated on the North East coast of England and its main urban areas (Middlesbrough, Hartlepool, Stockton on Tees) are some distance from other Northern urban areas such as Newcastle and Leeds.

By contrast, Shropshire is the largest land-locked county in England. It is also one of the most rural counties of England, nestled as it is between Wales to the West, Staffordshire to the East and Cheshire to the North. Nonetheless, it is still reasonably close to the large conurbation of Birmingham and the West Midlands. Buckinghamshire, meanwhile, whilst still seeking to retain the air of a rural 'home' county, is just North West of the Greater London conurbation and within easy access of London itself. In Chapter 2, further detailed consideration is given to charting the changing fortunes of Teesside and comparing and contrasting it with the two other regions.

## The nature of the problem

Chapter 2 also provides a useful backdrop for understanding the potential contribution that new businesses can make as a route out of particular economic and social predicaments. The specific contribution of Chapter 2 is to create an entrepreneurial index. Where this index differs from other indices is that it uses historical information derived from the contemporaneous population censuses of 1981, 1991 and 2001 and appropriate supplementary material. Such data are subsequently regionally disaggregated to expose how the regional economies have fared over a thirty-year period. Ultimately, the contribution of the index is its ability to show how little regional entrepreneurship has changed in the face of profound economic change.

## An experimental region

Besides the advantage of concentrating on *de novo* businesses, the second aim of this book is to look at how such businesses fare under differing policy contexts. The background for this is detailed more fully in Chapter 3. What this chapter shows is that in the 1970s there was effectively no public policy towards new businesses or small businesses in the United Kingdom. This was a position the UK shared with virtually all other developed nations. Indeed, the only major country with a long history of state involvement in supporting small businesses is the United States which began formally and publicly to support smaller businesses in the 1950s with the creation of the Small Business Administration.

Chapter 3 contrasts the "policy off" 1970s with the desperate policy flounderings of the Thatcher administration in the 1980s to increase the number of new businesses in the UK economy and create an 'enterprise culture'. The chapter argues that the increase in the rate of new business creation was not so much brought about by the urge to create do-it-yourself capitalism but because of the structural problems in the UK economy – reflected in close to unprecedented rates of unemployment. The chapter then highlights how the situation changed in the 1990s and has continued to subsequently evolve.

What is novel about Chapter 3 is that, other than detailing the flip-flop nature of specific interventions, it itemises, from available information, the nature of enterprise policy in Teesside over the three decades. This is important because it shows that Teesside in the 1980s was almost a laboratory for successive interventions that sought to establish an 'enterprise culture'.

Conceptually, it has proved difficult to ground a distinctive meaning out of the phrase 'enterprise culture'. Like enterprise, entrepreneur and entrepreneurship, enterprise culture has shown itself to be extremely malleable to differing agendas. Unsurprisingly, it might be taken to mean starting a business, developing a growing business, having a set of skills and behaviours or that there is some entrepreneurial 'animal spirit' (Keynes, 1936) in the air, pervading institutions and communities.

What is clearer empirically from Chapter 3 is that a range of soft (e.g. training and mentoring) and hard support (e.g. grants, loans) mushroomed in the 1980s and was sustained in the 1990s. This might suggest the development of an infrastructure to support a burgeoning enterprise culture. The more cynical might suggest, following on from MacDonald and Coffield (1991) – that it only represents the development of an 'enterprise industry' of policy and support providers.

## Examining the new businesses

In Chapters 4 through to 9, the emphasis is on looking at various aspects of the new businesses. The first of these empirical chapters (Chapter 4) considers the sorts of people who set up a business across the three decades and across the three regions. It begins by providing an analysis of prior studies that focus upon the types of people who set up in business. What is advantageous about this is that, surprisingly, there are very few actual studies that are about general entrepreneurship. Most of the actual research in this area either focuses upon particular groups such as the young or seeks to identify the macro-economic influences bearing down on the entrepreneurial choice.

Based upon this literature, Chapter 4 moves on to compare and contrast evident differences across the three regions and three decades. Where also the chapter differs is that it does not seek to see how entrepreneurial attributes impact on business performance. This is left to Chapters 8 and 9. What Chapter 4 does is to test if entrepreneurial attributes influence sectoral choices. This is of interest because a successful business or a successful economy is likely to be influenced by its sectoral composition. For instance, it is interesting to speculate on how many of the richest computer business leaders would have been as successful if they had chosen an alternative sector.

The issue of entrepreneurial choice is also important in Chapter 5 which looks at how entrepreneurs approach business. Because of the limited business strategy factors available from the 1970s and 1980s, Chapter 5 concentrates upon data for the 1990s. It uses the three regions to first identify particular strategic orientations held by the entrepreneur and, second, what determines such profiles. The value of this approach is to examine the relevant choices available to entrepreneurs, particularly in terms of the high, medium and low enterprise areas.

Chapter 6 continues the examination of the environment by investigating the use and quality of business support both prior to start-up and post start. The comparison is made across the three decades and between the three regions. In so doing, it raises issues about the value of such support, in terms of improvements over time and the impact of such support on new business performance.

Finance issues form the focus of Chapter 7. The background here is the suggestion that because new businesses have no track record, it is likely – for some of the time, for some sorts of finance and for some sorts of people – that new businesses will be unfairly treated by financiers. This chapter discusses the likely sources of this viewpoint but also contrasts it with other theoretical evidence which suggests that such finance gaps are modest. Empirically, Chapter 7 examines the three decades in terms of the finance preferences of the entrepreneurs, the relative importance of equity finance and the types of people who are discouraged or rejected for funding. The chapter also empirically examines finance differences between the three regions.

Overall, what clearly emerges is that even if finance and advice gaps were present in the 1970s, they were reduced or eliminated by the 1990s. This is a surprising finding since the expectation might have been that such 'gaps' were crucial elements in explaining why some regions had lower rates of new business formation. Instead, although finance and advice support has improved, a region like Teesside remains firmly rooted to the bottom of the 'enterprise league' (Chapter 2).

The value of new businesses both across the three decades (Chapter 8) and between the three regions (Chapter 9) forms the final part of the empirical evidence. To support these two chapters, Chapter 8 begins by looking at the thorny issue of performance and how it has been managed in previous studies. What emerges is that there still remains some conceptual confusion around the notion of performance. Nonetheless, Chapter 8 goes on to provide an original account of 54 multivariate studies that have looked at survival and employment growth as measures of performance. The central question that this chapter seeks to investigate is whether there are business performance differences between the three decades once a host of entrepreneurial attributes, business characteristics, finance, business support and strategy factors are considered.

Chapter 9 presents the growth and survival data on new businesses in the 1990s. It then links this to data on the capabilities of the entrepreneur, their finance arrangements, their business strategy, business support and business characteristics. It concludes that these factors have a very modest ability to predict the 'success' of a business. Instead, chance plays a major role.

Chapter 10 is the final chapter. Its main function is to review the empirical and theoretical evidence presented in this book. In so doing, its focus is on the value of actual interventions to support new businesses. One view of entrepreneurship is that what really matters for a society is to ensure that the correct incentives are in place for 'productive' entrepreneurship (Baumol, 1990). The Baumol perspective is that the entrepreneur is always with us – there is no shortage of such individuals. Their apparent absence in some contexts is because they have found better – from their viewpoint – ways of spending their time. If society wishes to change this it has to change 'the rules of the game' to make legitimate entrepreneurship more attractive. What is almost certainly a waste of time is to seek attitudinal change since that is not the root cause of the problem. Instead, society should align its incentives (i.e. taxation and regulatory frameworks) to support legitimate and socially beneficial entrepreneurs.

A theoretical alternative to this is that new business entry is shaped by the nature of prior beliefs held by people (Jovanovic, 1982). If these are strong, then more are likely to enter. One role for interventions, then, is to have entrepreneurship policies that promote the entrepreneurial capacity and propensity of individuals (Lundstrom and Stevenson, 2005). Jovanovic (1982) also theorises that entrepreneurs only really gain a sense of their entrepreneurial ability once they are in business.

Such contrasting views raise important policy issues such as what role, if any, should policy makers play in supporting new businesses. Are they really that well placed to provide managerial solutions to new businesses or, if they have a role at all, are they not better off providing governance structures that signal to entrepreneurs the nature of available incentives?

Chapter 10 broadly concludes that whilst Teesside has been a laboratory for enterprise culture experiments for thirty years, it has not resulted in any clear acceleration of entrepreneurial activity. This cannot be blamed upon an inability to limit or close finance and advice gaps. These gaps have been either addressed or mitigated. Equally, there appear limits to entrepreneurship policy making: those business that are a 'success' are often just lucky.

# 2
# Regional Differences in England and the Case of Teesside

## Introduction

In any economy there are likely to be widespread differences between particular regions. In Europe, one of the countries with the greatest evident differences is the United Kingdom. Indeed, it has one of the highest variations of GDP per capita in the European Union (HM Treasury, 2001). Inner London had a purchasing power parity of 315.3 in 2002 (EU25 = 100), making it the most prosperous economic area in the EU. At the other end of the scale is Cornwall, a county in the extreme South West of England. This had a purchasing power parity of 72.6 which means that, on average, people in Cornwall had only one-quarter the purchasing power of people who lived in inner London (Source: EU, 2005).

The aim of this chapter is to detail the wide variability of economic performance in England. This is done in two ways. In the first part, an index of the nine English regions of the UK is presented. This index is largely descriptive in that it seeks to rank the nine English regions against one another in terms of 15 factors that are commonly thought to be associated with entrepreneurship. What is novel about this index is that it charts changes in the regional economic performance over three decades using census data for 1981, 1991 and 2001. Hence, although the index is unable to offer a causal explanation for entrepreneurial behaviour in the English regions (see: Reynolds et al., 1994; Roberts, 2004), it is important because it demonstrates that little has changed in the economic condition of the English regions over the last three decades.

In the second part of the chapter, the aim is to compare Teesside with Buckinghamshire and Shropshire. This is important because Teesside lags behind Shropshire and Shropshire lags behind Buckinghamshire in terms of economic performance. These differences now seem permanent even if, during the early 1970s, Teesside was, arguably, at the forefront of economic development in the UK.

## Entrepreneurship in the English regions

There is nothing new about indexing the performance of particular areas against each other (Dunning et al., 1998), but there is considerable debate about what should be included in any such index (Kitson et al., 2004). Available indices, which either list the achievements of one nation compared to another (IMD, 2004; World Economic Forum, 2004) or one region against others (e.g. European Commission, 2000; Deas and Giordano, 2002; Porter, 2003; Parkinson et al., 2004), essentially weigh what should be considered against what data is available. This chapter is no different.

In Table 2.1, 15 factors that are often commonly associated with levels of regional entrepreneurship are identified (Storey, 1982). These are divided into four areas: features of the individual (human capital attributes); entrepreneurial activity; access to finance; and regional wealth. Table 2.1 also shows the suggested associations between individual factors and levels of entrepreneurship.

Before turning to the four themes, discussing the research evidence or presenting components of the index, we have to be clear that these factors were also shaped by pragmatic considerations of data availability. Ideally, what would have been appropriate is longitudinal data that tracked regional performance over the last 30 years. Unfortunately, detailed time-series data is largely unavailable for two main reasons.

First, it is often difficult to compare one region with another over time. For example, in the 1960s, England was divided into eight Standard Statistical Regions (SSRs) with the left-hand side of Figure 2.1 showing, for example, that London was part of the South East (region 8) whilst the 'Northern' region (no. 1) included major cities on the Eastern coast such as Newcastle and Middlesbrough and rural counties such as Cumbria on the Western coast. This regional division into SSRs remained after the local government reorganisation of 1974 which saw the six major metropolitan cities of England (Leeds and Sheffield (Yorkshire), Liverpool and Manchester (North West), Birmingham (West Midlands) and London) given their own local government. By 1994, it was decided to further reorganise the regional administrative boundaries into nine Government Office Regions (GORs). As the right

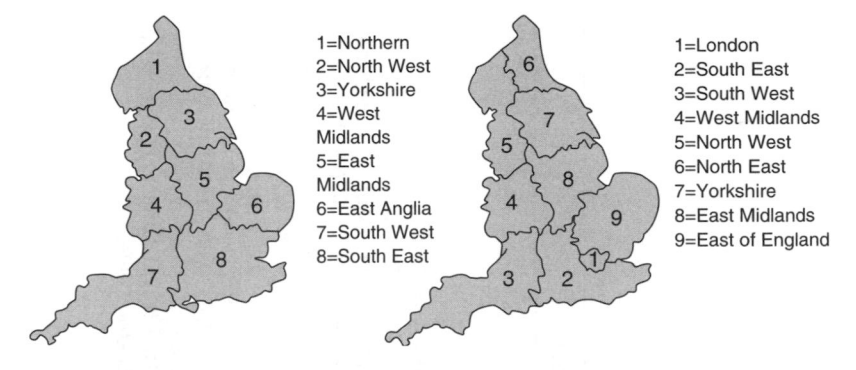

1=Northern
2=North West
3=Yorkshire
4=West Midlands
5=East Midlands
6=East Anglia
7=South West
8=South East

1=London
2=South East
3=South West
4=West Midlands
5=North West
6=North East
7=Yorkshire
8=East Midlands
9=East of England

*Figure 2.1*   The eight SSRs (1960–1994) and the nine GORs (1994 onwards).

hand of Figure 2.1 shows, this principally meant that London was recognised as a region in its own right, that the country of Cumbria moved from the Northern SSR to the North West GOR and the East Anglia SSR expanded to include counties such as Essex and Hertfordshire.

The second difficulty with much of the available regional data is that it remains patchy. Typical of this are sources such as the Labour Force Survey (LFS). Although the LFS goes back to 1975, it has seen major changes in how and what data is collected. Initially, it was collected on a biannual basis (1975–1983), then on an annual basis (1984–1991) and subsequently on a quarterly basis. Equally, there have been many changes to what data is collected. For instance, unemployment in the UK stood at 1½ million in July 1981 but less than two years later, in January 1983 it stood, supposedly, at more than 3 million individuals. What this neglects, however, is that the unemployment figures were revised more than 30 times by the Conservative government of the period (Coles, 1995).

Central to the construction of the present historical index of English regional entrepreneurship is the use of census information for 1981, 1991 and 2001. Using these censuses has a number of advantages. The most obvious is that, as a census, it is more likely to give a fuller picture of socio-economic conditions than surveys such as the LFS. Also important was that the 1981 data, which arguably looks back to conditions in the 1970s, is available for GOR regions. This is also true for the 1991 and 2001 censuses. Equally, factors such as unemployment are perhaps less prone to political interference since individuals self-report their own economic status and ethnicity. A final reason for choosing to look at regional entrepreneurship in 1981, 1991 and 2001 is that it

Table 2.1 Factors commonly associated with entrepreneurship

| Factors | Index | Expected sign | Research evidence |
|---|---|---|---|
| **Human capital** | | | |
| Ethnicity | % of ethnic minorities in the population | + | Le (1999) |
| Age & gender | % of 'prime age' males in the population | + | Cooper et al. (1994), Burke et al. (2000), (Henley, 2004), Greene (2002) |
| Unemployment | % of unemployment in the working population | ? | '+' Robson and Shah (1989), Evans and Leighton (1989), Blanchflower and Oswald (1990), Bogenhold and Staber (1991) '-' Blanchflower (2000) '?' Parker and Robson, (2004) |
| Education | % with degrees in the population | ? | '+' Rees and Shah (1986), Evans and Leighton (1989), Borjas (1992) '-' Evans (1989), de Wit (1993), Kidd (1993) |
| Labour market experience | % in managerial occupations in the working population | + | Storey (1982), Bates (1995), Gimeno et al. (1997), Robinson and Sexton (1994) |
| **Entrepreneurial activity** | | | |
| Self-employment | % self-employed in the working population | + | |

| | | | |
|---|---|---|---|
| Business birth | rate of VAT registrations/10,000 population | + | Love (1996), Disney et al. (2003), Scarpetta et al. (2002) |
| Business death | rate of VAT deregistrations/10,000 population | + | |
| Business stock | stock of VAT businesses/10,000 population | + | |
| Industrial structure | % employed in large businesses | − | Audretsch and Fritsch (1994) |
| | % employed in manufacturing | − | |
| *Access to capital* | | | |
| House ownership | % owner occupiers/total housing stock | + | Evans and Leighton (1989), Evans and Jovanovic (1989), Holtz-Eakin et al. (1994a, b), Bernhardt (1994), Laferrere and McEntee (1995), Lindh and Ohlsson (1996), Black et al. (1996), Cowling and Mitchell (1997), Blanchflower and Oswald (1998) |
| House prices | Price of average house | + | |
| *Regional wealth* | | | |
| Personal Income | Personal disposable income per head | + | Reynolds et al. (1994), Audretsch and Fritsch (1994) Robson (1996), Hart and McGuinness (2003), Porter (2003), Roberts (2004) |
| GDP per capita | GDP per head | + | |

coincides more or less with timing of the data collection for our empirical research on Teesside.

There are, though, drawbacks with such an approach. The most obvious of these is that the index is essentially three snapshots in time which has the potential to miss radical changes in economic conditions over the decade. Indeed, successive censuses make use of new categorizations to include economic developments. For example, between the 1981 and 2001 censuses there was a radical shift in the structure of house ownership in England. Particularly in the 1980s and 1990s, successive Conservative governments encouraged home ownership through schemes such as the 'right to buy' which allowed social housing occupants to buy their house. Equally, there has been a general increase in the numbers of individuals obtaining tertiary level qualifications and the ethnic characteristics of the English population have been redefined over the last 30 years to account for social changes (e.g. 'Indian' in 1981 and 'Indian' or 'Asian Whites' by 2001).

For this reason, the index reports unweighted averages for each of the factors. For each of the nine GOR regions both their raw score and their rank compared to the other regions are reported. Regions with high scores for each individual factor will be positively associated with high levels of entrepreneurship. For example, an area with the highest relative level for a particular factor scores nine whilst the lowest scores one.

A third consideration with using census information is that it fails to give a rounded picture of regional economic conditions. We, therefore, supplemented census information by making use of other publicly available data on house prices and business data (VAT data). Again, this has to be treated with some caution. For instance, the house price data is organised in terms of the 'old' regional SSRs which is another reason why we use an unweighted average of factors to compare regional entrepreneurial factors.

The aim of this index, though, is to merely describe changes in regional entrepreneurship over the last 30 years. We do not claim that a region with high scores overall – or for a particular factor – represents a causal explanation for their relative entrepreneurial prowess. Instead, what we are seeking to do with the index is simply capture intra-regional changes over time. We are interested in how regions have fared over the 30-year period and what changes have occurred in their relative rankings over this period. In the next part, therefore, we look at each of the four sets of indicators in turn before providing an overall index of their relative entrepreneurial strength.

## Human capital

Ideally, the aim here is to capture the extent of entrepreneurial ability that an individual possesses. This remains a perhaps unattainable measure since there is no obvious or direct measure of entrepreneurial ability. Instead, what Table 2.1 showed is there are a number of potential proxies for entrepreneurial ability. Le's (1999) review of self-employment studies showed that ethnicity was generally positively associated with high rates of entrepreneurship. For example, in the UK, those from Pakistani backgrounds are the most likely to be in self-employment. It is also commonly held that prime age and gender are reasonable proxies for entrepreneurship since males are more likely to be self-employed than females. Equally, 'prime' age males (34–44 years old) are more likely than other age groups to be self-employed (Greene, 2002).

The impact of education would seem to have a more ambiguous impact on new business formation. Lucas (1978) argued that individuals with increased education were more likely to consider entrepreneurship because they had the greater capacity to cope with the demands of running a new business. On the other hand, increased educational attainment, like increased managerial experience, increases the attractiveness of individuals to wage employers and may, thereby, decrease the likelihood of business start-up. This is reflected in Table 2.1. Similar arguments can be made about the influence of prior labour market experience with, on balance, the evidence suggesting that older individuals are more likely to start-up a business.

Also ambiguous is the impact of unemployment. Knight (1921) suggests that in the absence of wage employment individuals may seek out self-employment opportunities rather than settle for unemployment. Evidence for this 'push' hypothesis is, however, mixed (see Table 2.1).

What Tables 2.2a, 2.2b and 2.2c show are the five human capital factors for 1981, 1991 and 2001, respectively. These tables are organised in terms of GORs. The tables are ordered from the region with the lowest average ranking (where 1 is the lowest) to the region with the highest average ranking (where 9 is the highest). Table 2.2a shows that for 1981 Southern regions predominate, with the South East at the top, followed by the East of England and London. At the bottom are the three Northern regions: the North East, the North West and Yorkshire & Humberside, respectively. Regions such as London and

*Table 2.2a* Human capital variables for 1981

| | Ethnicity | | Prime age | | Unemployed | | Education | | Occupation | | Average |
|---|---|---|---|---|---|---|---|---|---|---|---|
| | % | Rank | % | Rank | % | Rank | % | Rank | % | Rank | score |
| South East | 6.28 | 3 | 6.00 | 5 | 5.77 | 1 | 1.67 | 9 | 13.71 | 1 | 3.80 |
| East of England | 5.78 | 4 | 6.27 | 4 | 6.36 | 2 | 1.42 | 7 | 12.62 | 3 | 4.00 |
| West Midlands | 6.65 | 2 | 6.35 | 2 | 10.70 | 7 | 1.14 | 2 | 9.84 | 8 | 4.20 |
| London | 18.20 | 1 | 5.99 | 6 | 7.78 | 5 | 1.54 | 8 | 11.77 | 2 | 4.40 |
| South West | 4.01 | 8 | 6.37 | 1 | 7.34 | 3 | 1.39 | 6 | 11.50 | 4 | 4.40 |
| East Midlands | 5.10 | 5 | 5.96 | 7 | 7.75 | 4 | 1.21 | 4 | 10.08 | 6 | 5.20 |
| North East | 1.88 | 9 | 6.32 | 3 | 12.72 | 9 | 1.13 | 1 | 8.28 | 9 | 6.20 |
| North West | 4.15 | 6 | 5.87 | 8 | 10.71 | 8 | 1.25 | 5 | 9.86 | 5 | 6.40 |
| Yorkshire & Humberside | 4.09 | 7 | 5.82 | 9 | 9.49 | 6 | 1.21 | 3 | 9.88 | 7 | 6.40 |

*Table 2.2b* Human capital variables for 1991

| | Ethnicity | | Prime age | | Unemployed | | Education | | Occupation | | Average score |
|---|---|---|---|---|---|---|---|---|---|---|---|
| | % | Rank | % | Rank | % | Rank | % | Rank | % | Rank | |
| South East | 4.47 | 7 | 7.21 | 1 | 8.66 | 3 | 8.91 | 2 | 31.13 | 1 | 2.80 |
| East of England | 4.59 | 6 | 7.19 | 2 | 7.36 | 1 | 7.11 | 3 | 28.27 | 3 | 3.00 |
| London | 23.99 | 1 | 6.75 | 9 | 9.34 | 4 | 11.81 | 1 | 30.63 | 2 | 3.40 |
| East Midlands | 5.83 | 3 | 7.13 | 3 | 12.50 | 8 | 5.73 | 6 | 25.40 | 5 | 5.00 |
| South West | 2.38 | 8 | 6.84 | 7 | 7.79 | 2 | 6.87 | 4 | 27.82 | 4 | 5.00 |
| Yorkshire & Humberside | 5.27 | 4 | 6.93 | 5 | 11.01 | 5 | 5.53 | 7 | 24.27 | 8 | 5.80 |
| West Midlands | 10.01 | 2 | 6.88 | 6 | 12.04 | 7 | 5.45 | 8 | 24.82 | 7 | 6.00 |
| North West | 5.18 | 5 | 6.83 | 8 | 11.44 | 6 | 5.82 | 5 | 25.09 | 6 | 6.00 |
| North East | 1.93 | 9 | 6.95 | 4 | 15.02 | 9 | 4.67 | 9 | 21.92 | 9 | 8.00 |

*Table 2.2c* Human capital variables for 2001

| | Ethnicity | | Prime age | | Unemployed | | Education | | Occupation | | Average score |
|---|---|---|---|---|---|---|---|---|---|---|---|
| | % | Rank | % | Rank | % | Rank | % | Rank | % | Rank | |
| London | 28.85 | 1 | 7.86 | 1 | 4.87 | 4 | 30.99 | 1 | 32.44 | 1 | 1.60 |
| South East | 4.90 | 6 | 7.56 | 2 | 3.81 | 3 | 21.75 | 2 | 29.55 | 2 | 3.00 |
| East of England | 4.88 | 7 | 7.45 | 3 | 3.31 | 1 | 18.14 | 4 | 27.08 | 3 | 3.60 |
| South West | 2.30 | 9 | 7.08 | 9 | 3.76 | 2 | 18.84 | 3 | 24.87 | 4 | 5.40 |
| East Midlands | 6.51 | 4 | 7.38 | 4 | 6.45 | 8 | 16.63 | 6 | 24.33 | 5 | 5.40 |
| North West | 5.56 | 5 | 7.24 | 7 | 5.69 | 6 | 17.17 | 5 | 24.18 | 6 | 5.80 |
| West Midlands | 11.26 | 2 | 7.14 | 8 | 5.68 | 5 | 16.19 | 8 | 24.04 | 7 | 6.00 |
| Yorkshire & Humberside | 6.52 | 3 | 7.24 | 6 | 5.73 | 7 | 16.38 | 7 | 22.94 | 8 | 6.20 |
| North East | 2.39 | 8 | 7.37 | 5 | 7.39 | 9 | 14.97 | 9 | 21.11 | 9 | 8.00 |

the South East owe their low average ranking to the high proportion of ethnic minorities, degree educated individuals and managers and professionals within their respective regions. London, for example, had the highest percentage of ethnic minorities of all the regions in 1981 (18.2 per cent) whilst the South East scored best in terms of managerial experience (13.7 per cent), education (1.67 per cent) and its relatively low rates of unemployment (5.8 per cent) (unlike the other four factors a high unemployment level attracts a high score). The same cannot be said of the North East. If the relative ranking for 'prime age' is discounted, the average score for this region would move from an already poor 6.20 to 7.00. Enhancing this, perhaps, is the fact that the North East had an unemployment rate, according to the 1981 census, of double that of the South East and nearly 50 per cent fewer individuals from a managerial or professional background.

Similar rankings are evident when we consider census data for 1991 (Table 2.2b). The South East, the East of England and London remain the top three regions. Below them, the East Midlands switch from 6th in 1981 to 4th in 1991 whilst Yorkshire & Humberside move from joint 8th (with the North West) in 1981 to 6th in 1991. The North East is rooted at the bottom with an average ranking of 8.00 which is nearly three times higher than that of the South East. What is also noticeable about Table 2.2b is that although there has been a general increase in individuals reporting being unemployed, highly educated or in managerial and professional occupations, the disparities evident in 1981 between the North East and South East persist.

By the 2001 census (Table 2.3c), it is possible to discern particular features of the human capital attributes of the English regions over time. London, for example, has remained the most ethnically diverse region of England. What is also apparent is that it contains the highest percentage of 'prime' age males. This is in sharp contrast to 1991 when it had the lowest percentage of such males. This seems to indicate that there has been a population shift amongst 'active' workers towards the capital principally from the West Midlands (ranked 2nd in 1981) and from the South West (ranked 1st in 1981). However, the South West has become a favoured location for retired people over the last 20 years.

The only human capital factor that London, with an average ranking of 1.6, does badly on is unemployment. This reflects that certain areas of London (e.g. Tower Hamlets, Hackney and Islington) are amongst the top 10 most deprived areas of England (ODPM, 2004).

Table 2.2c also shows there has been some alteration in the relative average rankings of the English regions: London goes ahead of the

South East and the East of England whilst Yorkshire and Humberside, previously 6th in 1991, swaps places in 2001 with the North West. The North East remains firmly rooted to the bottom with an average ranking more than four times higher than that of London.

## Entrepreneurial activity

This part looks at six further factors that indicate levels of entrepreneurial activity. Three of these variables are derived from sales tax data (Value Added Tax data) collected by the UK government. The three measures of VAT data are registrations (births), deregistrations (deaths) and stocks. It is well understood that some uncertainty persists about the use of such data, largely because registrations and deregistrations do not always equate to business birth and death (Partington and Mayell, 1998). For example, businesses may be 'born' many years before they register. Equally, deregistration does not necessarily mean the closure of a business due to a buyer being already registered for VAT. VAT data is also likely to miss many businesses since it excludes certain exempt goods and services, zero rated businesses, group registrations, or divisional registrations as well as those operating in the 'hidden' economy (Dale and Kerr, 1995).

Another major problem is that there is some dispute about whether a business stock or a labour market denominator should be used. Essentially, this is a measurement issue. Dividing the number of new businesses by total number or stock of businesses is one way in which it is possible to compare rates of new business formation in different sized geographical areas. Hence, if 100 new businesses are created per year and the existing business stock is 1,000, the annual rate is obviously 10%. The alternative measure is to normalise the number of new businesses by the population or by the number of working age individuals in the area. This is called the labour market approach. Table 2.1 uses a labour market denominator since, as Garofoli (1994) emphasises, it is primarily people, not businesses, who create new businesses and so people are the appropriate denominator.

We further supplement this VAT data by using census information on self-employment for each of the three decades. Besides being a more likely indicator of overall entrepreneurial activity, the census information is also likely to be a useful proxy because businesses only have to register once they reach a certain threshold of VAT sales. This is likely to miss individuals and businesses below that threshold.

The final two factors that we consider are measures of industrial structure: the percentage of manufacturing businesses as a proportion of total businesses; and the dominance of large businesses in the region. These two factors are proxies of likely entrepreneurial activity because, in terms of the prevalence of large businesses, it has long been held (Storey, 1982) that regions dominated by large businesses are unlikely to be fertile seed beds for individuals to set up their own business (The data for this factor is derived from government sources which present a slight problem in that prior to 2001, a large business is defined as 500 employees, but for 2001, it is considered to be large if it has 250 employees.).

The rationale for including some measure of sector (the percentage of manufacturing businesses) is because of evidence that business formation rates differ between services and manufacturing (Keeble et al., 1992; and Bryson et al., 1997). Similarly, it is also recognised that there has been considerable industrial restructuring not only of the English or UK economy but worldwide. Ideally, therefore, we would have liked to provide more finely granulated data on sectoral distribution but, unfortunately, such information is largely unavailable for 1981.

Tables 2.3a, 2.3b and 2.3c detail the relative rankings of each of the nine English regions. What is perhaps a little surprising is that the South West, although ranked relatively modestly in terms of human capital factors (6th (1981), 5th (1991) and 4th (2001)), has the lowest average ranking in 1981 for the entrepreneurial activity factors. About one in eight of the active population in 1981 was self-employed, whilst in terms of VAT data the region had high stock levels and a high rate of business birth and death. The relevant tables here treat high rates of business death as a positive outcome. The reason for this is that although such outcomes are potentially ruinous for individuals (Whyley, 1998), there is increasing evidence that high rates of 'churn' (high rates of births and deaths) have a favourable impact upon the productivity of businesses either because they shift resources to more efficient businesses or threaten incumbent businesses with failure if they do not improve their efficiency or innovatory capacity (e.g. Disney et al., 2003).

Table 2.3a also shows that below the South West region is the procession of the usual suspects: London, the East of England and the South East whilst, at the other end, are the North West and North East. The average rankings for these two regions are 7.17 and 7.83, respectively. The North East, for example, performs particularly poorly: its self-employment

*Table 2.3a*  Entrepreneurial activity in 1981

| | Self-employment | | Births | | Deaths | | Stock | | Manufacturing | | Large businesses | | Average rank |
|---|---|---|---|---|---|---|---|---|---|---|---|---|---|
| | % | Rank | % | Rank | % | Rank | % | Rank | % | Rank | % | Rank | |
| South West | 12.93 | 1 | 39.45 | 2 | 30.95 | 2 | 380 | 1 | 38.81 | 3 | 20.4 | 1 | 1.67 |
| London | 9.61 | 4 | 48.09 | 1 | 40.17 | 1 | 350 | 2 | 32.96 | 1 | 25.5 | 3 | 2.00 |
| East of England | 10.12 | 3 | 39.43 | 3 | 29.88 | 4 | 328 | 3 | 45.17 | 4 | 23.4 | 2 | 3.17 |
| South East | 10.45 | 2 | 39.16 | 4 | 29.96 | 3 | 310 | 5 | 37.27 | 2 | 25.5 | 3 | 3.33 |
| East Midlands | 8.77 | 5 | 34.61 | 6 | 27.14 | 7 | 312 | 4 | 55.27 | 8 | 32.5 | 7 | 6.17 |
| Yorkshire & Humberside | 8.00 | 7 | 32.44 | 8 | 26.80 | 8 | 285 | 7 | 49.10 | 6 | 25.9 | 5 | 6.83 |
| West Midlands | 7.91 | 8 | 36.12 | 5 | 28.14 | 5 | 297 | 6 | 62.13 | 9 | 33.7 | 8 | 6.83 |
| North West | 8.23 | 6 | 33.01 | 7 | 27.89 | 6 | 278 | 8 | 53.15 | 7 | 33.8 | 9 | 7.17 |
| North East | 5.45 | 9 | 24.54 | 9 | 18.96 | 9 | 192 | 9 | 47.20 | 5 | 31 | 6 | 7.83 |

Table 2.3b  Entrepreneurial activity in 1991

| | Self-employment | | Births | | Deaths | | Stock | | Manufacturing | | Large businesses | | Average rank |
|---|---|---|---|---|---|---|---|---|---|---|---|---|---|
| | % | Rank | | Rank | | Rank | | Rank | % | Rank | % | Rank | |
| London | 11.83 | 4 | 53.12 | 1 | 54.11 | 1 | 369 | 1 | 10.57 | 1 | 26.6 | 3 | 1.83 |
| South East | 13.10 | 2 | 44.32 | 2 | 45.89 | 2 | 342 | 3 | 14.72 | 2 | 26.6 | 3 | 2.33 |
| South West | 15.20 | 1 | 37.61 | 4 | 42.07 | 3 | 359 | 2 | 16.51 | 3 | 26.8 | 5 | 3.00 |
| East of England | 12.68 | 3 | 38.96 | 3 | 41.66 | 4 | 334 | 4 | 17.89 | 5 | 25.9 | 2 | 3.50 |
| East Midlands | 11.26 | 5 | 34.05 | 5 | 34.01 | 5 | 293 | 5 | 24.21 | 8 | 25.3 | 1 | 4.83 |
| West Midlands | 10.44 | 8 | 32.31 | 7 | 32.99 | 6 | 281 | 6 | 24.96 | 9 | 26.9 | 6 | 7.00 |
| North West | 10.48 | 6 | 33.19 | 6 | 32.83 | 7 | 257 | 8 | 20.29 | 7 | 30.7 | 8 | 7.00 |
| Yorkshire & Humberside | 10.48 | 6 | 30.98 | 8 | 31.10 | 8 | 264 | 7 | 19.35 | 6 | 29.7 | 7 | 7.00 |
| North East | 7.61 | 9 | 21.60 | 9 | 21.92 | 9 | 184 | 9 | 17.69 | 4 | 39.1 | 9 | 8.17 |

*Table 2.3c* Entrepreneurial activity in 2001

| | Self-employment | | Births | | Deaths | | Stock | | Manufacturing | | Large businesses | | Average |
| | % | Rank | % | Rank | % | Rank | | Rank | % | Rank | % | Rank | rank |
|---|---|---|---|---|---|---|---|---|---|---|---|---|---|
| South East | 13.68 | 2 | 33.80 | 2 | 29.15 | 2 | 350 | 2 | 12.13 | 2 | 41.6 | 3 | 2.17 |
| South West | 14.94 | 1 | 29.00 | 4 | 26.04 | 4 | 337 | 3 | 13.95 | 3 | 35.2 | 1 | 2.67 |
| London | 13.28 | 4 | 46.54 | 1 | 42.89 | 1 | 397 | 1 | 7.63 | 1 | 57.0 | 9 | 2.83 |
| East of England | 13.35 | 3 | 30.58 | 3 | 27.85 | 3 | 333 | 4 | 14.47 | 4 | 44.4 | 5 | 3.67 |
| East Midlands | 11.50 | 5 | 26.71 | 5 | 23.29 | 6 | 289 | 5 | 19.91 | 8 | 43.2 | 4 | 5.50 |
| North West | 11.12 | 7 | 24.17 | 7 | 22.48 | 7 | 251 | 8 | 16.89 | 5 | 40.6 | 2 | 6.00 |
| West Midlands | 11.22 | 6 | 26.47 | 6 | 23.48 | 5 | 283 | 6 | 20.80 | 9 | 45.8 | 7 | 6.50 |
| Yorkshire & Humberside | 11.11 | 8 | 23.34 | 8 | 22.16 | 8 | 256 | 7 | 17.35 | 7 | 45.7 | 6 | 7.33 |
| North East | 8.59 | 9 | 16.28 | 9 | 16.06 | 9 | 177 | 9 | 16.99 | 6 | 46.0 | 8 | 8.33 |

rate is less than half that of the South West in 1981. It fares little better in terms of its birth rate, death rate (about 40 per cent below the South West) and its business stock is around 50 per cent of the South West.

Some changes are evident for both 1991 (Table 2.3b) and 2001 (Table 2.3c). First, in Table 2.3b, London and the South East go above the South West in terms of average rankings. This situation persists for 2001 (Table 2.3c) as the South East remains above that of the South West in the average rankings (London, also, would be above the South West except that the shift from measuring the percentage employment share of large businesses as 250 to measuring it as 500 employees means that London looked as if it had a far greater percentage of its employees in larger businesses in 2001).

There is also some movement at the bottom end of the average rankings. The North West for example is ranked 8th in 1981 but climbs up to 7th in 1991 and on to 6th in 2001. Yorkshire & Humberside, meanwhile, slides from 6th in 1981 down to 8th in 1991, a position it still occupies in 2001. What is abundantly clear from each of the three tables is the relative position of the North East. It is rooted to the bottom of the average rankings for each of the three decades.

In terms of individual factors, the three tables also point to other interesting features. For example, rates of self-employment increase across all of the regions. Similarly, for regions such as London and the South East business birth and death rates are n-shaped, indicating heightened levels of business churn, particularly for 1991. Overall, though, London ends up over the 1981–2001 period with a business stock some 50 points higher.

This cannot, though, be said of the North East. Here rates of business birth and death actually fall in 1991 compared with 1981. Business birth and death rates for the North East fall further in 2001 (Table 2.3c). Overall, therefore, the business birth rate for the North East slips from 25 in 1981 to 16 in 2001. It is little wonder, therefore, that the business stock falls from 192 to 177 over the same period. This represents a percentage drop in the business stock of about 8 per cent in a period (1999–2003) where the total number of all UK enterprises held steady at around 3.8 million. Much the same can be said of Yorkshire & Humberside. Here birth rates fall from 32 to 23 and the business stock decreases from 286 to 256 (about 9 per cent) over the same period.

## Access to finance and regional income

It is frequently argued (see: Chapter 7) that lack of access to finance plays a central role in constraining the take-up of the entrepreneurship option. For this reason we now review two factors that may influence regional access to finance issues. The first of these is the percentage of home owners. Home ownership might be thought important to entrepreneurs because they can use it as collateral against any finance they may receive from an outside financier. Home ownership data are derived from the three censuses and relates to the GORs. The second factor used is average house prices from the Nationwide Building Society. Again, the presumption here is that those with more expensive houses are more able to access greater pools of finance. These data are organised in terms of the old SSRs and – since London was not a SSR – London is treated as being the same as the South East. This is likely to underestimate the house prices in London.

Besides the potential wealth of people, there is always their income. To assess this, two factors are presented. One of these is GDP per head (1981) or GVA per head (1991 and 2001). Although these two measures are slightly different (GVA measures the contribution to the economy of each individual producer, industry or sector whilst GDP is derived from GVA by adding taxes and subtracting subsidies on products), practically and in terms of intra-regional ranking, these differences are not likely to be significant. Whilst some measure of GDP is often included in other studies (see Table 2.1) a second measure of regional wealth (personal disposable income (PDI for 1981) or gross household disposable income (GHDI for 1991 and 2001)) was included. This is because, as the House of Commons ODPM Select Committee (2003) also suggests, such measures take better account of regional price differences and demographic factors (e.g. there are more retired people in the South West region). Again, the way these two measures are calculated differ and we also have the added problem that PDI data in 1981 relates to the SSRs. Hence, London is treated as being the same as the South East.

Tables 2.4a, 2.4b and 2.4c all show a similar picture to earlier tables: London and the South East dominate the rankings for each of the three time periods followed by more southern areas of England such as the South West, the East of England and the East Midlands. In each of the three tables, whilst there is an overall increase in house ownership, house prices, personal income, and GDP per head, there also seems to be a widening gulf between levels of regional demand (income). Take,

*Table 2.4a*   Access to finance and regional income in 1981

| | Owner-occupiers | | Average house prices | | Average personal income | | GDP per head | | Average rank |
|---|---|---|---|---|---|---|---|---|---|
| | % | Rank | | Rank | | Rank | | Rank | |
| South East | 64.60 | 1 | 29,379 | 1 | 3,474 | 1 | 4,271 | 1 | 1.00 |
| London | 48.60 | 8 | 29,379 | 2 | 3,474 | 1 | 4,271 | 1 | 3.00 |
| East of England | 60.77 | 3 | 24,204 | 3 | 3,019 | 5 | 3,541 | 4 | 3.75 |
| South West | 63.76 | 2 | 24,168 | 4 | 3,114 | 3 | 3,420 | 7 | 4.00 |
| East Midlands | 59.84 | 4 | 20,692 | 7 | 3,100 | 4 | 3,555 | 3 | 4.50 |
| North West | 59.56 | 5 | 20,112 | 8 | 2,953 | 6 | 3,460 | 5 | 6.00 |
| Yorkshire & Humberside | 56.26 | 7 | 23,885 | 5 | 2,873 | 8 | 3,381 | 8 | 7.00 |
| West Midlands | 57.56 | 6 | 21,959 | 6 | 2,815 | 9 | 3,329 | 9 | 7.50 |
| North East | 45.30 | 9 | 18,546 | 9 | 2,907 | 7 | 3,438 | 6 | 7.75 |

*Table 2.4b*   Access to finance and regional income in 1991

| | Owner-occupiers | | Average house prices | | Average personal income | | GDP per head | | Average rank |
|---|---|---|---|---|---|---|---|---|---|
| | % | Rank | | Rank | | Rank | | Rank | |
| South East | 73.76 | 1 | 72,741 | 1 | 7,387 | 2 | 9,850 | 2 | 1.50 |
| London | 57.19 | 9 | 72,741 | 2 | 8,254 | 1 | 11,631 | 1 | 3.25 |
| South West | 72.80 | 2 | 59,805 | 3 | 6,827 | 4 | 8,310 | 5 | 3.50 |
| East of England | 70.96 | 3 | 58,523 | 4 | 6,360 | 5 | 9,805 | 3 | 3.75 |
| East Midlands | 70.62 | 4 | 51,853 | 8 | 7,242 | 3 | 8,499 | 4 | 4.75 |
| North West | 68.11 | 5 | 55,513 | 6 | 6,292 | 7 | 8,135 | 7 | 6.25 |
| West Midlands | 67.65 | 6 | 52,371 | 7 | 6,298 | 6 | 8,228 | 6 | 6.25 |
| Yorkshire & Humberside | 65.90 | 7 | 57,384 | 5 | 6,150 | 8 | 8,094 | 8 | 7.00 |
| North East | 58.95 | 8 | 47,979 | 9 | 5,843 | 9 | 7,568 | 9 | 8.75 |

again, the North East. In terms of house price differentials, prices were some 40 per cent lower than that of the South East in 1981 but the level of disparity reached 60 per cent in 2001. Similarly, personal income in the North East was some 20 per cent lower in 1981 but 30 per cent lower than London in 2001. Finally, GDP per head in the North East was some 20 per cent lower than London in 1981. This differential increased to 40 per cent by 2001.

*Table 2.4c*   Access to finance and regional income in 2001

| | Owner-occupiers | | Average house prices | | Average personal income | | GDP per head | | Average rank |
|---|---|---|---|---|---|---|---|---|---|
| | % | Rank | | Rank | | Rank | | Rank | |
| South East | 73.96 | 1 | 139,140 | 1 | 13,460 | 2 | 17,518 | 2 | 1.50 |
| London | 56.52 | 9 | 139,140 | 2 | 14,484 | 1 | 19,265 | 1 | 3.25 |
| South West | 73.06 | 2 | 99,606 | 3 | 11,947 | 4 | 13,216 | 5 | 3.50 |
| East Midlands | 72.18 | 4 | 93,289 | 4 | 12,813 | 3 | 13,431 | 4 | 3.75 |
| East of England | 72.71 | 3 | 74,805 | 6 | 10,919 | 5 | 15,994 | 3 | 4.25 |
| North West | 69.26 | 6 | 82,978 | 5 | 10,879 | 6 | 13,060 | 7 | 6.00 |
| West Midlands | 69.56 | 5 | 65,241 | 8 | 10,862 | 7 | 13,171 | 6 | 6.50 |
| Yorkshire & Humberside | 67.61 | 7 | 71,469 | 7 | 10,791 | 8 | 12,596 | 8 | 7.50 |
| North East | 63.62 | 8 | 56,983 | 9 | 10,112 | 9 | 11,132 | 9 | 8.75 |

## Regional differences in England 1981–2001

The picture that emerges from the individual tables is confirmed when we consider the cumulative average rankings for each of the English regions for each of the three census years. As Table 2.5 shows the South East of England and London have the lowest average scores. Below them there is some slight movement as the South West slips from 3rd to 4th between 1981–1991 and the West Midlands slips underneath the North West. Two other features are evident. The relative ranking in 1991 is identical to that in 2001. Second, at the bottom of this index, there is the constant presence of Yorkshire and Humberside and the North East.

*Table 2.5*   Cumulative regional rankings

| | 1981 | | 1991 | | 2001 |
|---|---|---|---|---|---|
| South East (1) | 2.87 | South East (1) | 2.27 | South East (1) | 2.27 |
| London (2) | 3.07 | London (2) | 2.73 | London (2) | 2.53 |
| South West (3) | 3.20 | East of England (3) | 3.40 | East of England (3) | 3.80 |
| East of England (4) | 3.60 | South West (4) | 3.80 | South West (4) | 3.80 |
| East Midlands (5) | 5.33 | East Midlands (5) | 4.87 | East Midlands (5) | 5.00 |
| West Midlands (6) | 6.13 | North West (6) | 6.47 | North West (6) | 5.93 |
| North West (7) | 6.60 | West Midlands (7) | 6.47 | West Midlands (7) | 6.33 |
| Yorkshire & Humberside (8) | 6.73 | Yorkshire & Humberside (8) | 6.60 | Yorkshire & Humberside (8) | 7.00 |
| North East (9) | 7.27 | North East (9) | 8.27 | North East (9) | 8.33 |

This perhaps is not a surprise. Foreman-Peck (1985) argued that the beginnings of the economic decline of the Northern periphery of England have their roots in the inter-war period when new business formation rates in the North of England were much lower than that of London and the South East. He suggests that the chief reason for this was the lack of regional demand in the Northern regions brought about by lower employment levels and lower levels of overall regional wealth and income.

Little seemingly has changed since the inter-war period. Figure 2.2 demonstrates this by showing the rates of regional unemployment for the North East, the South East, the West Midlands and Great Britain, 1923–1980. What this chart clearly shows is that in 1923 the three regions were all around the British average of 10 per cent unemployment rate. Over the inter-war period unemployment rose markedly in all three regions but in the mid 1930s, fewer than 15 per cent of workers in the South East were unemployed. In the North East this rate stood at a figure approaching 30 per cent. Unsurprisingly, there was little regional unemployment differences during the Second World War but subsequent to this and, despite the 'golden' years of economic prosperity of the 1950s and 1960s in England, Figure 2.2 clearly demonstrates that unemployment in the North East has always been greater than that of Great Britain, that of the West Midlands but, most markedly, when compared to the South East of England.

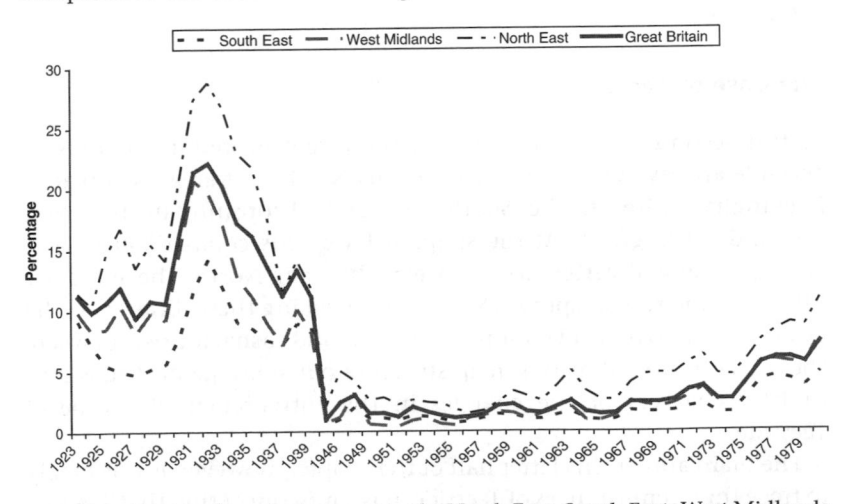

*Figure 2.2*  Regional unemployment in the North East, South East, West Midlands and Great Britain, 1923–1980.
*Source*: Mitchell, 1998.

## Summary

In this first part of the chapter, the aim was to explore the economic position of English regions. We presented an index comprising 15 different factors commonly associated with entrepreneurship. We then showed changes in those factors across three decades. The evidence points to widespread regional differences between the South East regions of England and the peripheral Northern regions. These differences have remained remarkably consistent over the three decades with regions such as the North East scoring relatively poorly in terms of human capital, entrepreneurial activity, access to finance and regional income.

Although the bulk of the evidence relates to the three decades, further evidence suggests that these regional differences have existed perhaps as far back as the 1920s. Such empirical promptings give little succour to those who believe that somehow or other regional convergence is likely to occur as businesses realise that land and labour are cheaper in poorer areas of England. Of course, our results are largely descriptive and tell us little in the way of factors that are likely to explain why such sharp regional differences persist over such a long period of time. Roberts' (2004) evidence, however, tends to confirm such findings for the English regions. Looking at the period 1977–1993, he finds little evidence of economic convergence at the regional level. Instead, his evidence has it that those already with the most are the ones most likely to continue to get the most.

## The Case of Teesside

In this second part of the chapter, the recent economic changes in Teesside are reviewed by comparing this North East area with that of Buckinghamshire in the South East and Shropshire in the West Midlands of England. At the simplest level, this comparison reflects clear subregional differences between the poor North, the middling Midlands and the prosperous South. In describing these differences the desire is both to remind seasoned observers and casual tourists of where these places are but also to help structure our subsequent discussions in later chapters of the changes in the entrepreneurial profile of Teesside.

The main aim of this latter half of the chapter, however, is not simply to trace the circumstances of Teesside. It is a misconception that Teesside has always been a poorly performing area. What we shall see is that Teesside, up until the last thirty years or so, was 'in the North but not of the North' (Benyon et al., 1994).

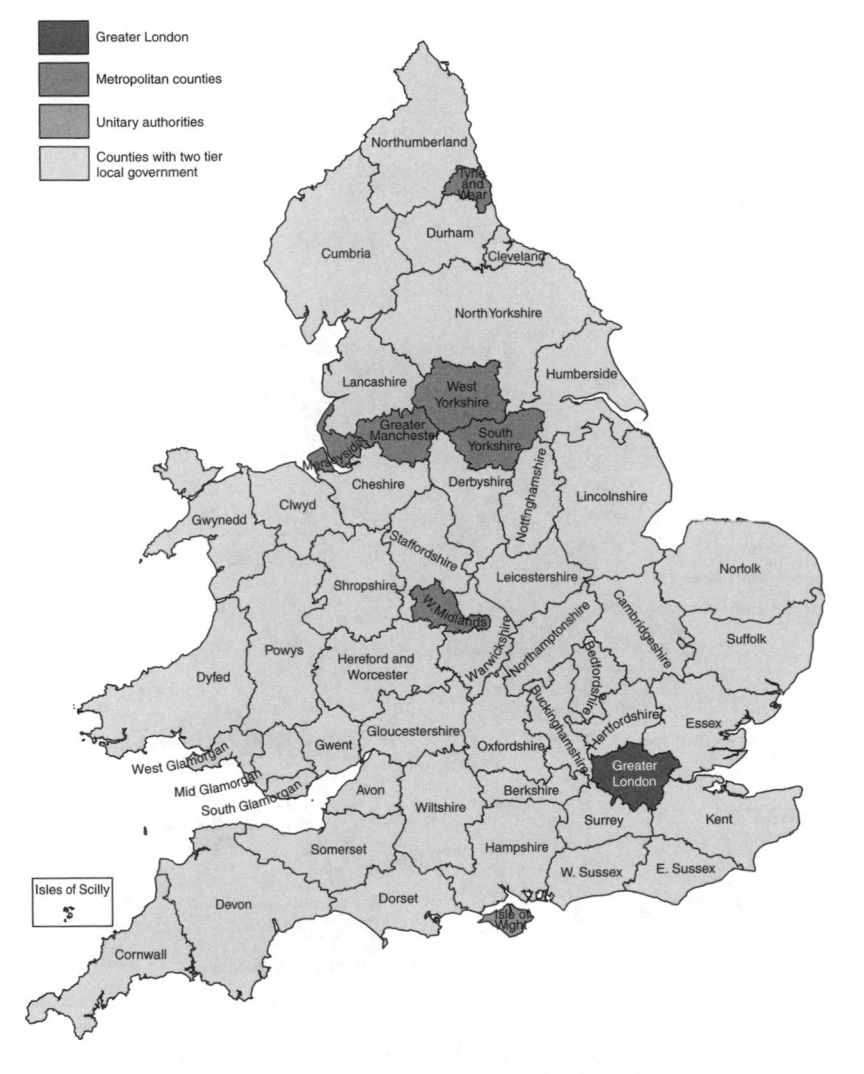

*Figure 2.3*  Map of former English and Welsh counties (post 1974).
*Source*: ONS, 2005.

## The three English counties

Teesside is located in the South East corner of the North East of England. To the North is the broadly rural county of Durham. Beyond this is the metropolitan conurbation of Tyne and Wear (the cities of Newcastle and Sunderland) and Northumberland. To the South and East is North Yorkshire (see Figure 2.3). Teesside has undergone two major administra-

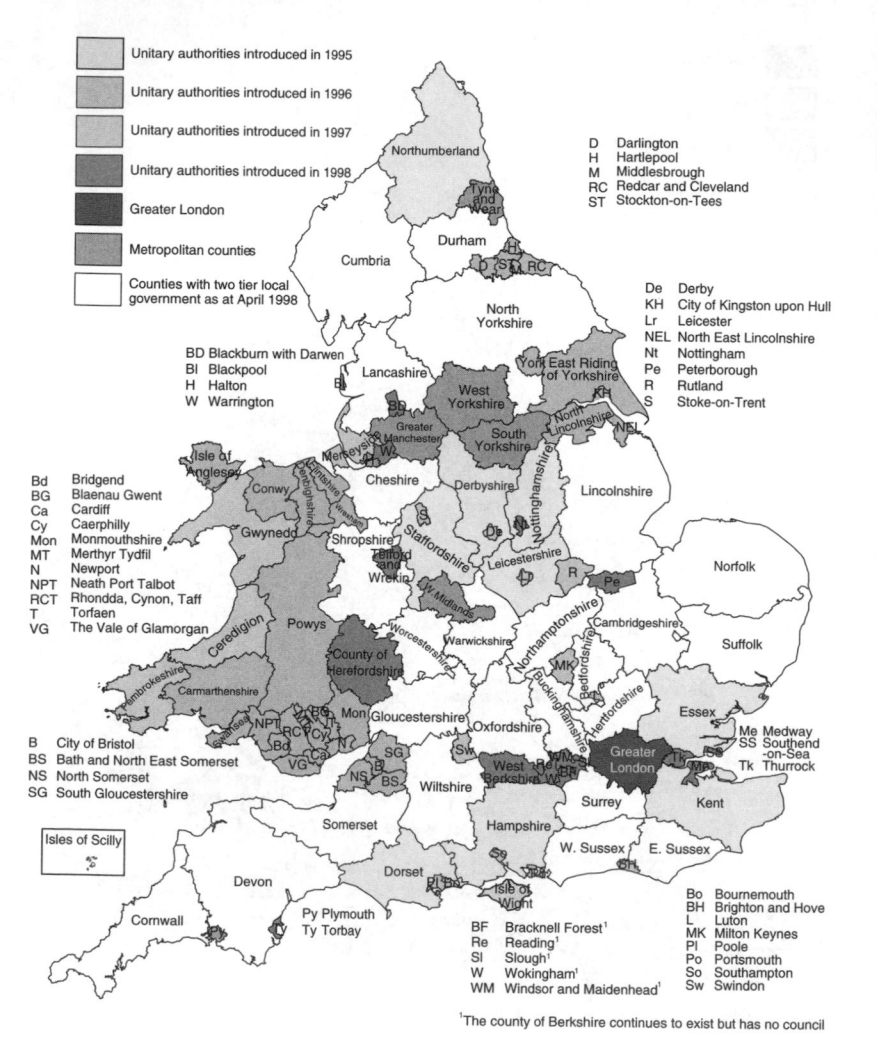

Unitary authorities introduced in 1995

Unitary authorities introduced in 1996

Unitary authorities introduced in 1997

Unitary authorities introduced in 1998

Greater London

Metropolitan counties

Counties with two tier local government as at April 1998

D    Darlington
H    Hartlepool
M    Middlesbrough
RC   Redcar and Cleveland
ST   Stockton-on-Tees

De    Derby
KH    City of Kingston upon Hull
Lr    Leicester
NEL   North East Lincolnshire
Nt    Nottingham
Pe    Peterborough
R     Rutland
S     Stoke-on-Trent

BD Blackburn with Darwen
Bl  Blackpool
H   Halton
W   Warrington

Bd    Bridgend
BG    Blaenau Gwent
Ca    Cardiff
Cy    Caerphilly
Mon   Monmouthshire
MT    Merthyr Tydfil
N     Newport
NPT   Neath Port Talbot
RCT   Rhondda, Cynon, Taff
T     Torfaen
VG    The Vale of Glamorgan

B     City of Bristol
BS    Bath and North East Somerset
NS    North Somerset
SG    South Gloucestershire

Isles of Scilly

Me   Medway
SS   Southend-on-Sea
Tk   Thurrock

Bo    Bournemouth
BH    Brighton and Hove
L     Luton
MK    Milton Keynes
Pl    Poole
Po    Portsmouth
So    Southampton
Sw    Swindon

BF    Bracknell Forest[1]
Re    Reading[1]
Sl    Slough[1]
W     Wokingham[1]
WM    Windsor and Maidenhead[1]

[1]The county of Berkshire continues to exist but has no council

*Figure 2.4*   Map of English and Welsh counties and unitary Authorities (post 1998).
*Source*: ONS, 2005.

tive reorganisations in the last 30 years. First, after 1974, four of its five areas (Hartlepool, Stockton-on-Tees, Middlesbrough and what is now Redcar & Cleveland) were brought together to form the county of Cleveland, with Darlington remaining as part of County Durham. This structure is shown in Figure 2.3. The second reorganisation occurred in 1996 when four unitary councils were created (Middlesbrough,

Hartlepool, Stockton-on-Tees and Redcar & Cleveland). To the west of these councils was Darlington which was deemed another unitary council area. The Darlington area was brought into the area to form Teesside. The reformed structure is shown in Figure 2.4.

The county of Buckinghamshire, ringed by the counties of Berkshire, Oxfordshire, Northamptonshire, Bedfordshire, Hertfordshire as well as Greater London (see Figure 2.3), is firmly located in the South East 'Home' counties. Like Teesside, it too saw its boundaries redefined after 1974 with the former Buckinghamshire towns of Slough and Eton becoming part of the neighbouring county of Berkshire whilst the county gained the 'new town' of Milton Keynes in 1967. Following the administrative reorganisation of the 1990s, Milton Keynes was granted unitary council status (see Figure 2.4).

Shropshire, like Buckinghamshire, has also no direct access to the sea. Located in the West Midlands, it was, subsequent to the 1974 local government reorganisation, surrounded by the Welsh counties of Powys and Clwyd to the West and North West, Cheshire to the North, Staffordshire to the East and Hereford & Worcester to the South (Figure 2.3). Like Buckinghamshire, Shropshire also gained a new town with the creation of Telford in 1968 and this new town was also given unitary authority status following the administrative reorganisation in the 1990s (Figure 2.4).

In terms of the population of these three areas, the populations of Shropshire (including Telford & Wrekin) and Buckinghamshire are roughly the same with populations of 447,000 and 478,000, respectively. Teesside is somewhat larger at 652,800 (source: ONS, 2003). What this masks, however, is the population density of these areas. Of all the areas, Teesside had the highest population density of 828 people per sq. km which was far greater than that of both Buckinghamshire (306) and

*Table 2.6*  Distance travelled to work, census 2001

|  | Teesside | Shropshire | Buckinghamshire |
|---|---|---|---|
| <20 km | 79.75 | 67.52 | 60.83 |
| 20km+ | 9.08 | 16.76 | 22.08 |
| Working from home | 7.18 | 11.37 | 11.65 |
| Other | 3.99 | 4.35 | 5.44 |
| Total | 100 | 100 | 100 |

*Source*: ONS, 2005.

Shropshire (89). This indicates that there are different degrees of rurality evident in these areas: Teesside is definitely urban, Buckinghamshire semi-rural and Shropshire distinctly rural by UK standards. Further information from the 2001 census (Table 2.6) also indicates that these three areas differ in terms of travel-to-work patterns. For example, more than one-fifth of Buckinghamshire workers travel more than 20 km to work. This may be explained by its close proximity to London. Some 17 per cent of Shropshire workers also commute similar distances, presumably either because the relatively large size of the county or because it is close to the Birmingham (West Midlands) conurbation. Only 9 per cent of Teesside (Tees Valley) workers travel sizeable distances indicating its relative geographic isolation from the nearest alternative conurbations (Newcastle and Leeds). It is also noticeable from Table 2.6 that relatively few Teesside workers work from home.

A possible explanation for these travel-to-work patterns is the types of work undertaken in the three areas. Figure 2.5 shows that Buckinghamshire is markedly different from the either the West Midlands or North East areas in that a quarter of all its workers (including the self-employed) are employed in finance, IT and other business activities. The county is also strong in terms of distribution, hotels and restaurants rather than construction or manufacturing. Shropshire,

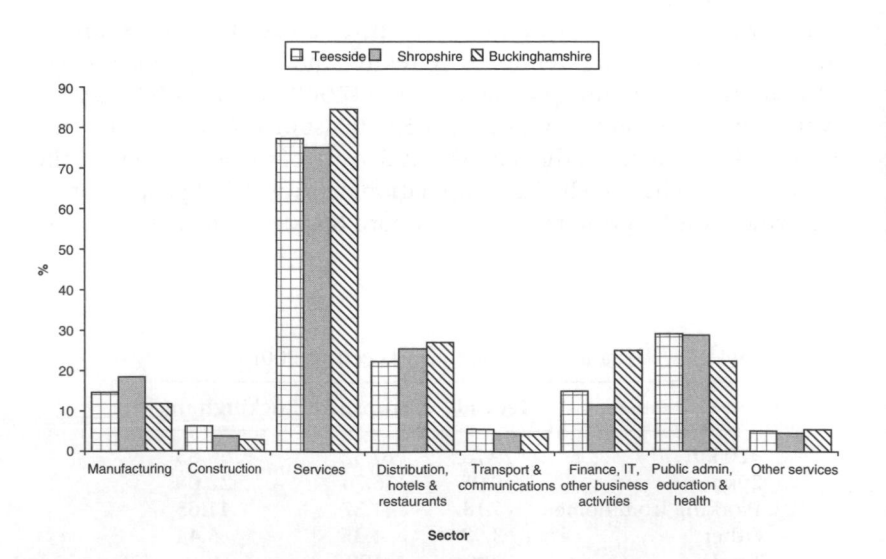

*Figure 2.5*   Employment structure of the three counties, 2003.
*Source*: Nomis, 2005.

however, has a comparatively greater percentage of its workforce in manufacturing but is relatively weak in terms of business services. What is particularly pronounced in Figure 2.5 is the marked reliance of both Shropshire and Teesside on the public sector in terms of administration, health or education jobs.

Similar data confirms that there are also apparent differences in the human capital attributes of the workforce of the three counties. Over half (51 per cent) of Buckinghamshire workers were in 1–3 SOC (2000) occupations (managers, professionals and associate professionals/technicians). By comparison, 40 per cent of Shropshire workers were in similar occupations. This figure dropped further for Teesside (34 per cent). Where Teesside did score highly is in the lower SOC (2000) occupation groups. In terms of groups 8 and 9 (machine operative and elementary occupations), it had the same percentage as Shropshire (24 per cent) but this was nearly double that of Buckinghamshire (13 per cent).

Table 2.7 continues this theme. It shows that people in Buckinghamshire were more highly educated, less likely to have no qualifications but more likely to be self-employed. On the other hand, Teesside had nearly 20 per cent of its working age population with no qualifications and a self-employment rate of about one-third of that of Buckinghamshire. Between these two extremes sits Shropshire.

What Table 2.7 begins to indicate, echoing the earlier part of this chapter, is the deep divisions in the economic outcomes for individuals who live in these three counties. A measure of this is shown in Figure 2.6. This shows the GVA per head for each of the areas (UK = 100). Unfortunately, official UK statistics have since 1995 further reordered the constituent areas into NUTS 3 areas. For this reason Figure 2.6 shows GVA rates for the following six areas: 1) South Teesside (Middlesbrough and Redcar & Cleveland); 2) Hartlepool & Stockton-on Tees; 3) Darlington; 4) Shropshire, 5) Telford & Wrekin; and 6) Buckinghamshire.

Figure 2.6 shows that GVA in Buckinghamshire over the period 1995–2002 was distinctly above the UK average (=100) by around 20 per cent. It also shows that there are similarities in the fortunes of both

*Table 2.7* Education qualifications in the three counties

|  | Tees Valley | Shropshire | Buckinghamshire |
| --- | --- | --- | --- |
| NVQ4 and above | 17.82 | 22.80 | 34.80 |
| No Qualifications | 18.07 | 15.08 | 10.20 |
| Self employed | 4.52 | 9.19 | 12.00 |

*Source*: Nomis, 2005.

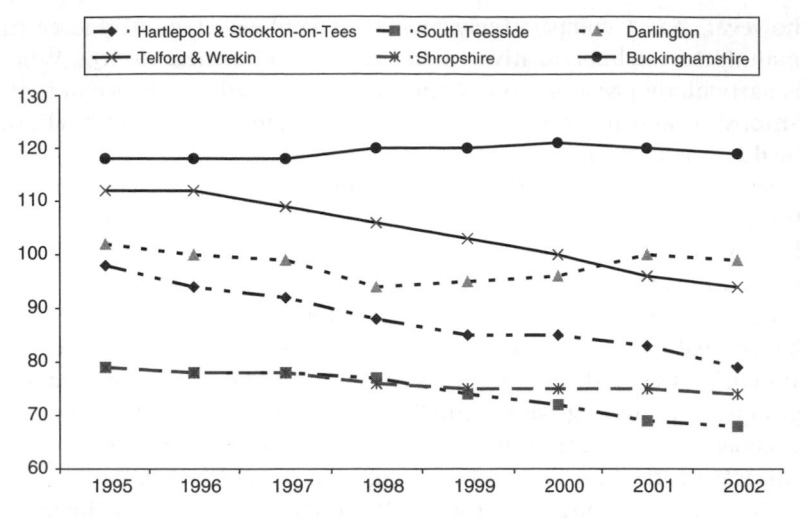

*Figure 2.6*    GVA rates for the three areas, 1995–2000 (UK = 100).
*Source*: ONS, 2005.

Telford & Wrekin and Shropshire. Although Telford & Wrekin has a GVA rate well above that of Shropshire, it slipped over the intervening seven years from being well above the UK average in 1995 to below the UK average in 2002. A similar story, albeit less dramatic, is apparent for Shropshire which was some 20 per cent below that of the UK average in 1995 but had fallen to around 25 per cent below the UK average by 2002. Similar differences are also evident for Teesside. Whilst Darlington has, more or less, remained around the UK average, Figure 2.6 shows that Hartlepool & Stockton-on-Tees have slipped from just below the UK average in 1995 to some 20 per cent below this by 2002. In South Teesside, the area was similar to Shropshire in 1995 at circa 20% below the UK average but since that time has a GVA rate approaching only two-thirds of the UK average.

In total, therefore, Figure 2.6 emphasises the marked differences in GVA rates between the areas. Rates in Buckinghamshire were consistently high and, in 1995, were 50 per cent higher than that of Shropshire and South Teesside. By 2002, this differential increased to around 60 per cent for South Teesside. Overall, Teesside has seen a wholesale decline in its GVA rates during the period.

Hand in hand with poor economic outcomes are poor social outcomes. For each of the 354 administrative areas of England, the UK government calculated an index of deprivation based upon income, employment, health, education, housing, crime and the environment. This index showed (source: OPMD, 2004) that each of the five areas of Teesside are within the top 25 per cent of this index. Indeed, two of the areas, Middlesbrough and Hartlepool were ranked 10th and 14th, respectively making them within the top 5 per cent most deprived areas of England. Shropshire, meanwhile, sits in the middle of the distribution whilst Buckinghamshire has amongst the least deprived areas in the whole of England: Chiltern, for example, is ranked 349th out of 354.

## 'In the North but not of the North'

The evidence above, in some senses, simply reflects the regional disparities apparent in the first part of this chapter: if it is sunny in Buckinghamshire, it rains in Shropshire but pours in Teesside. This, however, is a misconception. Consider Figure 2.7. This shows similar information to that presented in Figure 2.6, albeit in terms of GDP per head rather than GVA per head and in terms of the former counties rather than in terms of NUTS 3 areas.

Figure 2.7 clearly shows that there has been a remarkable shift in the fortunes of the three counties. In 1977, Buckinghamshire was 10 per cent below that of the UK average, Teesside (Cleveland) 10 per cent above. Since that time, we have seen the now familiar picture of the economic success of Buckinghamshire and the modest position of

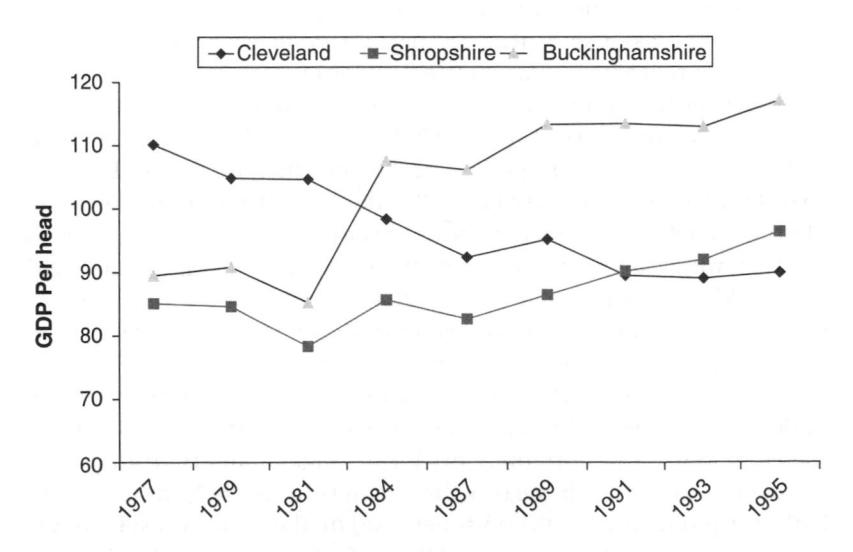

*Figure 2.7*   Three counties GDP per head (UK = 100), 1977–1995.
*Source*: ONS, 2005.

Shropshire. What Figure 2.7, though, shows is that every gain by Buckinghamshire has been matched by a decline in Teesside; the latter has inexorably slipped over the 18-year period from being 10 per cent above the UK average to some 10 per cent below the UK average. This trend, as the earlier Figure 2.6 showed, has continued.

It is, however, intriguing how a seemingly prosperous English county has slipped economically in just over one generation. For the rest of this chapter, the focus is on some of the general reasons for the economic decline of Teesside. This begins by examining a little of its economic history, before turning to the last 30 years.

## The British Ballarat

Teesside cannot claim to have been in the first wave of the Industrial Revolution. That distinction goes to Shropshire which was the site of Abraham Darby's use of coke rather than charcoal for iron smelting in 1709. Indeed, Teesside prior to the 1840s was dominated by the small rural towns of Stockton and Darlington which were to form, in 1825, the world's first public railway, the Stockton to Darlington railway.

This famous railway was designed to carry coal from the Durham coalfields to the sea at Stockton. To build it required an act of Parliament and the raising, then, of £125,000 (around £10 million at current prices) from financiers and industrialists such as the Pease family.

This family was also central to the development of Middlesbrough, Teesside's principal town. Briggs (1963) recounts that, prior to the 1830s, there were only 154 inhabitants in this small hamlet. The Pease family, however, bought the land for £30,000 (roughly £2¼ million) in 1828 and set about transforming it as a port from which to transfer Durham coal to London and elsewhere. By the mid-1840s, Ord described Middlesbrough as 'one of the commercial prodigies of the nineteenth century' whilst another Victorian historian, Ravenstein, documented that Middlesbrough's 'rapid growth, the heterogeneous composition of its population, and the preponderance of the male sex, recall features of the generally credited only to towns of the American West'.

But it was neither coal nor gold but iron ore that really made Middlesbrough seem similar to 'Dodge City' or Australia's Ballarat. In the early 1850s, two entrepreneurs John Vaughan and Henry Bolckow discovered iron ore in the nearby Cleveland Hills. By 1861, the Cleveland Hills was producing ½ million tones and, by the 1870s, Cleveland was producing nearly one-third of the UK's output of iron ore. With iron ore came the development of downstream iron and steel production. In

1860, the number of such furnaces reached 48. Eleven years later in 1871 this number had nearly doubled to 90 furnaces.

Alongside iron and steel production, Teesside quickly gained a significant market share of the world's engineering and shipbuilding industries. For example, by the end of the nineteenth century, Teesside produced one-tenth of the world's merchant shipping tonnage. Such success helped swell the population of Middlesbrough to 91,302 by 1901. In the early part of the twentieth century, Teesside continued to be pre-eminent particularly in bridge building (Victoria Falls, Tyne Bridge and Sydney Harbour Bridge were all built on Teesside). Indeed, even during the depressed inter-war period some 33,000 people were employed producing 1.5 million tons of iron and steel per annum. Also sheltering Teesside from the full impact of the inter-war depression was the development of chemical production in Billingham in 1903. Developments continued apace to the extent that ICI employed 11,000 workers just after the Second World War.

## Modernisation

Between 1950 and 1973, the UK enjoyed its highest rate of GDP growth in peacetime since prior to 1870 (Broadberry and O'Mahony, 2005). It was the 'golden age' (Cairncross and Cairncross, 1992) in which the UK caught up from the privations of the Second World War, enjoyed the stability of Bretton Woods international monetary regime and had an unemployment rate of around 3 per cent.

Teesside shared in this prosperity. Indeed, Teesside was seen as being pivotal to the regeneration of the North East and central to fortunes of the chemical, steel and engineering sectors. Pepler and MacFarlane, in a 1949 report for the UK government suggested that government policy should prevent workers from seeking other employment: "it would be unwise to prejudice the redeployment of Cleveland labour in heavy chemicals by offering it alternative male employment" (p. 76 quoted in Benyon et al., 1994: 60). Similar sentiments were also apparent in the 1960s. The Hailsham Programme for the North East (1963) and the National Plan (1965) both saw Teesside as a growth 'node', capable of leading the transformation of the North East region but, equally, having a clear role in reinvigorating and modernising the UK economy. The population of Teesside, for example, was forecast to grow to 700,000 by the 1990s and to have created an additional 120,000 new jobs.

Huge sums were invested. Already by 1945, the ICI Billingham complex was the world's largest single chemical production complex

(Beynon et al., 1994). ICI set about in the 1950s developing an alternative site at Wilton at the cost of £58 million (around a £1 billion today) which meant employment for around 9,000 workers. Further development occurred in the early 1960s with the opening of a new dock; the development of a huge 2,000 acre site; oil refinery developments both by Shell and BP; and the arrival of Monsanto in 1969 to create their largest non-US chemical plant. By 1976, ICI, alone, employed 23,000 people at its Teesside complex.

The fortunes of the steel industry were more varied. In 1951, steel was nationalised but then privatised two years later only to be returned to the public fold again in 1967. The newly created British Steel Corporation set about rationalising away its inland sites and concentrating upon five giant costal sites. One of these was at Redcar in Teesside which was supposed to become the largest integrated iron and steel production facility in Europe. Government investment was also huge: Robinson (1988) reckoned that fully one-quarter of all regional government grant expenditure was spent in Teesside in the mid 1970s.

All in all, the future of Teesside looked bright. Looking back, a Cleveland County Council report (1985) suggested that Teesside:

> ... was seen to be not only the major economic growth area of the North of England, but one of the most buoyant areas of the United Kingdom, and indeed the whole of Europe ... during the 1970s, the Tees Basin became the largest construction site in Europe ... with over £2,000 million being invested in the chemical, steel and oil industries the area could fairly claim to be Europe's most dynamic industrial centre.

## Economic retrenchment

> But this country cannot stay in the 1919s *[sic]*. It's got to come into the 1980s, it's got to think more about next week's pay packet, it's got to think about the industries for our children. (Margaret Thatcher, 1982)

Teesside may have appeared relatively prosperous in the 1960s and 1970s but, certainly by the mid 1970s, the success it had enjoyed was about to come apart spectacularly. In part, this was because the 1970s were a difficult decade for developed economies like the UK. The collapse of the Bretton Woods system of exchange controls, the quadrupling of oil prices in 1973, an inflation rate of 13.6 per cent (1970–1979), the calling in of the International Monetary Fund, continual industrial disputes (the three day week, the 'winter of discontent') and rising unemployment (1.3 million by 1976) were all symptomatic of ailments that were said to beset 'the sick man of Europe'.

The 1980s began and continued to be a very difficult period for the UK economy. In the late 1970s – early 1980s there was a major recession in the UK. Interest rates rose to 17 per cent in 1979, inflation reached 20 per cent in 1980 and the UK economy contracted by 3.5 per cent in the period 1980–1981. The UK was not alone in this. All of the major industrialised economies experienced a recession during this period due in part to another seismic increase in oil prices in 1979. However, everything changed with the arrival of a new government under Margaret Thatcher in 1979. She was committed to a repudiation of Keynesian demand side policies. Her agenda was to reduce the role of the state and the power of trade unions, to lower taxes and to move Britain away from what she viewed as a 'dependency culture' and instead to create an 'enterprise culture'.

One obvious consequence of her 'macroeconomic adventurism' (Tomlinson, 2004: 204) was a marked growth in unemployment. Although, unemployment had reached 1.3 million in 1976, it dramatically increased over the next seven years: 1½ million in July 1980, 2 million in December 1980, 2½ million by September 1981 and 3 million in January 1983 (about one-in-eight adults). It remained at this level, despite changes to the way unemployment figures were calculated, until March 1987. Unemployment only fell to below 2 million in April 1989.

The impact of unemployment was pernicious on Teesside in the early 1980s. This factor alone does much to explain the dramatic fall in GDP per head evident in Figure 2.7 throughout the 1980s. Bereft of government succour, British Steel curtailed its development plans for the massive Redcar plant. Employment fell from 23,000 in 1978 to around 7,000 in 1984. ICI also cut employment from 23,000 in 1976 to 14,500 in 1985. Beynon et al. (1994) believe that this process was exacerbated by the UK government. Regional grant assistance to Teesside was heavily concentrated upon providing support to both British Steel and ICI. Indeed, these two companies alone received some £153 million or 63 per cent of such assistance over the period 1980–1987 (Wren, 1989). Beynon et al. (1994) suggest that these two companies used this money to substitute capital for labour which meant that whilst productivity increased actual employment declined.

British Steel and ICI were not alone in closing branch plants in Teesside. There were 32 major closures between 1974 and 1985. Over a similar period (1975–1986) one-quarter of all jobs in Teesside were lost

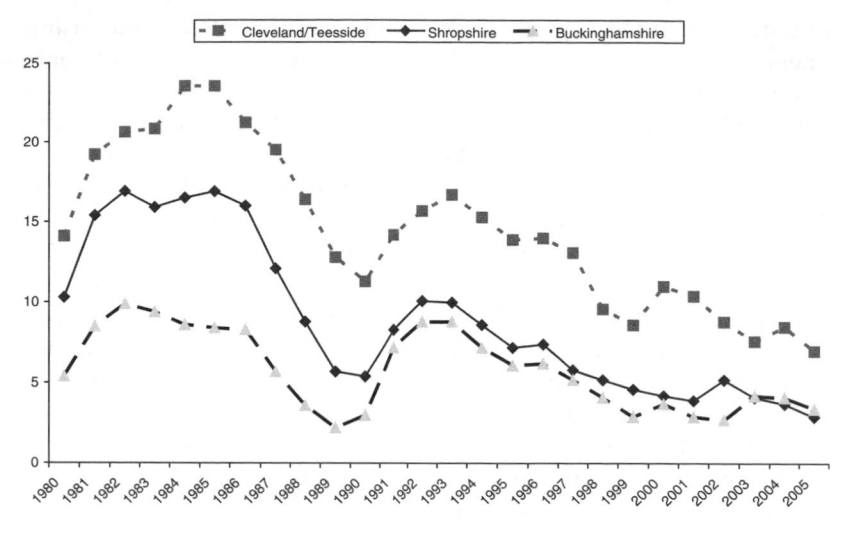

*Figure 2.8*   Unemployment in the three counties, 1980–2005.
*Source*: Employment gazette, various years and Nomis, 2005.

and nearly half of those employed in manufacturing and construction lost their jobs (MacDonald and Coffield, 1991). Indeed, between 1981 and 1984, 18,000 jobs were lost. Unemployment increased from 4.3 per cent in 1974 to 12.3 per cent in 1980 and then on to 23.5 per cent in 1984 (Cleveland County Council, 1985). In some inner city wards, unemployment reached 40 per cent (Beynon et al., 1994).

Teesside has never really recovered from the Thatcher medicine of the early 1980s. Consider Figure 2.8. This shows the official rates of unemployment for each of the three counties, 1980–2005 (figures prior to 1996 refer to the 1974 counties, figures after this refer to the new areas). On the left-hand side, is the percentage unemployment rate. In 1980, this rate stood at 5 per cent in Buckinghamshire, 10 per cent in Shropshire and nearly 15 per cent in Teesside. Such differences persist into the 1990s when the unemployment rates in both Shropshire and Buckinghamshire begin to follow each other much more closely. Teesside, though, has never approached or even come close to that of the other two counties.

A key reason for the high unemployment is the dramatic reduction in the numbers of individuals employed in Teesside's manufacturing industry. Table 2.8 shows that in the period 1971 to 2003, nearly 89,000 jobs or 69 per cent of the 1971 workforce have been lost in manufacturing with a further fifth being lost in construction. Table 2.8 shows that

*Table 2.8* Employees in employment Teesside

|  | 1971 | 1981 | 1991 | 2001 | 2003 | Change 2003 from 1971 | % Change 2003 from 1971 |
|---|---|---|---|---|---|---|---|
| Primary | 8,560 | 9,657 | 3,518 | 4,497 | 4,977 | −3,583 | −41.86 |
| Manufacturing | 128,028 | 85,585 | 60,041 | 39,288 | 39,219 | −88,809 | −69.37 |
| Construction | 21,629 | 18,259 | 20,536 | 15,866 | 16,730 | −4,899 | −22.65 |
| Services | 119,346 | 138,994 | 159,587 | 193,119 | 207,415 | 88,069 | 73.79 |
| Total | 275,592 | 250,514 | 243,681 | 252,768 | 268,341 | −7,251 | −2.63 |

*Source*: TVJSU, 2005.

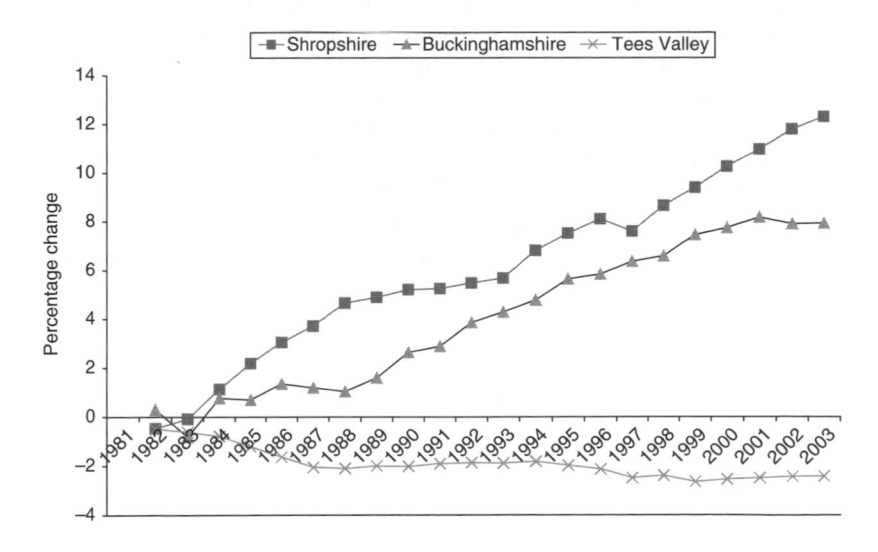

*Figure 2.9* Population change in three counties, 1981–2003.
*Source*: Nomis, 2005.

these jobs have seemingly been replaced by the growth of the service sector which has grown by 88,000 jobs over the period. What this, however, ignores is the quality of very many of these jobs. One of the growth sectors in the Teesside economy has been the advent of call centres through the major banks and other large corporations. Such employment, however, is relatively low skilled and easily transferred to other regions (Richardson et al., 2000).

It is perhaps unsurprising, therefore, that some people in Teesside have tended to 'get on their bike'. Figure 2.9 shows an index of population changes in the three counties (1981 = 100) over the period 1981 to 2003. Over this period, it is clear that Shropshire has seen the biggest growth in population, with Buckinghamshire in close attendance. The Teesside area has continued to lose population since 1981. Recent projections also suggest that by 2021, Teesside will lose a further 3 per cent of its population with an 8 per cent reduction in its working population (TVJSU, 2005).

## Summary

This second part of the chapter has traced the economic evolution of Teesside. Set against Buckinghamshire and, to some extent, Shropshire, Teesside does appear a failing region racked by a weak economy, leaden entrepreneurial performance and unfortunate social outcomes.

The chapter has also shown, though, that this was not always the case. In the 1960s and 1970s, there was tremendous investment in Teesside and real optimism in its ability to rejuvenate not only the North East but contribute favourably to the wider economic growth of the UK. The deep recession of the late 1970s and early 1980s now makes such optimism look rather like a sardonic joke. Teesside's 'mistake' was to rely upon core growth sectors such as steel and chemicals. After this employment went, the Teesside economy has never been able to recover from the shock of the Thatcher medicine intended to 'cure' the patient.

# 3
# Enterprise Policy in the UK

## Introduction

If you stand on Newcastle's train station, in the early evening, you will often see orthodox Jews. Dressed in their sombre suits with their black Homberg hats, you might think that they are just in Newcastle on business. Go again and you might see them there again. This seems incongruous: you might expect to see orthodox Jews in London, but in Newcastle?

According to Loebl (1978), one reason for this was due to the dark days of the 1930s. Persecuted by the Nazis, German Jews sought refuge in Britain. To get in, they were asked four simple questions. The first was *Have you or a family member ever run a business?* The second was *Do you have access to finance?* The third was *Are you willing to start a business?* and the final question was *Are you prepared to go to the North East or another area of high unemployment?* If the refugee was able to answer yes to all four of these questions, they were allowed in.

These four issues – entrepreneurial experience, access to finance, entrepreneurial propensity and geographic mobility – have long dominated the UK's enterprise policy. This chapter charts these developments from the 1930s through to the 2000s. From this, it will be seen that the enterprise policies targeted at smaller enterprises have dramatically grown over this 70-year period. For instance, some £5 million was spent in the 1930s on small enterprise policies. This equates to around £207 million in 2002 prices. In 2001–2002, however, small enterprise policy expenditure had grown to nearly £8 billion.

What this chapter argues is that there have been four main types of (small) enterprise policy over this period. For the bulk of the time (1930s–1970s), there was effectively no small enterprise policy. Instead, what can be broadly seen was a policy akin to that of the dirigiste Gaullism of France. This effectively emphasised support for corporate enterprises. In the 1980s, though, a different path was followed in the UK. Generally, it is possible to discern that the 1980s was a time when entrepreneurship policy equated to increasing the 'quantity' of enterprises in the UK. The third major policy period is the 1990s, which saw attempts to improve the 'quality' of smaller enterprises. The final period suggests that in the years around the new millennium, we have seen a 'balanced portfolio' approach to enterprise policy which balances a focus on increasing start-up activity – particularly amongst those groups that were under-represented amongst the entrepreneurial population – with a concern for improving the competitiveness of enterprises.

Running through this discussion of these four periods, the chapter maps the nature of public support provision in Teesside and the North East of England over the period 1980 to 2006. This exercise identifies the range and type of enterprise support over our four enterprise policy periods. This information is derived from various guides to enterprise support produced either for Teesside or the North East of England. Such information illustrates, in line with these periods, that there have been huge shifts in the nature and intensity of support over the period.

One way of reading these developments is to say that the evolution of enterprise policy from corporate capitalism through to increasing the quantity (1980s), quality (1990s) or adopting a balanced portfolio (2000s), represents a steady maturing of such policies. This is not what the bulk of this chapter demonstrates. Instead, it indicates that virtually every enterprise policy from the tentative and speculative to the targeted and concentrated has been attempted over these four periods. In detailing these various forms of support, the picture that we present is not one where money or effort was necessarily deficient.

One point of this chapter, then, is to provide some context for the empirical evidence on new businesses detailed in Chapters 4 to 9. The second point, dealt with more fully in Chapter 10, is to raise the important point of what form should enterprise support take? It is possible to see this as a spectrum of views, ranging from no involvement, through to governance and then into micro-management. At one end, there is no need for any government intervention. Barnett (1996), for example, argues for junking any policy that impairs the freedom and ability of the free market. For him, the free market should decide and, if this means the suffering of '... species at the end of their evolutionary line, unwilling or unable to adapt' (Barnett, 1996: 323), then so be it.

A little removed from this, is a suggestion that there is a need for governance that allows for the creation of appropriate incentives (either through the regulatory or taxation system) that fosters entrepreneurial propensities. Baumol (1990), for instance, argues that there is rarely a shortage of entrepreneurs. What is lacking in societies which appear to exhibit a shortage is that entrepreneurial individuals do something else from which they gain higher utility than from being a productive entrepreneur. This may mean they become a bureaucrat, a lawyer, a regulator or a gangster/drug dealer and the only way to shift them is to change the rules of the game in such a way as to make these 'occupations' less attractive and make productive entrepreneurship more attractive.

This approach is compatible with policies to raise awareness of, or performance in, entrepreneurship, but not compatible with policies that seek to change attitudes. Classic problems here are poor skills (Chapter 4), limited business strategies (Chapter 5) or access to finance problems (Chapter 7). Support may then be necessary to rectify particular problems or issues faced by entrepreneurs (Chapter 6).

Finally, perhaps at the end of this spectrum, at least in developed economies, is that (state) support is so total that it is more appropriate to talk about an enterprise dependency culture than any free-standing enterprise culture.

The next section of this chapter begins by tracing the first enterprise policy (1930s–1970s) and some of the reasons why it was so prominent until the 1980s. It then looks at the 'radical' departures of the 1980s and argues that, although a seemingly instinctive reaction to the 1970s, UK entrepreneurship policy in this period was a function of political necessity as much as political belief. For the third period (1990s), the concentration on improving the 'quality' of enterprises is traced. This feeds into the fourth period (2000s) but what is distinctive about this period is the influence of endogenous economic growth ideas on (small) enterprise policy.

## The era of corporate enterprise policy: 1930s–1970s

Suppose one part of the economy is depressed. What are the options? The first is to simply ignore the issue in the belief that there is no help like self help or, buttressed by neoclassical economic theory, concur with the view that if a region is depressed it is likely to see its factor costs (land and labour) fall. This will, in turn, attract businesses into depressed areas and bring down any evident regional disparities. Versions of such views have always been held but perhaps never so completely as in the inter-war years (1918–1939).

Such views, though, did struggle in the face of high unemployment rates and wide regional differences (See Chapter 2). For those who were fearful that the UK economy was close to calamity in the 1920s and 1930s, there was also increasing consciousness that those in peripheral areas could not simply be ignored. Fuelled by *The Road to Wigan Pier* (Orwell, 1937), *English Journey* (Priestley, 1938) and *In Search of England* (Morton, 1927), there was a burgeoning sense of the desperate poverty in communities such as Merthyr Tydfil in South Wales where unemployment reached 62 per cent in 1932.

In the 1930s, the two alternatives were either to promote labour mobility or provide incentives for businesses to locate in these areas. The UK government tried both of these approaches in the 1930s. First, the Industrial Transference Board was set up in 1928 to relocate unemployed workers to the more prosperous parts of the UK and the 'colonies'. The Board managed to relocate some 200,000 individuals by 1938.

The second option was inducements. One form of financial sweetener was the Special Areas Act (1934) which sought to alleviate the plight of four particularly depressed areas: Clydeside (Scotland); South Wales; Durham and Tyneside; and West Cumberland (Cumbria). Support largely revolved around improvements to the infrastructure (e.g. reclaiming derelict land), incentives for businesses to move to the depressed areas or, in terms of small business policy, the creation of the Special Areas Reconstruction Association (SARA) which was a loan fund designed to support small enterprises. SARA, as Scott (2000) and Wren (1996) relate, had £1 million at its disposal. SARA was not the only such scheme. The Nuffield Trust provided £2 million for businesses that were seeking to create employment in depressed areas. A third fund, the Treasury Fund, was set up in 1937, again with £2 million and, again, with a specific remit to maximize employment creation.

Such policies can be judged as being largely ineffectual. Given the size of the unemployment problem, it was very unlikely that the limited nature of the Industrial Transference Board or the spatial narrowness of the four special areas would have much of an impact on general unemployment. In any case, the Second World War intervened.

The war allowed, strange though it may seem, pause for reflection. Two key reports (the Beveridge Report, 1942 and the Barlow Report, 1944) reflected the determination to move away from the deprivations of the inter-war period. The rationale, derived from the bitter experiences of the 1930s, was that evident economic disparities, either in terms of unemployment or income, produce poor economic outcomes. Low employment levels equate to lower levels of national demand. The key in the post-war period was to manage demand so that both sales (output) and employment were maximised. Post-war governments, armed with the general sense of running a successful war time economy, believed in of government intervention. Whole industries were subsequently nationalised. Starting in 1946, airlines were taken into public ownership, followed by telecommunications and coal (1947), electricity, buses, ports and railways (1948) and gas (1949) (see Hannah, 2004 for a fuller view of nationalisation).

There were also sustained attempts to redress evident regional imbalances in the UK. After the war, the onus was on telling manufacturers where they could locate their plants; providing tax allowances on capital depreciation to encourage investment; and setting up schemes to support small businesses (the Industrial and Commercial Finance Corporation) or large businesses in new industries (Finance Corporation for Industry). Wren (1996) shows that such support varied according to prevailing economic conditions. For example, the mild recession of the late 1950s saw direct involvement in supporting ailing industries such as shipbuilding and steel. Reconstruction aid was also given to other industries like cotton to help rationalise the industry. Further support was provided to the aircraft industry in the form of 'Launching Aid'. The scale of such support rose quickly and by the mid 1970s, £747million had been spent by the UK government.

The halcyon days of these interventions, however, were the late 1960s. Wren (1996) estimates that 'direct subsidy payments to private firms amounted to five per cent of national output at their peak in the late 1960s' (p. 1). A blizzard of regional planning policies were introduced and extended during this period. Nine new towns were introduced, there was the redrawing of 'assisted areas' to take in the 40 per cent of the land mass of Great Britain (Scotland, Wales, Northern Ireland, Merseyside, Cumbria, the North East, Yorkshire, Cornwall and North Devon), a considerable increase in sectoral subsidies; employment premiums designed to subsidise jobs in depressed areas; and investment incentives.

One dominant leitmotiv of this period was an emphasis on the 'white heat of technology'. Here enterprise policy was delivered by a newly created Ministry of Technology which sought to shift the balance away from Research & Development expenditure in military projects and towards civilian projects. The emphasis was on 'big science' whether this was in atomic energy, aviation, 'bridgehead industries' such as machine tools, computers, electronics or telecommunications (Edgerton, 1996). Alongside this, another recurring theme was for the UK to reach the 'commanding heights' by direct intervention. Picking winners, therefore, meant spatial specialisation and rationalisation in particular sectors (e.g. steel and chemicals) to ensure that UK businesses were large enough to compete against the 'giants' of the United States and (West) Germany.

Merger activity was particularly intense with the UK government, through the Industrial Reorganisation Corporation, taking an active involvement in supporting the increased size of British businesses. For example, the merger of Leyland Motors and British Motor Holdings into the ill-fated British Leyland was supported with a government loan of £25 million pounds in 1968 (about £290 million in 2005 prices).

Equally symptomatic was the provision of public subsidies to established businesses wishing to open or transfer factories in deprived areas. Fothergill and Guy (1990), estimate there were some 5,100 inter-regional moves, involving some 800,000 jobs, over the period 1945–1980.

This emphasis upon increased business size to reap economies of scale left little room for the smaller enterprise. There was a seeming consensus that the market was dead, replaced by the 'visible hand of managerial direction' (Chandler, 1992: 95). Illustrating this was the decline in the number of small manufacturing businesses from 136,000 in 1938 to just 58,000 by 1968: a fall of nearly 60 per cent (Bannock, 1981). Small enterprises were seen, despite the efforts of the Bolton Report (1971), as being 'inimical to progress and professionalism' (Boswell, 1973: 19) or run by individuals at the margins of society (Stanworth and Curran, 1973). Indeed, even the Bolton Report suggested that the actual contribution of smaller enterprises had remained static whilst total output in manufacturing had increased by a quarter (1958–1963).

The wholesale intervention of the UK government in the 1950s and 1960s did not last the 1970s. The early 1970s saw the first efforts by a UK government to deregulate the UK economy. The Heath government (1970–1973) sought, for example, to reduce regional assistance expenditure (Figure 3.1). This was not to last. The UK economy was beset by labour market rigidities (trade unions), poor levels of investment, weak management, stagnant growth, rising costs (the oil shocks of 1973 and 1979) and the ignominy of having to call in the International Monetary Fund in 1976. Such general ailments did little to curtail regional spending: indeed, the 1970s saw sustained public expenditure of circa £10 billion (at 1995 prices) over the five-year period 1974–1976.

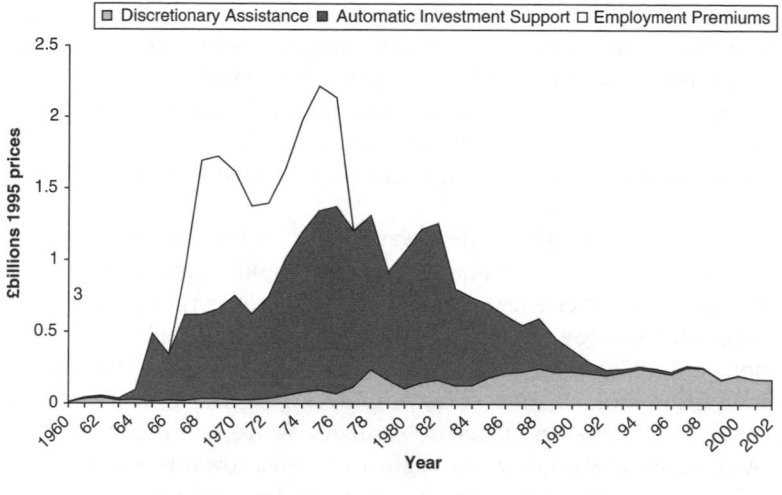

*Figure 3.1* Expenditure on regional industrial assistance, 1960–2002.
*Source*: Wren 2003.

Support for smaller enterprises, however, did begin to emerge during the 1970s. At a national level, and following the Bolton Report (1971), there was an increased recognition of the 'uneven playing field' faced by smaller enterprises. As Johnson (2005) suggests, these arguments have long revolved around three aspects where policy makers have felt that small enterprises are discriminated against (see Bolton, 1971). The first of these is imperfect competition which can prevent market entry through the exercising of monopoly power. New small enterprises, therefore, may require support to ease their entry into new markets.

A second issue is the presence of information asymmetries which may prevent the smaller enterprise from getting appropriate levels of support. In the 1970s, this was tackled, following on from the Bolton Report's recommendation, by creating a Small Firms Service which had centres and area counselling offices to signpost and support the information needs of post start-up enterprises (Wren, 1996). Also, information asymmetries have long been thought to be most acute in small enterprise finance where – because of the difficulties and cost of distinguishing between good and bad investments – banks are often said to under-supply finance to smaller enterprises. In response to this, the Wilson Committee (1979) was set up to investigate, amongst other things, mechanisms for bridging the 'finance gap' through the provision of loan guarantee and investment incentive schemes.

The third issue is that in any economy there are likely to be externalities. These are the unintended (unpriced) consequences of private (business) activity on social (usually consumers) activities. Typically, these externalities come in two forms: negative externalities which may be the cost to society of a chemical producer (pollution). Alternatively, externalities may be positive. For example, the invention and commercialisation of penicillin provided greater benefits to society than that which accrued to the original businesses involved in the production and distribution of the drug.

By the end of the 1970s there was a view – albeit held only by a minority of people – that smaller enterprises could be pivotal to creating jobs since the experience of the 1970s was that corporate enterprises effectively took government subsidies to substitute capital for labour. Appleyard (1978) in the *Times* suggested, for instance, that 'if all Britain's small firms took on one extra employee something over a million people would be taken off the dole queues overnight' (p. 16).

A small business policy did begin to emerge towards the end of the 1970s. Besides the creation of a Minister for Small Firms and the Small Firms Service, Beesley and Wilson (1984) charted an increased pace of government intervention. In the period 1946–70, there were only 15 state interventions to support small enterprises: this compares with 15 between 1971 and 1975; and a further 18 between 1976 and 1981.

On the ground, this translated into a modest supply of support to smaller enterprises in Teesside/the North East of England in 1980. What Figure 3.2 shows is that, based upon the guide the DTI's *Aid for Enterprise* (1980) and Storey (1980), there were 19 providers of support. These were split between eight local providers (to Teesside), seven regional providers (the North East) and four national providers of support. The main national providers were the Confederation of British Industry, the Council of Small Industries in Rural Areas (CoSIRA), the Department of Industry (forerunner to the DTI) and British Steel who set up a scheme in 1975 to support the transition of former steel workers into self-employment.

Both locally and regionally, the vast bulk of the initiatives – whether this was to pre or post start-ups or in terms of soft (guidance, advice, counselling) or hard support (grants, loans, capital allowances) – were provided by the councils or government-sponsored agencies designed to promote regional development. Thirty-five initiatives were available, with the vast bulk of these, save local self help groups (Teesside Small Business Club or the local Chamber of Commerce) being publicly resourced grants from central government. Similarly, Figure 3.2 shows that the focus of much of this support was on post start-up enterprises. Indeed, only three providers (CoSIRA, British Steel and DUBS) offered any hard support to pre start-up enterprises.

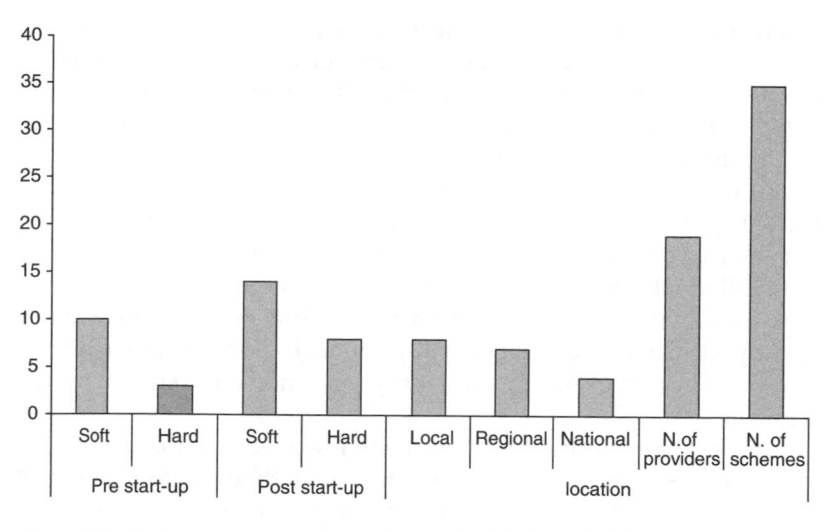

*Figure 3.2*  Enterprise support providers and initiatives, 1980.

## Enterprise policy in the 1980s: the rise of the smaller enterprise

The essence of the previous section was that successive UK governments throughout the post-war period indulged in increasingly more futile attempts to manage the UK economy. The emphasis was on 'picking winners' from amongst the UK's corporate enterprises in the hope that these larger businesses would be big enough to compete with the economies of scale enjoyed by European and US competitors. There was no real policy towards smaller enterprises either to correct any market failures or to encourage entrepreneurial aspirations. By the end of the 1970s, it was evident that such policies had failed.

We now turn to the ways in which the British government of the 1980s sought to reignite entrepreneurial capacity. Prior to examining these policy interventions, it is first of all worth noting two points.

First, it would be unwise to suggest that the election of the first Thatcher administration in 1979 constituted a seismic shift away from past policies. For example, the earlier Conservative administration under Prime Minister Edward Heath in the early 1970s could be, in some senses, described as being more 'Thatcherite' in its aims and orientation. Second, ideas do not come from nowhere. In the late 1970s, there was a general sense that smaller enterprises could be the real motor of recovery. One illustration of this was the publication of an influential report by Birch in 1979 which suggested that smaller enterprises provided the vast majority of new jobs in the United States. Whilst such results were subsequently queried on methodological grounds both by Armington and Odle (1982) and Storey and Johnson (1986, 1987), Birch (1979) chimed with a view of the importance of the small business (Appleyard, 1978).

This was particularly true for key intellectuals within the Conservative Party. They regarded the industrial sclerosis of UK manufacturing as being best resolved by a return to free-enterprise fundamentals. Central to this is the intellectual promptings of economists such as von Hayek, the Institute of Economic Affairs and the Centre for Policy Studies. All sought a return to the principles of economic liberalism through the promotion of the efficacy of free markets, sound money and non-intervention in the economy.

Two illustrations will suffice. First, Keith Joseph, chastened by the trade union induced defeat of the Heath government in the early 1970s, switched from a belief in the power of government intervention to a belief, like Aladdin, that all we had to do was to rub the magic lamp and the genie of enterprise would be forthcoming (Joseph, 1976). So, when Joseph did get into power as the Minister for the Department of Industry (what was formerly the DTI and is now the Department for Business, Enterprise and Regulatory Reform), he had two aims. The first was to enthuse his civil servants by asking them to read his work and that of other free-enterprise thinkers. His second aim was to encourage them to think of ways in which they could effectively do themselves out of a job.

The second major rider on any claim that an enterprise culture was either born or regained in the 1980s is that the Conservative government continued to intervene quite extensively in many areas of the economy. For example, labour market 'rigidities' were attacked. The rights of unions to enforce 'closed shops' (where all workers had to be unionised) was removed, as was, secondary picketing and wildcat strikes. The privatisation of the utilities (e.g. gas, electricity, telecommunications) was also designed to increase product market competition by changing the boundaries of ownership so that such utilities were managed by the private sector rather than the government. Privitization also had the benefit of raising some £33 billion (Economist, 1990).

Such money was sorely needed since the early 1980s saw some of the most miserable economic indicators of the century: inflation stood at 18 per cent (1980); the economy contracted by 3.35 per cent (CSO, 1981: GDP at market prices change average of 4 quarters – 1980/1981); interest rates stood at 16 per cent (October, 1980); labour productivity fell by nearly 4 per cent; and gross domestic capital formation fell by nearly

6 per cent. The biggest change, however, was in unemployment. In July 1980, unemployment stood at 1½ million. Five months later (December 1980), unemployment was more than 2 million. It subsequently reached 2½ million by September 1981 and 3 million in January 1983. It remained at this level, despite over 30 changes to the way unemployment figures were calculated, until March 1987.

Faced with such figures, it is perhaps unsurprising that besides attempts to remove product and labour market rigidities, the Thatcher administration actually increased regional expenditure in the early 1980s (see Figure 3.1 above). This was not the only cost. Figure 3.3 shows the cost of unemployment payments, 1980–2004. Expressed in terms of GDP, Figure 3.3 shows that unemployment payments represented 0.6 per cent of GDP in 1979–1980. Two years later, this had doubled and a further two years later (1984–1985) it reached 1.6 per cent of GDP. Indeed, there was vast expenditure on unemployment payments throughout the 1980s: the total amount spent, in 2004–2005 prices was nearly £94 billion.

Unemployment payments were not the only form of transfer payment either to poorer areas or to poorer individuals. For example, building on the previous Labour government's 'new deal for the young unemployed', (Youth Opportunities Programme (YOP)), the Conservative government sought to massively increase youth training. For example, in 1979–1980, about 200,000 young people were on YOP. The following year, this

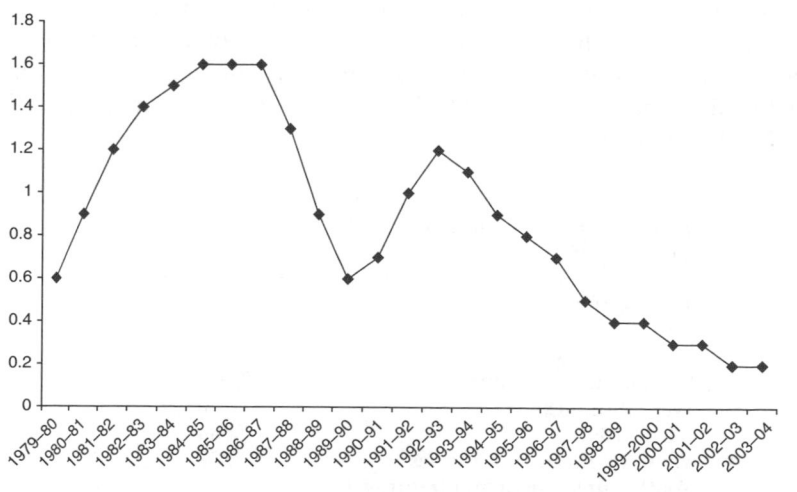

*Figure 3.3*   Cost of unemployment payments as a percentage of GDP, 1979–2004.
*Source*: Hansard, written answer, Tuesday, 7 September 2004.

increased to 360,000. In the two subsequent years, over half a million young people participated, so that there were actually more young people (aged 16–17) on YOP than in work. YOP's replacement, the Youth Training Scheme (YTS) was also a mass training scheme for young people. In its six years of existence (it was replaced by Youth Training in April 1990) the number of young people on the scheme never fell below 370,000. Indeed, the numbers were generally higher than this, peaking at 420,000 in 1986–1987. In other words youth training, once the province of industry (apprenticeships), was effectively nationalised.

The cost of this was prodigious. Based upon Wren (1996) figures, the total cost of these youth employment and training programmes was £8.3 billion over the decade. Table 3.1 also shows that the government continued to intervene heavily in the provision of regional assistance (£6.5 billion). A further £2.4 billion was given to shipbuilding and labour supply reduction programmes (e.g. encouraging early retirement), respectively. £7.8 billion was also spent on job creation schemes over the 1980s. The vast bulk of this money (nearly £6.5 billion) went to the Community Programme which was a scheme designed to allow unemployed individuals the opportunity to work on schemes to improve the environment of their locality.

Wren (1996) also indicates that considerable sums were spent on various other initiatives. For instance, between 1978 and 1991, some £1.7 billion (current prices) was spent on urban policy measures (mostly the Urban Programme and Urban Development Corporations) and the DTI spent £822 million on industrial innovation programmes between 1981/82 and 1987/88. Membership of the EU also brought considerable financial support between 1980/88: some £4.2 billion in loans and £4.7 billion in grants.

*Table 3.1* Cost of subsidies, 1979/80 to 1989/90 in £m (current prices)

| Type of subsidy | £m in current prices |
| --- | --- |
| Regional assistance | 6,588 |
| Shipbuilder's assistance | 2,383 |
| Wage subsidies | 100 |
| Job creation | 7,884 |
| Youth recruitment subsidies | 220 |
| Youth employment and training | 8,331 |
| Labour supply reduction | 2,441 |
| Total | 34,888 |

The level of such spending is important because it places into context the efforts made to create an enterprise culture in the 1980s. Wren (1996) identifies that there were four main enterprise measures in that decade. The most important of these was the Enterprise Allowance Scheme. This was introduced in 1983 and gave unemployed people a payment of £40 a week for a year. The numbers on the scheme steadily increased year-on-year, reaching a peak of 106,000 in 1987–1988. In total, during the lifespan of EAS (1983–1991), 565,700 people made use of it at a direct cost (cost of benefits) of £1,177 million.

Albeit radical and innovative, it would be misleading to think that the EAS was more than an updated form of job creation. For example, the original idea for the EAS came from Lord Vinson who thought it a mechanism 'to legitimise moonlighting' (quoted in Cockett, 1994: 301). EAS also had other benefits: it cost little or no more than unemployment benefit; there was a possibility that the business may take off and create further employment; and, once on the EAS, individuals no longer counted towards the unemployment total.

The second main scheme, launched in Chancellor Geoffrey Howe's 1980 budget was Enterprise Zones. These were urban areas in which capital tax allowance and development tax relief was offered. This cost, between 1981/91, at current prices, some £301 million. The third scheme, to overcome any finance gaps faced by smaller enterprises, was the Small Firm Loan Guarantee Scheme. This cost £271 million (1981/91). The fourth main scheme was the Business Expansion Scheme which was designed to give full qualifying tax relief on investments in new unquoted companies. Such stimulation cost £543 million over the ten-year period. In total, these schemes cost £2,292 million. In context, if the ten-year period saw some £34,888 million spent on subsidies of one sort or another (Table 3.1), the total expenditure on small enterprise policies only represented about 6.6 per cent of such spending.

For all the talk then of the enterprise culture (e.g. Gibb, 1987; Keat, 1990; Ritchie, 1991; and Carr, 2000), much of the enterprise policy of the 1980s appears a victory of style over substance. At best, there was an increased awareness of the entrepreneurial option. For a politician – interested in avoiding the gloomy unemployment figures, the transparent futility of schemes like Community Enterprise or downplaying the huge transfer payments to depressed regions – the entrepreneurial option represented an opportunity to recast the UK. Nowhere is this rhetoric better expressed than by Margaret Thatcher herself:

I came into office with one deliberate intent: to change Britain from a dependent to a self-reliant society – from a give-it-to-me to a do-it yourself nation. A get-up-and-go, instead of a sit-back-and wait-for-it Britain. This means creating a new culture – an enterprise culture – which accords a new status to the entrepreneur and offers him the rewards to match; which breeds a new generation of men and women who create jobs for others instead of waiting for others to create jobs for them. (Thatcher, 1984: 11)

Such DIY capitalism was reflected in attempts to reduce the distance between the world of work and education (e.g. 'Compacts' between schools and business, Mini Enterprise in Schools Project and Enterprise Awareness in Teacher Education) and a range of not-for-profit schemes designed to encourage new start-ups (e.g. Prince's Trust, Local Enterprise Agencies).

Earlier in Figure 3.2, it was shown that there were 19 providers and 35 initiatives born out of the efforts in the 1970s to support smaller enterprises in Teesside. This position had already begun to change by the early 1980s. Using information from the DTI guide *Sources of Assistance to Small Firms in the North East of England* (1982) and Spicer and Pegler's *Financing your Business in the North East* (1983), it is possible to establish that the number of support providers had increased from 19 to 24. Many of these had existed in 1980 (e.g. the local authorities, Durham University Business School British Steel, CoSIRA), but there were also new providers. The biggest difference, however, is in the proliferation of initiatives: up from 35 initiatives to 125. Moreover, whilst the support for post start-up enterprises still dominated, Figure 3.4 clearly shows an increased impetus behind pre start-up support.

The nature and intensity of support, however, had changed markedly by the end of the 1980s. Figure 3.5 is based upon three other more contemporaneous guides: the DTI's *Sources of Assistance to Small Firms in the North East of England* (1988c); CCVS's *Community Enterprise Directory* (Teesside) (1988); and the county council's *Financial Assistance in Cleveland* (1989). Based upon these guides, Figure 3.5 shows that the number of support providers had increased from 19 in 1980 to 68 by the end of the decade. Equally, the number of initiatives for smaller enterprises had increased to 279. Over the decade, then, there had nearly been a ten-fold increase in the number of initiatives designed to support smaller enterprises.

Figure 3.5 also shows that the balance of support had also changed. Although the guides upon which this identification of support provid-

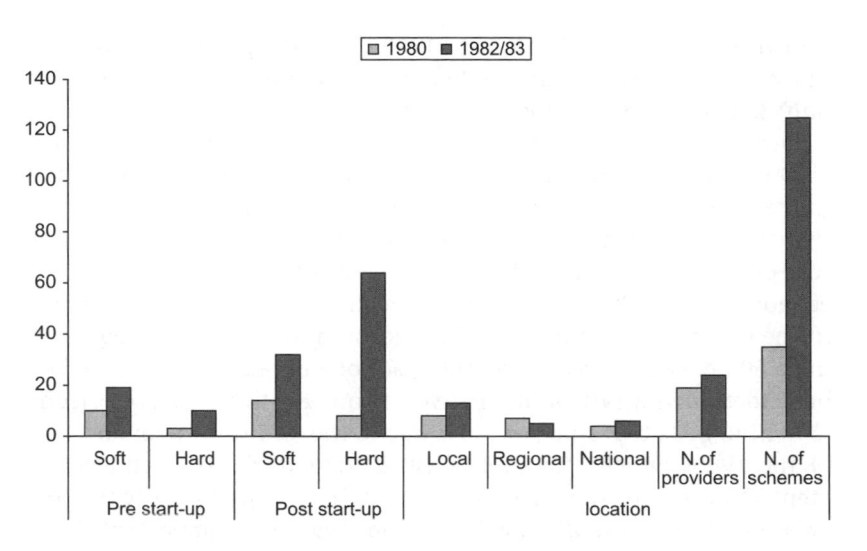

*Figure 3.4*   Enterprise support providers and initiatives, 1980–1982/83.

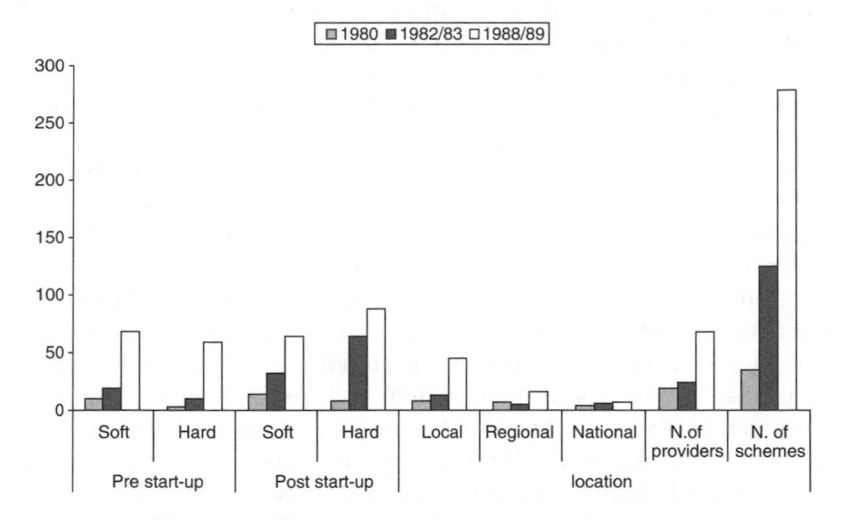

*Figure 3.5*   Enterprise support providers and initiatives, 1980–1988/89.

ers and initiatives are likely to be incomplete, Figure 3.5 shows that the provision of support and initiatives had tilted much more towards local initiatives. Similarly, even though one of the publications – *Financial Assistance in Cleveland* – is specifically about hard support, it is discernable from Figure 3.5 that the balance between support for pre start-up and post start-up enterprises had changed over the period. Indeed, 46 per cent of the initiatives in the late 1980s were designed to focus upon individuals seeking to start-up their own business. This compares with only 23 per cent of initiatives in 1982/83.

Such evidence chimes in with the evidence of Curran and Blackburn (2000). They argue that there were some 103 national policy initiatives in the 1980s focussed on small enterprises. It is tempting here to assert that there is a close union between the discernable increase in policy support and the increased number of small businesses in the UK economy in the 1980s. There were, after all, only 2.4 million enterprises in the UK in 1980 but by 1989 this had risen to 3.6 million, representing a 50 per cent increase over the space of a decade. Others, however, have identified a raft of alternative reasons for this increase. Greene (2005) suggests that some of it was due to the rampant unemployment of the 1980s which effectively pushed individuals into self-employment. Others argue that macro-economic changes, particularly the slow or negative rate of GDP growth (Robson, 1996) were important. Shutt and Whittington (1987), along with Harrison (1994) believe that much of the growth in the enterprise population was due to the activities of larger businesses who wished to transfer the risks of a more uncertain environment on to smaller enterprises. Indeed, Hart and Hanvey (1995) argued that the activities of larger enterprises were entwined with the fortunes of their smaller counterparts.

Keeble et al. (1992) and Bryson et al. (1997) argued instead, that an important factor determining the rise in the enterprise population was the growth of the service sector: Curran and Blackburn, (1991), for instance, point to the absence of economies of scale in many service operations. It may also be explained by technological change (Acs et al., 1991) since the 1980s saw the introduction of new technologies (e.g. computer aided design, robots), organisation processes (e.g. 'just in time') and management techniques (e.g. total quality management) which allowed enterprises to operate at lower optimal sizes (Acs and Audretsch, 1990). Along with this 'de-scaling', (smaller sized optimal plants), new technologies allowed for greater flexibility (Kaplinsky, 1990). This meant it became possible to produce smaller batches of manufactured goods much more efficiently (Carlsson, 1989). Fraser and Greene (2004, 2006) found in their analysis of British Social Attitude surveys of the 1980s an increased level of optimism: '... rates of optimism are high and uncertainty in self-employment choices is rising in the 1980s ... The empirical analysis also lends support to the popular view that entrepreneurship in the

Thatcher era was driven predominantly by the prospect of financial gain' (2004: 29).

The evidence here, therefore, suggests that the quantity of smaller enterprises increased in the 1980s for a combination of reasons that comprised both stereotypes of that decade – the brooding 'giz a job' and the euphoric 'loads-a-money' mentalities. It is much harder, however, to find evidence that government interest in new small enterprises was directly responsible for the increased number of UK enterprises in the 1980s. Nonetheless, if the policy objective was to increase the number of smaller enterprises in the UK economy, this objective was achieved.

This, however, tells us nothing about whether such policies were reflected in the attributes of new businesses (Chapters 4 to 7) or the outcomes they experienced (Chapters 8 and 9). For the moment, though, the emphasis is on continuing to chart the evolution of UK enterprise policy by considering the 'quality' era of the 1990s.

## Enterprise policy in the 1990s: down quality street?

If the focus of enterprise policy in the 1980s was upon increasing the quantity of smaller enterprises, then the following decade sees an important change. The 1990s it is argued is a decade marked by an emphasis on improving the quality of new and small enterprises.

The roots of this suggestion rest in the 1980s policy environment. In the late 1980s, one early signal of the shift in enterprise policy was the White Paper (Cm. 278) *DTI – the Department of Enterprise* (1988a). This represented a return to traditional UK concerns with the 'productivity gap' between the UK and OECD competitors (particularly the US and Germany) and the continued need to open markets, deregulate and privatise. In terms of enterprise policy, what was distinct was the need for an 'Enterprise Initiative' that would overcome market failures in the provision of support and advice to smaller enterprises. The DTI wanted a 'national quality campaign' (p. 14) that sought to increase the use of consultancy services by SME owner/managers so that, fundamentally, they were better able to manage their business.

Central to this was the Consultancy Initiative which ran from 1988 to 1994 at a cost of £275 million (see Wren and Storey, 2002). Alongside this, there was the 'Managing into the '90s' programme launched in 1989 which sought to improve the provision of business services to smaller enterprises. Aiding this shift towards the support of existing businesses was the changing macro-economic environment. After the 'feast' of the boom of the mid-to-late 1980s, the UK returned to the famine of a short and very sharp recession in the early 1990s. There were also doubts about any strategy focused solely upon start-ups. In simple arithmetic terms, it was difficult to see how new small enterprises could effectively replace the jobs shed by larger enterprises. Robinson (1988) suggests that

> To replace the 16,000 redundancies in BSC [British Steel] on Teesside since 1976 would require the creation of between two-and-a-half thousand new businesses in the county, of which nearly 1,500 would not survive anyway (and half of these would fail within two or three years). (p. 101).

Besides the established evidence of the high failure rates of new enterprises (see: Mata and Portugal, 1994; Nucci, 1999; and Headd, 2003), other concerns about deadweight and displacement were also evident. Schemes such as the Enterprise Allowance Scheme were shown to attract people who would have started without financial assistance (deadweight). Similarly, displacement effects were pronounced. What the EAS's subsidy of £40 a week for a year gave individuals was the opportunity to displace existing businesses. These 'survivors' would then either exit when their subsidy came to an end or be faced by another cohort of individuals who would subsequently displace them because they had access to the subsidy. In effect, a high rate of business churn (entry and exit) had little impact on productivity (prosperity).

Such views are confirmed by the empirical evidence of van Stel and Storey (2004) who examined the relationship between new business formation rates and subsequent (lagged) employment change. What they found was that there was no positive link between new business formation rates in low enterprise areas and employment creation in the 1980s. Their second finding was that Scotland – which followed a business birth rate strategy in the 1990s (Scottish Enterprise, 1993) – failed to raise its business birth rates (Fraser of Allander Institute, 2001).

Supporting the new found policies were two changes in the governance arrangements of enterprise policy. The first of these was the replacement of centrally determined enterprise support (Manpower Services Commission) by tailored local support delivered by Training and Enterprise Councils (TECs) in England and Wales and Local Enterprise Companies in Scotland (Deakin and Edwards, 1993). This occurred in 1989. The changes to Training/Local Enterprise Companies were seemingly radical:

they were companies limited by guarantee; employer led; sought to be responsive to local needs; and contract, rather than grant, funded (see: Vickerstaff and Parker, 1995; Bennett, 1995; Bennett and Robson, 2003).

The second main initiative in the early 1990s, was the introduction of the 'Business Links' concept. This began with six pilot areas in April 1993. To aid the development of these bodies, which were often partnerships between the TECs, Chamber of Commerce and Local Enterprise Agencies, some £53.8 million was spent setting them up and a further £412m on operationalising them. In total, by 1998, some 83 Business Link partnerships and 240 outlets were created. What was new about the programme is that they sought to develop on from earlier programmes (e.g. the Consultancy Initiative) by offering a single point of contact for smaller enterprises and, crucially, by offering the services of 'Personal Business Advisors' (PBAs).

These PBAs were there to encourage the growth and development of existing enterprises: 'There was also to be a shift in emphasis from start-ups and micro-businesses towards established businesses with the potential to grow' (Trade and Industry Select Committee, 1996: xi).

Indeed, perhaps for the first time, there was an explicit DTI target. The explicit target was to concentrate on businesses with between 10 and 200 employees which had the potential to grow.

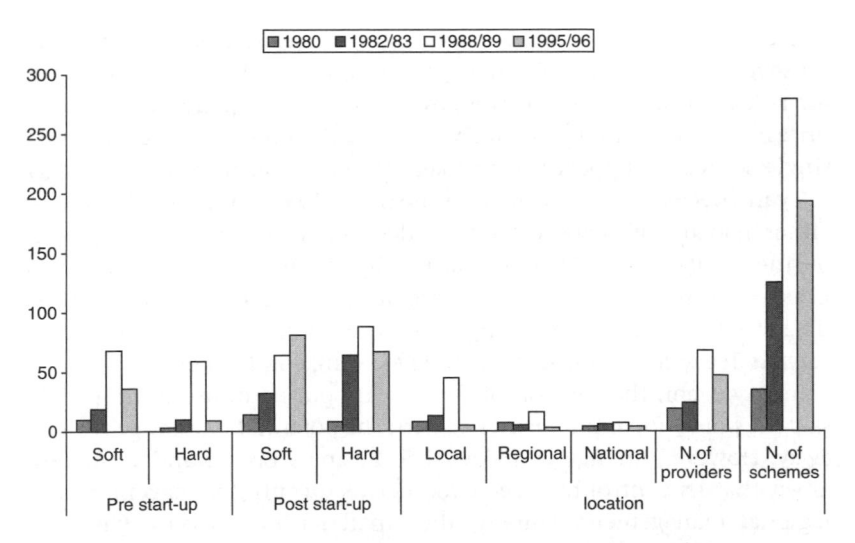

*Figure 3.6*  Enterprise support providers and initiatives, 1980–1995/96.

We can begin to measure the effect of any such transitions from a quantity to a quality-based approach by considering two guides: the DTI's *A Guide to Help for Small Firms* (1995) and *Business Link Teesside: Directory of Business Services* (1996). Again, these two guides are illustrative (see Figure 3.6) and we do not claim these to be a census of business support in Teesside/the North East of England.

Figure 3.6 shows, for the first time since 1980, there was a contraction in the number of small enterprise support organisations in Teesside. Nonetheless, of the 47 identifiable support providers, there were still 14 partners and 22 service providers involved in Teesside Business Link. Equally, although there was a decline in both the number of providers (down from a peak of 68 in 1988/89) and support initiatives (down from 297 in 1988/89), Figure 3.6 does show some 197 initiatives available in 1994/95. Whilst this is a clear reduction it can hardly be described as a 'one stop shop'. This is important because one of the main aims of the policies of the 1990s was to concentrate support in the hands of a few providers so as to minimise the confusion of multiple provision of such support. Nonetheless, Figure 3.6 does demonstrate a rebalancing of support towards post start-up enterprises. Indeed, the relative level of soft and hard support given to pre start-up enterprises fell to 23 per cent. This is equivalent to the 1982/83 percentage level.

## The balanced portfolio: New Labour's approach

The explicit emphasis upon growing businesses did not survive long for several reasons. First, Bennett (1996) complained that it was difficult for risk neutral agents like the government to properly advise enterprises when they took no equity stake in the enterprise. Second, one single source of support was unlikely to supply business with all their relevant needs (Forum of Private Business, 1996); and the PBAs were either inadequately experienced or failed to identify and support growth businesses (Sear and Agar, 1996). Finally, because TECs and Business Links were supposed to be localised forms of support, it was just as likely that instead of supporting growing enterprises, the focus in areas such as Teesside was on safeguarding existing employment.

In any event, the election of the first Labour administration in 1997 saw the policy focus on businesses with the potential to grow gently ebb away. However, change was slow. The Business Link brand continues, albeit that its control has see-sawed between central management and regional management. Equally, the Small Business Service (SBS) did begin to see a role for itself in providing strategic direction and guidance to enterprise policy. Indeed, in line with other government policy throughout the late 1990s and 2000s, there has been a general explosion in the number of targets that government wishes to meet. SBS (2004), for example, identified 21 'key measures' amongst its 'seven pillars' of enterprise policy.

Principally, this is because the UK government returned to the issue of productivity ("making markets work better" – DTI, 1998: 11) rather than focus on creating jobs to limit the economic and social impact of unemployment. Hence, besides the emphasis on macro-economic stability, there has also been the usual raft of new regulations either to remove market imperfections (Competition Act, 1998) or to reduce regulation burdens (e.g. changes to insolvency law).

Other features, derived from the 1980s, still also remain. The Small Firm Loan Guarantee Scheme persists and, by 2005, had guaranteed £4 billion worth of loans. So, too, do schemes such as Shell STEP (a programme encouraging undergraduates to spend 8 weeks in a small business) Shell Livewire, the Prince's Trust and the various iterations of attempts to increase graduate entrepreneurship (Enterprise in Higher Education, Science Enterprise Challenge, National Council for Graduate Entrepreneurship). Indeed, judging from the 2002 review of small business expenditure (DTI/HM Treasury, 2002) the sense is that government whether national, regional or local, has always been heavily involved in enterprise policy. This review suggested that some £8 billion was spent on smaller enterprises in 2001/02. More recent figures (Table 3.2) suggest that this has increased to £10.3 billion by 2003/04. This is more than was spent on policing in the UK during this period. Of this, some £2.4 billion (Table 3.2) is related to agricultural businesses. A further £3.6 billion went on tax credits whilst another £1.7 billion was spent by the Learning and Skills Council. In essence, enterprise support is skewed to particular sectors (agriculture) and is largely in the form either the provision of financial or skills support.

It is also incorrect to think that enterprise support is either delivered or even formulated by the ministry charged with industrial policy (the Department of Trade and Industry or what became the Department for Business, Enterprise and Regulatory Reform). Although the DTI appears to have the single biggest budget of any government department (£425 million), it is evident that the Department of Environment, Food and Rural Affairs (£297 million), the Department for Culture, Media and Sport (£336 million) Department of Work & Pensions/Job Centre Plus (£331 million) all play a significant spending role. Even when the Small Business Service (£271 million) is added to the Department of Trade and Industry budget of £425 million, this only totals £696 million which is 17.7 per cent of the total for Central Government Programme Budgets or

*Table 3.2*   Support for smaller enterprises in 2003/04

| Central government programme budgets | Cost (£ million) |
|---|---|
| Arbitration and conciliation advisory service | 46 |
| Department of environment, food and rural affairs (excluding CAP) | 297 |
| Department for culture, media and sport | 336 |
| Department for education and skills | 126 |
| Department of trade & industry | 425 |
| Department of work & pensions/job centre plus | 331 |
| Home office | 6 |
| Learning and skills council (national) | 1,672 |
| Office of science and technology | 49 |
| Office of the deputy prime minister | 10 |
| Small business service | 271 |
| UK trade international | 81 |
| European commission (structural funds) | 276 |
| TOTAL | 3,926 |
| *Regional development agencies & local authorities* | 360 |
| Tax Incentives | |
|    Corporation tax (20% rate) | 2,300 |
|    Corporation tax (zero rate) | 350 |
|    SME R&D tax credit | 260 |
|    Enterprise investment scheme | 180 |
|    Venture capital trusts | 15 |
|    EMI | 60 |
|    VAT small traders | 450 |
| TOTAL EXPENDITURE ON TAX INCENTIVES | 3,615 |
| Common agricultural policy production subsidies | 2,398 |
| GRAND TOTAL | 10,299 |

*Source*: PACEC, 2005.

just 6.8 per cent of the overall total spent on supporting smaller businesses.

Given the diffused nature of enterprise support, it is difficult to see how any one government department, on its own, has much influence or control over non-agricultural enterprise policy. Indeed, to illustrate this further Table 3.3 shows a breakdown of the spending by the Small Business Service. What, again, is clear is that most of its money is spent on access to finance issues, helping existing businesses (Business Link initiatives, management best practice) rather than the promotion of enterprise. Hence, for all the political agreement about the importance of entrepreneurship, the Small Business Service spent £6.1 million or 0.06

*Table 3.3* Breakdown of Small Business Service expenditure (2005/06)

| | £ million |
|---|---|
| Access to finance/enterprise in under-represented groups | |
|     Access to finance | 110.1 |
|     Phoenix Fund | 40.6 |
| Enterprise, encouraging start-ups and capability for growth | |
|     Management best practice | 8.5 |
|     Promotion of enterprise | 6.1 |
|     Other | 1 |
| Supporting business link | |
|     Businesslink.gov (including call handling and website) | 29 |
|     Business link marketing | 3.6 |
|     Business link university | 2.1 |
| Policy development/research and evaluation | 1.6 |
| Administration | 10.4 |
| Total | 213 |

Source: NAO, 2006.

per cent of the total expenditure on smaller businesses on the promotion of enterprise.

Two distinctive policy flavours were, nevertheless, evident in the new millennium. First, there has been another distinct change in intellectual tastes. As we have seen earlier in this chapter, the emphasis prior to the end of the 1970s was on corporate capitalism which meant a role for the state in rationalising and concentrating on industry and commerce. Put simplistically, if an economy wanted economic growth then the government had a role in supporting the development of bigger plants and helping industry make more use of capital and labour. By the early 1980s, faith in such interventions had evaporated. The focus, therefore, shifted towards supply-side reforms to both labour and product markets.

In the 1990s, however, there was a distinctive turn in the intellectual understanding of how economic growth occurs. Various economic theorists (e.g. Romer, 1986, 1990; Aghion and Howitt, 2000) suggested that economic growth is dependent not just upon the productivity of labour or capital but upon the quality of a society's ideas (innovation) and its people (e.g. human capital attributes). Hence, in the DTI's (1998) White Paper it was suggested:

'Our competitiveness depends on making the most of our distinctive and valuable assets, which competitors find hard to imitate. In a

modern economy these distinctive assets are increasingly knowledge, skills and creativity rather than the traditional factors such as
land and other natural resources' (p. 14).

Such views lie behind many of the attempts to improve the education
and skills of the population, improve the pathways by which skilled
individuals can commercialise their innovations and modernise the
science base. It has also witnessed a quiet change in the way regional
assistance was provided. For instance, Regional Selective Assistance
(RSA) was changed following the DTI's (1998) White Paper to be 're-
focused more on high-quality knowledge based projects providing
skilled jobs' (IDA, 2001: 1). The cost of the RSA was £1¼ billion (2001/04
in Great Britain). Further tinkering subsequently occurred: Enterprise
Grants were first introduced in 2000 for England, again with the aim of
fostering innovation and enterprise. This cost £112 million (2000/04).
In 2004, these schemes were replaced by the Selective Finance for
Investment for England scheme (equivalent schemes were introduced
for Scotland and Wales).

Similar changes were also made to the various innovation schemes
that the Labour party inherited from the previous Conservative administration. Hence, schemes designed to support commercialisation of innovation such as the SMART and SPUR schemes were replaced by R&D
grants. Taxation changes also focussed upon innovative enterprises
with R&D tax credits introduced in 2000 (cost of £570 million
(2000/04)).

Much attention has also focussed upon the supposed equity gap between private sector providers of finance and smaller, innovative enterprises. The Labour administration instituted, therefore, a number of
schemes to close various supposed finance gaps: capital gains tax
business asset taper relief; the Enterprise Investment Scheme; the introduction of the UK High Technology Fund (£126 million venture capital
fund); Regional Venture Capital Funds (£74 million (2004)) and the
Early Growth Fund (£8.5 million).

Where, crucially, there seems to be a distinctive difference in terms of
the Labour government's approach is that we have seen a re-emergence
of a version of the 'commanding heights' policies of the 1960s. This, of
course, following the promptings of Porter and Ketels (2003), is not seen
in terms of industrial policy but rather industrial 'strategy'. Equally, it
differs from the earlier iteration by concentrating upon new and innovative industries. The role of government is also distinct. As Cooke
and Morgan (1998) suggests, the role of government is not to intervene

but to act as an 'animateur'. Hence, we have seen a number of initiatives to increase linkages between industry and the public universities (e.g. the Higher Education Innovation fund (£178 million for 2007/08)).

More importantly, a cluster policy has emerged which seeks to support enterprises through schemes such as the Knowledge Transfer Networks and Partnerships. These schemes rest upon the premise that economic growth is best developed through understanding 'the mechanisms by which networks, social capital and civic engagement affect competition' (Porter, 1998: 227). Hence, rather than traditional agglomeration analyses (see McCann and Sheppard, 2003) which emphasise capital and labour factor advantages, economic growth is dependent upon 'soft' positive externalities that result from knowledge or technology spillovers. The general idea here is that social networks of professionals (e.g. scientists, high-tech knowledge workers, financiers), with access to highly valuable specialist tacit knowledge, interact with each other to produce new forms of knowledge on the assumption that increased levels of investment in R&D lead to increased levels of innovation and output (Malecki, 1997). These knowledge spillovers subsequently confer competitive advantages since individuals and businesses are able to use this knowledge to discover, organise and undertake novel process and products.

Questions remain, however, about this 'emerging heights' policy focus. In particular, clusters remain a one-way bet: once you set up cotton mills in Manchester, steel mills in Sheffield or chemical plants in Teesside it is hard to reverse such investments. Second, if it is difficult to delineate the trajectory of an individual enterprise (picking a winner), it is difficult to see how a risk neutral government can support the idiosyncrasies of a 'cluster' – even if this could be reliably measured (Martin and Sunley, 2003). Finally, Lewis et al. (2002) suggest that the spectacular growth of US productivity in the late 1990s is not due to the emergence of new and innovative industries. Instead, they posit a 'Wal-Mart' effect where much of the productivity increase is due to retailers such as Wal-Mart being able to exploit traditional economic concerns such as economies of scale (bigger stores), wider ranges (economies of scope) and monopsonistic advantages (bulk buying to ensure 'everyday lower prices').

### Equity concerns

The concern with increased efficiency and the general competitiveness of UK enterprises has not been the only evident change. Recent UK policy has also sought to reflect differing understandings of the way that resources should be distributed. Prior to the 1980s, the emphasis was on transferring resources from the richer South East of England to the more peripheral regions in the expectation that this will at least dampen social and economic divisions. In the 1980s, such utilitarianism was supposedly swept away as the market mechanism delineated what was 'equitable'. This, of course, never occurred: government policy, as we saw, has remained strongly wedded to ensuring that 'weak' regions have a safety net. Indeed, the stated regional policy of the 1980s was to ameliorate social rather than economic disadvantage.

Where, however, matters have changed is in the increased emphasis on a new rhetoric rooted in the notion of equality of opportunity. Here, instead, of concentrating upon who are the winners and losers of entrepreneurship and then deciding whether such outcomes should be unequally shared, equally shared or partially shared, the policy aim has been to ensure that everyone has the opportunity to participate in enterprise. Hence, amidst continued transfer payments to the poorer regions, there have been attempts to improve opportunities for disadvantaged groups (e.g. women, ethnic minorities) by encouraging investments in disadvantaged areas (e.g. Business Volunteer Mentoring (£0.9 million in 2003), the Phoenix Development Fund (£30 million), Community Development Finance Institutions (£43.5 million), the Community Development Venture Fund (£40 million)). Another notable scheme was the creation of enterprise areas in 2000 of the UK's most deprived areas. This was designed to afford exemptions on stamp duty and on business renovation. Finally, there are schemes designed to ease the transition into self-employment (e.g. the self-employment stream in the New Deal programme).

These twin concerns of efficiency and equity are evident when we consider the rebalancing of enterprise support that has occurred since the emphasis upon improving the quality of enterprises in the mid 1990s. Using the SBS's (2006) database of enterprise support initiatives for Teesside, Figure 3.7 shows that there were 66 initiatives (46 per cent) targeted at pre start-up and 77 (54 per cent) at post start-up phases of business development. This virtually equal distribution, however, is not reflected in the types of support available to potential or existing enterprises. Instead, unlike the 1990s, there appears to be a return towards hard support since 76 per cent and 69 per cent of available support for both pre start-up and post start-up, respectively is orientated towards some form of grant, loan or award on Teesside.

Such data, as in previous Figures, are illustrative. Other available sources of information, however, indicate that there has been a (muted) return to quantity issues, mixed in with a concentration on innovation.

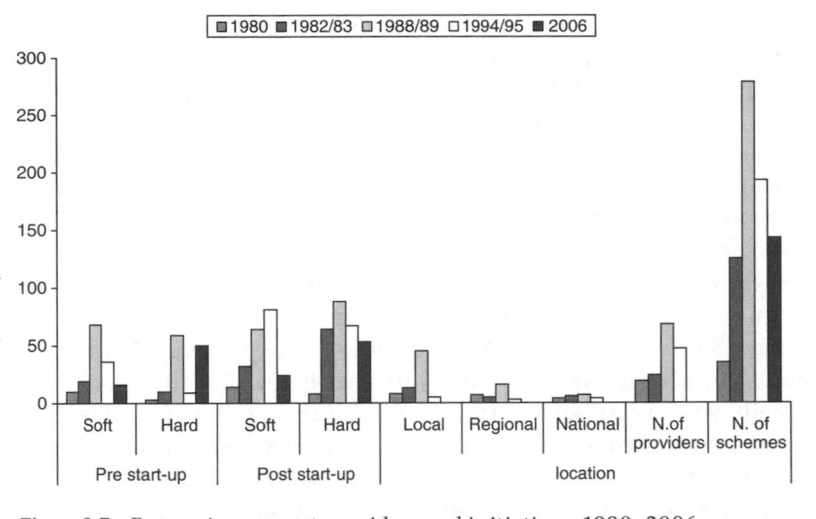

*Figure 3.7* Enterprise support providers and initiatives, 1980–2006.

For example, ONE North East's (the Regional Development Agency for the North East of England) regional strategy listed 28 'headline indicators' of regional development in 1999. Some of these were concerned with raising the skills base or improving the environment but, in terms of economic growth, the focus was on business survival, formation rates and increasing the incidence of innovative businesses.

Furthermore, PACEC (2003) conducted a survey of business support providers and initiatives in the North East. They found that there were 144 providers and some 550 initiatives to support smaller enterprises in the region. They suggest that the balance between these services still emphasises business development rather than pre start-up support. Using PACEC's categories, 198 of the region wide initiatives are orientated towards pre start-up businesses with the other 352 being for post start-up businesses.

## Conclusions

At the start of this chapter, four questions which were used to ration British citizenship in the 1930s (Loebl, 1978) were highlighted. These issues – entrepreneurial experience, access to capital, entrepreneurial propensity and geographic mobility – have been pivotal to the UK's enterprise policy. This chapter has also identified four distinctive periods of enterprise policy in the UK. The first of these, stretching between the

1930s and the late 1970s, was a period of 'corporate' enterprise policy. At its zenith, policy in this period was primarily focussed upon increasing the size of British enterprises to capture greater economies of scale. This meant a focus upon substituting capital for labour and an almost complete disregard for smaller enterprises. Even with the arrival of the Small Firms Service, the CBI (1980) was able to suggest that it 'suffers from a lack of status and a generally low public profile, both within government and outside of it' (p. 3).

There would appear to have been an almost complete change in support for smaller businesses in the 1980s. In part, this was rooted in the ideological concerns about the existence of a 'dependency culture' rather than an 'enterprise culture' in the 1970s. Equally important, though, was that small enterprise policy in the 1980s needs to be contextualised within a period of rampant and persistent unemployment. Policies in this decade that sought to increase the number of new businesses are justified on the basis of creating an 'enterprise culture' (Bannock and Peacock, 1989). However such policies are also acceptable to the government of the day because they constitute transfer payments to poorer individuals and regions.

The third period identified was a relatively short-lived attempt to improve the competitiveness of UK enterprises by explicitly concentrating on those businesses with the potential to grow. This largely meant the creation of governance structures (e.g. TECs, Business Links) that were designed to be responsive to the needs of individual communities. More recently, spurred on by endogenous growth theories, there has been an attempt to re-balance small enterprise support so as to both encourage the start-up market and growth businesses in particular sectors.

Running through the identification of these four policy periods has been historical information, largely derived from guides and factsheets, that have sought to chart the nature of provision in Teesside/the North East of England. Whilst this data is not perfect, it does lend itself to the suggestion that there is some merit in the identification of these four policy periods.

It is also useful for another reason. Based upon this historical information, it would seem apparent that every possible scheme from the speculative to the highly targeted has been attempted. Indeed, in general, what the chapter shows above all is the flip-flop nature of small enterprise policy. First, we had 'commanding heights' in the 1960s then, in the 2000s, we had the 'emerging heights' of cluster policy. Similarly, there was the 'new deal' (YOP) of the late 1970s/early 1980s which was replaced by the New Deal of late 1990s. Finally, quantity policies appeared to have sunk in the early 1990s but have experienced a re-emergence in the late 1990s. Overall, recent efforts by UK governments have revolved around two issues: first, attempts to push up the quantity of small enterprises and, second, trying to get an economically more vibrant small enterprise population.

Above all, though, what this chapter shows is that little has actually changed over the last 70 years, bar an unprecedented growth in the 'enterprise industry' made up of private, quasi-public and public agents. Hence, whilst we identify four distinct policy periods, one obvious complaint is that they are episodes of symbolic or totemic policy making. Indeed, what is abundantly clear is that UK enterprise policy has long been concerned with cutting off the corners of regional disadvantage by indulging in utilitarian attempts to manage resources towards the "archipelago of the provinces" (Dorling and Thomas, 2004: 7).

# Part II

# An Introduction to the Empirical Evidence on New Businesses

In Chapters 2 and 3, the focus was on providing an index of regional entrepreneurship, an overview of regional policy developments over the last thirty years and an explanation of why Teesside is important. In this second part, the focus shifts from these larger concerns to examining the particular features of new businesses.

There are three main ways that new business formation can be considered (Rotefoss and Kolvereid, 2005). One perspective is to consider the individual characteristics of the entrepreneur. This interest has, in turn, seen a development of the quest for some underlying psychological attribute to explain the entrepreneur (Carland et al., 1984; Stewart et al., 1999). Hence, entrepreneurs can be thought of as being people with a need to control (Rotter, 1966), achieve (McClelland, 1971), that are super optimists (de Meza and Southey, 1996; de Meza, 2002), very tolerant of ambiguity (Bhide, 2000) or who are naturally risk averse.

All of these appeal to common sense interpretations of what is needed to set up a new business. Empirically, there is also evidence to support such promptings. Central to being able to lead and achieve, is the ability to plan (Ajzen, 1991) and there is evidence that business planning promotes business performance (Delmar and Shane, 2003, 2004). Equally, some economists are happy to suggest that risk-taking is central to entrepreneurial endeavours (Knight, 1921; Kihlstrom and Laffont, 1979; Lazear, 2005). Fairlie (2002) has also shown that there was a distinctive association between being an illegal drug dealer in a person's youth and then going on to being in legitimate business later on. Finally, if a group of entrepreneurs are asked about their future prospects, the majority of them will respond that they will outperform most other entrepreneurs and certainly do better than the average entrepreneur (Ashworth et al., 1998; Arabsheibani et al., 2000).

Underlying all of this may be some kernel of truth. The problem is that despite a vast number of studies, investigations and 'war stories' told by this or that entrepreneur, nothing really stands out as being central to any 'entrepreneurial gene' (Gartner, 1988). Indeed, there is no real evidence to suggest that there are any particular individual traits for entrepreneurial ability (Delmar, 2000). For instance, entrepreneurs might appear to love risk, but are often found to be averse to risk, particularly if it is their own capital on the line (Sahlman and Stevenson, 1989).

Those interested in the individual have, therefore, sought to identify particular determinants of the individual such as age, sex or education characteristics which they believe may proxy for an individual's entrepreneurial ability. In the following chapter (Chapter 4), the aim is to look at the individual determinants of setting up a business. The first key focus here is on establishing a historical profile of the response to entrepreneurship over the last thirty years. The second key focus is on what are the main differences between low (Teesside), medium (Shropshire) and high entrepreneurship areas (Buckinghamshire). This builds upon the earlier review in Chapters 2 and 3 by explicitly examining entrepreneurial profiles both temporally and spatially.

The second main way of examining new business formation has largely been a reaction of the failure to accurately specify the psychological attributes of the entrepreneur. Instead of looking at the entrepreneur, attention has switched to investigating and understanding the entrepreneurial processes. Hence, what matters is not so much who they are, but what they do. Central to this is how entrepreneurs negotiate the potentially difficult early development – the pre start journey. In Chapter 5, therefore, the focus is on understanding the strategic orientation of the entrepreneur.

Clearly, one other implication of how new businesses do business is to recognise that the entrepreneur alone is not the only agent involved in the business. Chapter 6, therefore, considers how business support impacts on the new business. Equally, Chapter 7 looks at the finance underlying new businesses. As is the consistent approach, the interest is in how finance has changed over the thirty years and how a new business in a high, medium and low entrepreneurship area makes use of finance.

The emphasis on the individual and the organisation is likely to provide an incomplete understanding of the new business. One thing that is clear about new entrepreneurs is that in their struggle to legitimise themselves and their business, the external environment can often be pivotal. One view then is that such is the dominance of the external environment, the fortunes of the new business are largely a matter of chance. Others hold that the entrepreneur is not so impotent and that they make some strategic choices, which along with the attributes and skills of the entrepreneur, allow the individual new business to safely negotiate its way through the environment. Chapters 8 and 9 then syntheses the earlier empirical chapters by reviewing the factors – both individual and organisational – that potentially motivate business development. Chapter 8 considers the historical patterns whilst Chapter 9 examines the spatial patterns associated with the economic impact of new businesses.

# 4
## Individual Entrepreneurial Determinants

## Introduction

Let us presume that an individual wishes to set up their own business. How could they be helped? One suggestion is that he or she should undergo a battery of psychological tests to see if they were suited for this form of work. For example, an investigation could be undertaken of their risk propensities, tolerance of ambiguity and their need to succeed. Having established if they are enough of a maverick, the temptation might be to counsel them to go ahead.

Arguably, this might be a mistake. One trouble is that such tests might be working off an archetypal notion that entrepreneurship is fast paced and dynamic. This is clearly not the case for most businesses. In the United States – perhaps the country most associated with entrepreneurship – the most likely type of new businesses are ones that either sell us things we need to keep us going; or help us with keeping our houses in good repair. Hence, even if the routines of selling food, furniture or books are new to the individual, they are not unique events. Neither is it likely that the types of business set up in the US differ that much from businesses set up elsewhere. Another problem is that, even if the environment is dynamic, who is to say that these entrepreneurs would not earn more money and be as happy in their work if they were employees? The evidence is that it is extremely tricky to separate out these two groups (Lazear, 2005; Stewart et al., 1999), but what is clear is that, on balance, there is a financial penalty in being a business owner. Hamilton (2000) in a study of the US self-employed finds that individuals with the same levels of human capital earn significantly less in self-employment than they could earn as an employee.

Suitably chastised, one alternative is to say nothing. This seems again justifiable. After all, one of the main theories of entrepreneurship has it that an individual's suitability for entrepreneurship is largely unknown to them (or anyone else) until they actually start their own business (Jovanovic, 1982). Once they begin, they (and we) find out whether they are suited for it and if not, the expectation is that they will get out and do something else; although the reality is that they often persist in running their business even when it is past its sell-by-date (Gimeno et al., 1997).

However, saying nothing is only a strategy for those with no commitment to the aspiring business. Banks are often seen as a major source of external finance to the new business (see Chapter 7), so if the bank lends the money to start the business they have a vested interest in at least seeing their loan capital returned to them. Family and friends may also be asked to make investments either financially or in terms of effort (sweat equity). Prior to such investments, it may be entirely appropriate to find out about the entrepreneur's skills and experience. For example, if an aspiring entrepreneur seeks to run a construction business, it might be useful if they either know how to lay bricks or cut timber or can find people with such knowledge and skills. If this is absent, the suggestion might be that this business had very sorry prospects.

This issue of experience and skills has been central to many attempts to understand why it is that people set up in business. Even here, there is a spectrum of views. At one end, there has been a quest to identify if entrepreneurs are more likely to be those with prior exposure to particular skills or experiences such as having prior enterprise experience either directly by running their own business or indirectly because one of their family members was involved in running a business. Alternatively, it may be there is no one or unique skill or talent that an individual possess but, instead, what typifies the entrepreneur is having a range or balance to their skills (Lazear, 2005).

One aim of this chapter is to delineate the types of attributes that entrepreneurs possess. It might be thought that this is fairly well understood. For example, it is fairly clear that males are more likely to set up a business. Equally, those that set up in business tend to be around 35 to 45 years old.

Despite this, there are surprisingly few general studies of the attributes of existing entrepreneurs. For example, perhaps the two most well cited studies are by Evans and Leighton (1989) and Blanchflower and Oswald (1998). These studies look at individuals under 40 and 23 year olds, respectively.

Indeed, it is a fairly common pattern to focus on particular sub-samples of the adult population or particular areas of business creation.

In terms of particular areas, what empirically is evident is particular concentrations on the following:

1. the *young* (Blanchflower and Meyer, 1994; Dolton and Makepeace, 1990; Rosa 2003; van Praag, 2003; Williams, 2004);
2. *females* (Marlow, 2006; Cromie and Birley, 1992; Cowling and Taylor, 2001);
3. *ethnic minorities* (Basu and Goswami, 1999; Fairlie, 2004; Clark and Drinkwater, 2000; Fairlie and Meyer, 1996);
4. particular *industries* (Mason and McNally, 1997; van Oort and Atzema, 2004);
5. *single country studies of the external environment* (e.g. the US (Armington and Acs, 2002), Germany (Folster, 2002) Italy (Garofoli, 1994), France (Guesnier, 1994), Japan (Harada and Honjo, 2005), Ireland (Hart and Gudgin, 1994), and Finland (Ritsila and Tervo, 2002); and
6. *international comparisons* (e.g. Carree et al., 2002; Blanchflower, 2000; Reynolds et al., 1994).

Another development is to consider the 'might be' or 'could be' entrepreneurs. This focus on so-called nascent entrepreneurs has led, again, to a wealth of papers that try to explain why it might be that some people, at certain times, in particular contexts, whilst doing a range of related activities, might eventually get round – sometime – to setting up their business (Masuda, 2006; Reynolds et al., 2004; Davidsson and Honig, 2003).

Curiously it is, less common to examine the general determinants of individuals who actually set up a business. So, whilst there is lots of evidence on specific groups seeking to uncover their intentions of setting up a business, our interest is on those that actually start.

The focus in this chapter is on what are the individual determinants of individuals who have actually started a business. It embeds this investigating by tracing how the profile of entrepreneurs has changed historically. This is important because it is novel and affords the potential for investigating if, indeed, there are some structured features to the types of people who set up their own business.

Also, how is it that each of the particular circumstances in each of the decades influences the types of people who become entrepreneurs? In Chapter 3 we showed that there were distinctive policy and economic aspects to each of the three decades. In the 1970s, there was still the sense that Teesside was moving forward and support only needed to be focussed on its core 'growth' sectors. In the 1980s, such a strategy looked lamentable in the face of the urge to soak up unemployment by encouraging individuals into businesses. The Teesside economy has fared little better in the 1990s.

These three differing decades may also have influenced the sectoral choices of individuals. One of the main charges of Foreman-Peck's (1985) analysis (see Chapter 2) is that the North East has historically concentrated on businesses that were chaff businesses rather than businesses that would 'seed' economic benefits. This chapter investigates this relationship between individual characteristics and sectoral choice to see, if indeed, there have been historical changes.

The chapter also investigates how sectoral choices play out in relation to an area of high (Buckinghamshire), medium (Shropshire) and low entrepreneurship (Teesside). Again, the chapter seeks to identify if there are particular differences in the characteristics of the entrepreneurs in these three areas. This is also important because it allows for the identification of relative 'strengths' and 'weaknesses' of each area.

The chapter proceeds as follows. It begins by first providing a succinct overview of the relevant empirical literature on what general characteristics typify those who set up a business. It then proceeds to examine the empirical evidence on the three decades and the differences between the three areas.

## Background

There are generally three different sets of individual determinants typifying those that set up in business. First, there are demographic factors such as sex, age, being married and so on. These are largely intractable (at least in the short term). Second, there is 'general' human capital which is usually based upon the likely schooling and education that an individual experiences, particularly prior to entering the labour market. The third form is 'specific' human capital (Becker, 1994). This may be prior experience in a particular industry or prior managerial experience. Usually, however, in terms of entrepreneurship a further distinction is often drawn between those who *know* about business (e.g. worked as a manager) and those who have *done* or are *doing* business either because they used to run a business (serial entrepreneur) or because they have at least another business whilst they are setting up their current one (portfolio entrepreneur). Such distinctions should be thought to be important because the general view is that the greater the investment by the individual, the greater the likelihood of a higher return to them (Schultz, 1980) and that the more specific the human capital of the individual, the greater the likelihood that they will become involved in setting up a business (Vesper, 1996).

In an ideal world, all of these human capital proxies would be collected. In the first iteration of this study (1970s), there was a relatively weak understanding of the individual determinants of entrepreneurship. For example, the nearest factor to ethnicity in the 1970s data is whether an individual was born and bred in the county. This is in contrast to the now current understanding that an individual's ethnicity does clearly influence the likelihood of them setting up a business (Le, 1999). Equally, it has also emerged that finance is pivotal. Although this is discussed more fully in Chapter 7 when we turn to our historical and temporal data on this, it is sufficient to note here that in the 1970s it was not altogether clear what role windfalls (e.g. redundancy money, bonus or lottery winnings) played in increasing the likelihood of an individual becoming an entrepreneur (see: Evans and Jovanovic, 1989; Laferrere and McEntee, 1995; Lindh and Ohlsson, 1996; Blanchflower and Oswald, 1998).

In the 1970s, therefore, only a limited range of variables were collected (e.g. age, sex, education). These determinants were added to in the 1980s and the 1990s although the main aim of these studies was to remain consistent with the individual determinants of business entry. The data is detailed in Table 4.1 (columns 1–3).

Table 4.1 also shows the findings from 11 studies that have looked at the general characteristics of those that set up a business. What is unique about these studies is that they are the studies that were the *least* likely to primarily focus on a particular sub-sample of the population such as the young. Even here, though, very few of the studies sought just to look at the determinants of business entry. Instead, some studies compared business entrants with nascents (e.g. Parker and Belghitar, 2006), whilst others sought to embed an understanding of finance (e.g. Taylor, 2001; Burke et al., 2000), the environment (e.g. Carrasco, 1999; Henley, 2004) or entrepreneurial intentions (e.g. Arabsheibani et al., 2000) within their explanations of those that set up their own business. Necessarily, they are also focussed upon a particular country, although the coverage in Table 4.1 ranges from the Ivory Coast (Goedhuys and Sleuwaegen, 2000) to the United States (Parker and Belghitar, 2006).

The studies in Table 4.1 are grouped under three headings: those particular determinants that were found to be statistically more likely to be present amongst those who had set up their own business (+), those factors that were statistically less likely to be present (–) and those

*Table 4.1*   Synopsis of prior general profiles of entrepreneurs

| | 70s | 80s | 90s | (+) | (–) | n.s. |
|---|---|---|---|---|---|---|
| **Demographic determinants** | | | | | | |
| Age | X | X | X | 7 studies[2,3,4,5,8,10,11] | | 1 study[1] |
| Age[2] | X | X | X | | 4 studies[4,5,8,11] | |
| Male | X | X | X | 8 studies[4,5,6,7,8,9,10,11] | | 3 studies[1,2,3] |
| Disabled | | | | | | 1 study[4] |
| Married | | | | 1 study[4] | 1 study[1] | 4 studies[5,7,8,10] |
| Parents business owner | | | | 4 studies[7,9,10,11] | 3 studies[1,2,3] | |
| Children | | | | | 1 study[5] | 2 studies[1,7] |
| Indigenous | X | X | X | | 1 study[3] | |
| **General human capital** | | | | | | |
| Years of schooling | | | | 1 study[8] | 2 studies[7,9] | |
| Post degree | | | | | | 1 study[6] |
| Degree | X | X | X | 3 studies[3,5,11] | 1 study[6] | 3 studies[1,2,10] |
| Post compulsory schooling | X | X | X | 3 studies[1,4,11] | | 2 studies[6,10] |
| Secondary schooling | X | X | X | 2 studies[4,11] | | 2 studies[6,10] |
| Technical/ vocational | X | X | X | 2 studies[3,6] | | 2 studies[4,10] |
| **Specific human capital** | | | | | | |
| Prior entrepreneurial experience | X | X | X | 2 studies[2,10] | | 1 study[1] |
| Portfolio entrepreneur | | X | X | 1 study[2] | | |
| Sectoral experience | | X | X | 1 study[3] | | |
| Previously unemployed | X | X | X | 1 study[10] | | 1 study[1] |
| Full time | X | X | X | | | |
| Manager | | X | X | | | |

X attributes available in the data; [1] Parker and Belghitar, 2006; [2] Rotefoss and Kolvereid, 2005; [3] Goedhuys and Sleuwaegen, 2000; [4] Arabsheibani et al., 2000; [5] Carrasco, 1999; [6] Burke et al., 2000; [7] De Wit and Van Winden, 1990; [8] Rees and Shah, 1986; [9] De Wit, 1993; [10] Taylor, 2001; and [11] Henley, 2004.

that are immaterial (n.s.). The studies suggest several very stable features: older individuals are more likely to set up their business, though this tails off (age[2]) as people age. Parental background is also important. So, too, are males. Playing an insignificant role were other demographic factors such as having children or being married. In general, these findings are similar to those studies which considered various sub-samples of the adult population (Le, 1999).

The general view of education, however, is at odds with what is found in Table 4.1. Lucas (1978) argued that individuals with higher levels of schooling tend to have greater skills and so are more likely to increase their propensity to start their own business. At the same time, having greater skills makes individuals more attractive to employers, which suggests an ambiguous relationship between education and business entry. Such ambiguity is evident in Le's (1999) review of studies. He finds, particularly amongst studies that consider sub-samples of the adult population (e.g. Kidd, 1993; Borjas and Bronars, 1989; Evans and Leighton, 1990), that this relationship is, indeed, ambiguous. From Table 4.1, cumulatively, it would appear that education plays, at worst, a non-significant role in determining business entry. At best, it would appear that there is a positive relationship between education and business propensity. The influence of education is not confined to those with a trade or professional qualification but also permeates through to those with a university degree.

Table 4.1 also shows that there is a sense that more specific human capital determinants such as being in business before (serial entrepreneurship) increases the likelihood of setting up a business. However, the coverage of such human capital determinants is generally less intensive in the studies so perhaps less can be inferred about the likely relationship between specific human capital and business entry from Table 4.1.

What is clear, though, is that education and demographic determinants such as age and being a male do positively influence the likelihood of starting a business. In the following section, the emphasis turns to comparing and contrasting the individual determinants of business start-up over the three decades.

## Individual determinants of business start-up over the three decades

This section begins simply by looking at the profile of the three decades to tease out any evident similarities or differences. These are detailed in Table 4.2 which shows the simple statistics on the three decades and identifies if they are statistically significantly different from one another.

One obvious difference is that entrepreneurs have tended to age, both in terms of the mean and median age across the three decades. Unsurprisingly, therefore, very many more of them are of 'prime age' in the 1990s than they were in the 1970s. Equally, the vast majority of the entrepreneurs were male. Nonetheless, Table 4.2 demonstrates that this changed markedly between the 1970s and the 1980s: in fact the rate of female entrepreneurship doubled from around 15 per cent to 30 per cent over the period. This is much faster than can be explained by simple recourse to the average (for each decade) economic activity rates for females. The high rate of female entrepreneurship does subsequently slip to around a quarter in the 1990s.

If there are few differences in terms of indigenous (born and bred) or vocational qualifications, there were large differences in terms of educational attainment levels. At the high end (university degree), it would appear that graduates were much less likely to start-up their own business in the 1980s. Higher education, however, has increased its participation levels over the last 30 years which is reflected in increases in the national rate. Even controlling for this, businesses in the 1980s were less likely to be started by graduates. The 1980s also heightened numbers of individuals with no formal qualifications setting up their own business. This is despite, as is evident from the percentage of graduates, rising levels of formal qualifications.

*Table 4.2* Profile of entrepreneurs across the three decades

|  | 1970s | 1980s | 1990s | $F/X^2$ |
|---|---|---|---|---|
| Mean age at foundation | 34.7 | 39.5 | 40.8 | 21.932* |
| Median age | 33.0 | 41.0 | 40.0 | |
| Prime age (35–45) % | 28.9 | 39.2 | 40.5 | 6.138** |
| Male % | 84.0 | 70.2 | 75.9 | 8.925** |
| Average economic activity rate for females (decade) | 46.5 | 50.6 | 53.8 | |
| Indigenous (born and bred in county) % | 68.9 | 70.7 | 68.1 | 0.370 |
| Degree % | 5.3 | 5.1 | 11.6 | 8.691** |
| National rate | 7.0 | 10.2 | 16.3 | |
| Degree/national rate | 0.76 | 0.5 | 0.71 | |
| Vocational % | 27.3 | 34.5 | 34.4 | 2.621 |
| No qualifications % | 5.1 | 38.4 | 10.9 | 83.076* |
| Manager % | | 41.9 | 57.0 | 9.845* |
| Sectoral experience % | | 59.9 | 65.2 | 1.306 |
| Unemployed (immediately prior to starting up the business) % | 26.7 | 40.3 | 21.7 | 20.308* |
| Average unemployment (decade) | 9.9 | 18.7 | 11.6 | |
| Unemployment/average unemployment | 2.7 | 2.16 | 1.87 | |
| Prior entrepreneurial experience % | 31.7 | 17.3 | 30.6 | 12.907* |
| Portfolio entrepreneur % | | 6.7 | 17.3 | 11.499* |

*significant at 1 per cent level; ** significant at 5 per cent level.

Equally, the gross figure suggests that the 1980s was a decade marked by large numbers of individuals who were previously unemployed setting up their own business. Other indicators present a similar picture. Those with prior entrepreneurship experience (serial entrepreneurs) are more likely to be either found in the 1970s or the 1990s rather than the 1980s; managerial experience was more prevalent in the 1990s; as was those with more than one business (portfolio entrepreneurs).

## Comparing the three counties

Overall, the sense is that the human capital of those who set up a business in the 1980s was weaker than it was the 1970s. The crumb of comfort may be that the position at least improved in the 1990s. This looks particularly weak, though, when the human capital attributes of entrepreneurs in Teesside is compared with that of Buckinghamshire and Shropshire. Table 4.3 shows that entrepreneurs in Teesside are statistically significantly younger, despite – as was shown in Table 4.2 – an increasing age effect across the three decades. Such age differences do not, though, translate into statistically significant differences in the percentage that are prime age. Of note, also, is that there are no marked differences in terms of gender.

What is abundantly clear from Table 4.3 is that businesses in Teesside are much more likely, indeed more than twice as likely, to have entrepreneurs that were born and bred in the area. In both Buckinghamshire and Shropshire only around 30 per cent of entrepreneurs are from the county. This may suggest that in-migration enhances the likelihood of an individual starting a business. Table 4.3 also makes it clear that individuals in the 'high' and medium entrepreneurship areas are much more likely to be graduates, have managerial experience, and have either current or previous experience of entrepreneurship. Another difference is that Teesside entrepreneurs are much more likely to have vocational qualifications than those starting a business in Buckinghamshire or Shropshire.

The picture, however, is not completely uniform. Table 4.3 shows the three areas share similar proportions of individuals who are unqualified and who were unemployed immediately prior to starting their business. This implies there is considerable heterogeneity within the enterprise population. For instance, whilst Buckinghamshire may appear as an area where the 'average' entrepreneur has some managerial experience and may have a university degree, it is also home to those who have relatively limited human capital attributes.

Also of note in Table 4.3 is the non-significance of the 'same sector' variable. From this it would appear that business choice tends to be path dependent so that about seven out of 10 businesses are set up in a sector where an entrepreneur has prior experience. This is important for two reasons. First, it suggests that people often have limited choices when they decide to set up their own business. For many businesses, it is obvious that there are particular skill thresholds. For instance, those who wish to service motor vehicles might be anticipated to either have particular qualifications and/or training in this field. Equally, if the aim is to open a professional services business such as an accountancy practice, again some training or experience may be a pre-requisite.

Sectoral choice is also important for a second reason. As noted earlier, Foreman-Peck (1985) has argued that much of the economic malaise faced by more peripheral UK regions is the result of either investing in ultimately fruitless sectors or failing to catch up quickly with sectoral developments. A good example of this is the development of business, finance and professional service businesses since the 1980s whose numbers increased from 80,000 in 1980 to 160,000 by 1993 and subsequently reached – a decade later in 2003 – a stock of ½ million such businesses. Such growth has been attributed to changes in demand, specialist expertise, and personal attention to customer needs (Bryson et al., 1997).

*Table 4.3*   Profile of entrepreneurs across the three counties

|  | Teesside | Bucking-hamshire | Shrop-shire | $F/X^2$ |
|---|---|---|---|---|
| Mean age at foundation | 40.8 | 46.6 | 44.8 | 1.764* |
| Median age | 40.0 | 48.0 | 43.0 | |
| Prime age (35–45) % | 40.5 | 34.1 | 43.8 | 2.700 |
| Male % | 75.9 | 81.5 | 78.5 | 1.682 |
| Indigenous (born and bred in county) % | 68.1 | 26.8 | 31.8 | 83.342* |
| Degree % | 11.6 | 27.9 | 24.6 | 20.22* |
| Vocational qualifications % | 34.4 | 10.1 | 13.1 | 39.817* |
| No qualifications % | 9.2 | 13.1 | 8.5 | 1.955 |
| Manager % | 57.0 | 70.2 | 66.4 | 7.5** |
| Sectoral experience % | 65.2 | 74.2 | 67.8 | 3.243 |
| Unemployed (immediately prior to starting up the business) % | 21.7 | 28.1 | 22.0 | 2.206 |
| Prior entrepreneurial experience % | 30.6 | 35.7 | 46.1 | 9.353* |
| Portfolio entrepreneur % | 17.3 | 27.3 | 24.6 | 6.3** |

* significant at 1 per cent level; ** significant at 5 per cent level.

Despite this clearly being a buoyant sector, there seems little evidence of it attracting large numbers of new businesses in Teesside (Table 4.4). Columns 2–4 of Table 4.4 show that in the 1970s, one-fifth of businesses entered this sector whilst nearly 16 per cent entered in the 1990s. Just 5.6 per cent entered in the 1980s.

Moreover, despite the long term falling away of manufacturing which, as the previous chapter showed, began in the late 1970s, people still elected to enter this sector in the 1980s. However, in a prior study using the 1980s data (Storey and Strange, 1992), it was evident that there was a large number of Motor Repair and Beauty (e.g. car respraying, hairdressing) businesses set up in the 1980s. The number of these businesses doubled between the 1970s and the 1980s. The numbers of such businesses remained much the same in Teesside during the 1990s.

Turning now to a comparison between the three areas, what is immediately noticeable from Table 4.4 is that both Buckinghamshire and Shropshire have nothing like the same proportions of people who set up a business in Motor Repair and Beauty sectors. There are also marked differences in terms of the number of professional service businesses that are established. For both counties, the percentage of such businesses is nearly double that of Teesside.

Such differences may be thought to be unimportant. Most businesses are 'lifestyle' in that they are both there to provide a sustainable living for their owners and to meet the lifestyle needs of their customers. If Teesside has a greater *flow* of individuals seeking to repair cars or service the hair and beauty needs of individuals, this is surely not a concern. The rejoinder, of course, is that it does matter. One suspicion is that these types of businesses are more marginal than more dynamic busi-

*Table 4.4* Sectoral choices in the three decades and in the three counties

|  | Teesside | | | Bucking- hamshire | Shrop- shire |
|  | 1970 | 1980 | 1990 | | |
|---|---|---|---|---|---|
| Manufacturing | 19.3 | 24.2 | 15.6 | 15.4 | 22.3 |
| Construction | 20.7 | 4.0 | 8.1 | 9.2 | 9.2 |
| Professional services | 20.0 | 5.6 | 15.9 | 36.9 | 32.3 |
| Distribution | 10.7 | 20.2 | 18.0 | 18.5 | 15.4 |
| Other services | 16.7 | 21.7 | 18.6 | 16.2 | 16.2 |
| Motor repairs and beauty | 12.7 | 24.2 | 23.7 | 3.8 | 4.6 |
| $X^2$ | | | 58.26* | | 59.923* |

* significant at 1 per cent level.

nesses in other sectors. According to Foreman-Peck (1985), they are more chaff than seed. As a consequence, they a) are unlikely to sustain the entrepreneur over the longer term since the income from the business is both low and uncertain; b) such *flows* may be into a population that has already reached its capacity with the potential consequence that further flows just unnecessarily displace existing businesses in the local economy and; – most damaging of all – c) do little to enhance the competitiveness of the locality so that it can develop dynamic businesses that will challenge the existing economic poverty of the area. Sales are primarily to highly localised markets, compared with those selling overseas. The phrase 'taking in someone else's washing' seems an appropriate description.

In Chapters 8 and 9 the aim is to more fully explore these issues, but in terms of the present concerns, sectoral choice also points to another important area of interest. So far, the underlying assumption has been that individual entrepreneurs are able to choose what type of business they operate. The evidence, however, from Table 4.3 was that sectoral choice is largely path dependent: if an individual has experience in one sector, they are likely to set up their business in this sector. This, alone, may explain the sectoral choices of many individuals.

However, there may be other influences at play such as demographic, general or specific human capital differences which explain why it is that individuals choose a particular sector.

To test this, Table 4.5 compares each of the sectors – Manufacturing, Construction, Professional Services, Distribution, Other Services and Motor and Beauty Repairs – to see whether individuals with particular human capital characteristics are more likely to start businesses in certain sectors. Each sector is compared with Professional Services. The selection of Professional Services is deliberate: as has been shown, it is an important driver underlying some of the profound growth in the number of new small businesses.

There are three sets of models in Table 4.5. The first looks at a comparison between the 1970s, 1980s and 1990s using a range of determinants. The second model uses these same determinants (e.g. age, sex, serial entrepreneurship) but supplements them with prior managerial experience, same sector experience and concurrently running another business (portfolio entrepreneurship). Adding these further factors obviously means that it is no longer possible to compare the 1970s with the other two decades so the comparison is between the 1980s and 1990s. The third and final set of models uses these same variables but compares the three counties rather than the three decades.

For each of the determinants, a RRR statistic is given which equates to the 'Relative Risk Ratio' for that determinant. By the way of an example, suppose the comparison is between manufacturing with professional services. Are males more likely to choose manufacturing than professional services? Table 4.4 (model 1) shows the answer is yes at about 11.8 per cent (1.118–1) although this is statistically insignificant. Those with a degree, however, are much less likely (35.2 per cent i.e. 0.648–1) to choose manufacturing than professional services. Such a result is, however, again insignificant.

### The three decades

What is significant in model 1 (variables available from the 1970s onwards) is that those with a vocational qualification were 244.2 per cent (3.442–1) more likely to enter manufacturing. It also shows that people in the 1980s were 220.1 per cent more likely to elect to enter manufacturing when compared to those in professional services.

Model 2 indicates other determinants of entry (prior managerial experience, same sector experience and portfolio entrepreneurship) but those with a vocational qualification were still more likely to choose manufacturing. Moreover, relative to the 1980s, those from the 1990s were around 75 per cent less likely to choose manufacturing.

Compared with professional services, construction in both models 1 and 2 suggests, again, the importance of vocational qualifications. In construction, entrepreneurs brought with them no qualifications. In the 1970s–1990s model (model 1), they are 219.2 per cent more likely to have no qualifications and in the 1980s–1990s model (model 2), this is even more pronounced (390.7 per cent). There is also evidence that prior unemployment also influences the choice of construction with the unemployed in model 1 being 132.4 per cent more likely to enter this sector. Noticeably, however, there is no effect for any particular decade. Hence, those that enter construction tend to be primarily drawn from those with vocational qualifications but they also attract those with no qualifications and those who had experience of unemployment immediately prior to setting up their business.

The third sector considered in Table 4.4 is distribution. Here what is apparent is that males are much less likely to be in this sector than they are in professional services. Turned around, what both models 1 and 2 suggest is that females are around 64–68 per cent more likely to enter distribution. Vocational qualifications, again, are important as are the

Table 4.5 Multinomial comparison between the three decades and the three regions (omitted sector: professional services)

| | Model 1: 1970s/1990s | | Model 2: 1980s/1990s | | Model 3: 3 Regions | |
|---|---|---|---|---|---|---|
| | RRR | z | RRR | z | RRR | z |
| Manufacturing | | | | | | |
| *Demographics* | | | | | | |
| Male | 1.118 | 0.260 | 1.075 | 0.140 | 0.935 | −0.17 |
| Age | 1.028 | 0.220 | 0.975 | −0.160 | 1.104 | 0.77 |
| Age² | 1.000 | −0.200 | 1.000 | 0.230 | 0.999 | −0.77 |
| Indigenous | 0.574 | −1.690 | 0.692 | −0.890 | 0.847 | −0.49 |
| *Qualifications* | | | | | | |
| Degree | 0.648 | −0.890 | 1.144 | 0.230 | 0.569 | −1.47 |
| Vocational | 3.442 | 2.950* | 4.347 | 2.690* | 2.050 | 1.63 |
| Professional | 0.242 | −1.720 | 0.000 | 0.000 | 0.387 | −1.52 |
| None | 1.549 | 0.980 | 1.195 | 0.290 | 0.464 | −1.33 |
| *Specific experience/skills* | | | | | | |
| Previously unemployed | 1.828 | 1.680 | 1.096 | 0.200 | 0.860 | −0.43 |
| Prior entrepreneurial experience | 0.824 | −0.570 | 0.917 | −0.180 | 1.148 | 0.43 |
| Managerial experience | | | 0.718 | −0.830 | 1.063 | 0.19 |
| Sectoral experience | | | 0.722 | −0.800 | 0.547 | −1.85 |
| Portfolio entrepreneur | | | 0.594 | −0.910 | 0.902 | −0.28 |
| *Decade* | | | | | | |
| 1990s | 1.103 | 0.260 | | | | |
| 1980s | 3.201 | 2.510** | 0.251 | −2.780* | | |
| *Region* | | | | | | |
| Buckinghamshire | | | | | 0.556 | −1.51 |
| Shropshire | | | | | 0.698 | −0.95 |

**Construction**

| | | | | | | |
|---|---|---|---|---|---|---|
| *Demographics* | | | | | | |
| Male | 1.592 | 0.830 | 1.451 | 0.490 | 1.705 | 0.89 |
| Age | 0.866 | −1.020 | 0.885 | −0.580 | 0.897 | −0.75 |
| Age² | 1.002 | 0.950 | 1.001 | 0.590 | 1.001 | 0.81 |
| Indigenous | 0.941 | −0.150 | 1.713 | 0.930 | 1.225 | 0.49 |
| *Qualifications* | | | | | | |
| Degree | 0.000 | 0.000 | 0.000 | 0.000 | 0.652 | −0.75 |
| Vocational | 6.182 | 3.820* | 7.837 | 3.120* | 3.755 | 2.53** |
| Professional | 1.167 | 0.220 | 0.638 | −0.380 | 1.041 | 0.05 |
| None | 3.192 | 2.250** | 4.907 | 2.130** | 1.836 | 1 |
| *Specific experience/skills* | | | | | | |
| Previously unemployed | 2.324 | 2.060** | 2.406 | 1.570 | 1.689 | 1.3 |
| Prior entrepreneurial experience | 0.840 | −0.440 | 1.203 | 0.310 | 1.899 | 1.62 |
| Managerial experience | | | 0.791 | −0.470 | 0.818 | −0.51 |
| Sectoral experience | | | 3.235 | 1.820 | 0.957 | −0.1 |
| Portfolio entrepreneur | | | 0.598 | −0.670 | 0.641 | −0.85 |
| *Decade* | | | | | | |
| 1990s | 0.734 | −0.730 | | | | |
| 1980s | 0.564 | −1.000 | 1.245 | 0.340 | | |
| *Region* | | | | | | |
| Buckinghamshire | | | | | 0.549 | −1.25 |
| Shropshire | | | | | 0.633 | −0.94 |

**Distribution**

| | | | | | | |
|---|---|---|---|---|---|---|
| *Demographics* | | | | | | |
| Male | 0.357 | −2.620* | 0.326 | −2.330** | 0.501 | −1.87 |
| Age | 0.977 | −0.170 | 0.944 | −0.340 | 1.002 | 0.02 |
| Age² | 1.000 | 0.040 | 1.000 | 0.250 | 1.000 | −0.11 |
| Indigenous | 0.617 | −1.420 | 1.034 | 0.080 | 0.881 | −0.39 |

Continued

Table 4.5 (Continued)

| | Model 1: 1970s/1990s | | Model 2: 1980s/1990s | | Model 3: 3 Regions | |
|---|---|---|---|---|---|---|
| | RRR | z | RRR | z | RRR | z |
| *Qualifications* | | | | | | |
| Degree | 0.831 | −0.370 | 0.946 | −0.090 | 0.400 | −2.11** |
| Vocational | 2.468 | 1.980** | 3.674 | 2.300* | 1.710 | 1.16 |
| Professional | 0.735 | −0.490 | 0.722 | −0.450 | 1.154 | 0.29 |
| None | 3.925 | 3.030* | 3.381 | 2.060** | 1.771 | 1.27 |
| *Specific experience/skills* | | | | | | |
| Previously unemployed | 1.311 | 0.710 | 0.971 | −0.060 | 0.855 | −0.45 |
| Prior entrepreneurial experience | 1.436 | 1.050 | 1.892 | 1.410 | 1.187 | 0.53 |
| Managerial experience | | | 1.413 | 0.860 | 1.214 | 0.6 |
| Sectoral experience | | | 0.521 | −1.620 | 0.469 | −2.35 |
| Portfolio entrepreneur | | | 0.686 | −0.700 | 1.287 | 0.69 |
| *Decade* | | | | | | |
| 1990s | 4.146 | 3.170* | | | | |
| 1980s | 7.361 | 3.820* | 0.475 | −1.460 | | |
| *Region* | | | | | | |
| Buckinghamshire | | | | | 0.543 | −1.63 |
| Shropshire | | | | | 0.383 | −2.35 |
| Other Services | | | | | | |
| *Demographics* | | | | | | |
| Male | 0.541 | −1.570 | 0.590 | −1.100 | 0.567 | −1.54 |
| Age | 0.937 | −0.530 | 1.099 | 0.560 | 1.122 | 0.88 |
| Age$^2$ | 1.001 | 0.560 | 0.999 | −0.500 | 0.999 | −0.89 |
| Indigenous | 0.817 | −0.620 | 0.979 | −0.050 | 1.326 | 0.86 |

| | | | | | | |
|---|---|---|---|---|---|---|
| *Qualifications* | | | | | | |
| Degree | 0.763 | -0.580 | 1.008 | 0.010 | 0.530 | -1.62 |
| Vocational | 2.010 | 1.600 | 2.271 | 1.480 | 0.894 | -0.24 |
| Professional | 0.867 | -0.260 | 1.002 | 0.000 | 1.224 | 0.44 |
| None | 2.213 | 1.830 | 1.051 | 0.080 | 0.378 | -1.66 |
| *Specific experience/skills* | | | | | | |
| Previously unemployed | 1.330 | 0.770 | 0.746 | -0.640 | 0.664 | -1.11 |
| Prior entrepreneurial | 0.967 | -0.100 | 1.258 | 0.520 | 1.264 | 0.74 |
| Experience | | | | | | |
| Managerial experience | | | 0.742 | -0.780 | 0.802 | -0.71 |
| Sectoral experience | | | 0.553 | -1.540 | 0.491 | -2.23** |
| Portfolio entrepreneur | | | 1.065 | 0.130 | 1.229 | 0.58 |
| *Decade* | | | | | | |
| 1990s | 1.703 | 1.380 | | 0.253 | | |
| 1980s | 3.945 | 2.910* | | -2.760* | | |
| *Region* | | | | | | |
| Buckinghamshire | | | | | 0.506 | -1.81 |
| Shropshire | | | | | 0.415 | -2.23 |
| Motor Repairs and Beauty | | | | | | |
| *Demographics* | | | | | | |
| Male | 0.288 | -3.160* | 0.292 | -2.540** | 0.313 | -2.79* |
| Age | 0.836 | -1.350 | 0.958 | -0.240 | 0.991 | -0.05 |
| Age$^2$ | 1.001 | 0.850 | 1.000 | -0.170 | 0.999 | -0.36 |
| Indigenous | 0.805 | -0.610 | 0.980 | -0.050 | 1.279 | 0.6 |
| *Qualifications* | | | | | | |
| Degree | 0.341 | -1.500 | 0.422 | -0.990 | 0.161 | -2.25** |
| Vocational | 11.577 | 5.630* | 13.530 | 4.770* | 4.728 | 3.4* |
| Professional | 1.748 | 0.920 | 2.194 | 1.170 | 1.122 | 0.19 |
| None | 3.300 | 2.420** | 2.259 | 1.270 | 0.356 | -1.23 |

Continued

Table 4.5 (Continued)

| Specific Experience/Skills | Model 1: 1970s/1990s | | Model 2: 1980s/1990s | | Model 3: 3 Regions | |
|---|---|---|---|---|---|---|
| | RRR | z | RRR | z | RRR | z |
| Previously unemployed | 1.898 | 1.700 | 1.241 | 0.470 | 0.505 | −1.47 |
| Prior entrepreneurial experience | 1.027 | 0.070 | 1.314 | 0.580 | 0.971 | −0.07 |
| Managerial experience | | | 1.086 | 0.210 | 1.291 | 0.71 |
| Sectoral experience | | | 1.149 | 0.330 | 0.683 | −0.98 |
| Portfolio entrepreneur | | | 0.623 | −0.830 | 0.861 | −0.31 |
| *Decade* | | | | | | |
| 1990s | 5.306 | 3.800* | | | | |
| 1980s | 7.874 | 3.990* | 0.409 | −1.760 | | |
| *Region* | | | | | | |
| Buckinghamshire | | | | | 0.166 | −2.93* |
| Shropshire | | | | | 0.161 | −3.22* |
| N. | 621 | | 438 | | 498 | |
| LR chi² | 259.43 | | 202.24 | | 209.5 | |
| Sig. | 0.000 | | 0.000 | | 0.000 | |
| Log likelihood | −966.06 | | −656.29 | | −765.49 | |

* significant at 1 per cent level; ** significant at 5 per cent level.

absence of any formal qualifications. Relative to the 1970s, there also seems to be a greater likelihood of people choosing distribution in both the 1980s and 1990s. This effect disappears, however, when prior sectoral, managerial and current entrepreneurial experience is included (model 2).

In terms of Other Services, the only statistically significant determinant is that 1980s' businesses (model 1) were more likely to choose this sector and 1990s' businesses were less likely to choose it (model 2). Overall, controlling for the other determinants, this sector was more popular in the 1980s than either previously or subsequently. For Motor Repairs and Beauty, what emerges from Table 4.4 is that females are more than 70 per cent more likely to enter this sector. As with Manufacturing, Construction and Distribution, vocational qualifications were highly significant. For model 1 at least, those with no formal qualifications were more likely to select this sector. Also, compared to the 1970s, this was a much more favoured destination for those who set up in the 1980s or the 1990s. The non-significance (model 2) of any differences between the 1980s and the 1990s suggest that the popularity of this sector, evident from the simple results in Table 4.3, has continued unabated over the two decades.

In essence, then, this sectoral comparison points to the importance of vocational qualifications in determining sectoral choices. There is further evidence to suggest that there were differences between the decades and that gender and having no qualifications were partial determinants of sectoral choice.

**The three regions**

Model 3 in Table 4.5 suggests rather different results. Compared with Professional Services and controlling this time for region, what emerges is that there are no significant differences to be found for Manufacturing, but that entry into Construction is again influenced by vocational qualifications. There are also some differences in terms of Distribution since graduates are less likely to enter this sector. Those with prior sector experience are also nearly 50 per cent less likely to enter the Other Services sector. The most interesting results, however, lie in terms of Motor Repairs and Beauty sectors. Females, those with vocational qualifications and without degrees, are much more likely to enter this sector. However, what is also evident is that having controlled for a range of human capital determinants, this sectoral choice is clearly much less popular in either Buckinghamshire or Shropshire.

## Summary

This chapter began with the suggestion that there are three alternative strategies for helping someone interested in setting up their own business. The first was to provide a risk profile for them. The second was to do nothing. The third strategy was to look at their human capital attributes to see if these were a good guide to their likely propensity towards setting up a business.

The chapter reviewed a range of studies that examined business creation by the general population rather than by sub-samples of the population. These studies suggested several likely determinants of business entry (e.g. age and gender). These findings were largely confirmed in this chapter (Tables 4.2 and 4.3). Indeed, what comes out is the importance of education, with vocational qualifications being of particular note. Similarly, although the data looks at 'in-migration' rather than ethnicity, the latter could be an important factor in explaining the very different enterprise populations in the three counties.

One implicit interest of this chapter, however, has been to see how the entrepreneurial profile has shifted over the three decades. One of the issues that emerged from Chapter 3's discussion of enterprise policy was the efforts of the UK government in the 1980s to shift individual preferences towards increasing the number of entrepreneurs. The aim, therefore, was to create an enterprise culture by increasing the level of optimism people had about their likely success in entrepreneurship (Fraser and Greene, 2006).

The evidence from this chapter suggests that, on one level, such optimism policies worked more forcefully on those with lower levels of human capital. Indeed, the evidence from Table 4.2 is fairly stark: compared to the 1970s and 1990s, the average 1980s entrepreneur was more likely to have limited qualifications, more likely to have recently experienced unemployment, have less managerial experience and have less exposure to entrepreneurship.

Spatially, very many of these differences persist between the three regions. The correlation may then be that areas which have lower human capital attributes are the areas with poorer economic outcomes. At one level, this is absolutely true. At another level, it looks like a cheap association that belies issues about choice.

Hinting at this is the fact that around one-fifth of the businesses in Buckinghamshire were set up by individuals who were previously unemployed. Such a finding does at least point to the heterogeneous characteristics of entrepreneurs and that high entrepreneurship areas should not simply be equated with fast-paced dynamic new businesses.

Equally, the other implicit theme running through this chapter is the possibility that there may be a fourth reason why people choose entrepreneurship. Whilst many people set up in business for positive reasons, some recognise they have no alternative. This may be the reason for the distinctive sectoral patterns in Table 4.4.

The multinomial modelling in Table 4.5 sought to investigate, both historically and spatially, what factors are associated with these sectoral choices. Largely, it found that the most frequent human capital difference between the Professional Service sector and sectors such as Construction and Manufacturing was that they were more likely to be populated by individuals with vocational qualifications. This points to such educational qualifications acting as a threshold by screening out individuals. Indeed, having such qualifications was seemingly much more important than having specific human capital experiences such as running a business either in the past or concurrently.

These effects are just as prevalent for females as they were for males in the Construction and Manufacturing sectors. Females found themselves in Distribution and beauty, even after controlling for historical or spatial differences. Such findings again suggest the obvious point that sectoral choices, particularly for women, appear to be dependent upon prior skill accumulation.

These results do not, of course, indicate if these sectoral choices led to positive or negative performance outcomes. This is a matter for later chapters. Nonetheless, they do point to the sense, particularly in the 1980s, that entrepreneurship was not simply a matter of free choice or just a consequence of the heady optimism of the time. Instead, it alludes to the way that constrained environments may make entrepreneurship appear an economic necessity rather than an opportunity for individuals (Rosa et al., 2006).

Equally, evident is that sectoral choices are often path dependent: if an individual has a set of skills and experiences they do, on the whole, constrain the options available to an individual. This appears particularly constraining on Teesside where demand is less buoyant. Here, despite some improvement in the 1990s, the popularity of car repairing, hairdressing and beauty salons appears undiminished; suggesting that once an area has elected a set of sectoral choices it is often difficult to change to alternatives that might appear more economically productive.

# 5
# The Strategic Orientation of New Businesses

'Evaluating a marketing strategy to those actually in business is a bit hypothetical. And SMEs are there, they're more intent on surviving and earning a living than they are to considering theoretical and hypothetical marketing strategies' Technology counsellor quoted in Mole (1999: 156).

## Introduction

From the above quote, it might be thought that the concept of strategy is somewhat esoteric for smaller businesses. However, those who write on small business strategy suggest that everyone starting a new business has to choose 'where' and 'how' to compete (Hofer, 1975; MacDougall and Robinson, 1990; O'Gorman, 2000). Strategy is then two sets of decisions: first, the decision to compete in a particular industry (the where), and second, the decision concerning what aspects of the business to emphasise (the how). Rumelt (1991) compared the proportion of profits of large business accounted for from the industry structure compared with that from individual business. Although both factors were significant, the biggest contribution proportionately to the profitability of a particular business was from factors that were individual to the business rather than the contribution of the industry. Moreover, for writers on strategy there is an implicit belief in a positive and causative relationship between strategy and performance. The purpose of strategy is to confer competitive advantage so that greater profits accrue to the business with the 'best' strategy (Katz and Green, 2007).

This chapter examines the strategy of the new business. It identifies the elements of strategy as: on being close to the customer, price, innovation, cost, and the skills of the workforce, entrepreneur and administration, and having a better location. For each criterion it compares how entrepreneurs see themselves in comparison with their competitors. The chapter shows that the choice of strategy is in part conditioned by the location of the business and that it has a major impact on the new business's chances of survival.

The chapter starts with a discussion of the generic strategies of small businesses and then links this to the resource-based view of the business. We then present the results and discuss their implications. Since issues of business strategy were not asked of new businesses in the 1970s and 1980s, the empirical material in this chapter is derived entirely from the 1990s. We begin initially with generic strategies.

## Generic strategies

According to Porter (1980), there are three generic strategies available to a business seeking to respond to their competitive environment: price, differentiation and focus. Price concerns the ability to compete with a comparative quality but at a lower price to the buyer. Researchers have suggested that this mode of competing requires economies of scale to spread fixed costs over a greater output and use production processes that are, if not automated, then highly prescribed (Sutton, 1991). Consequently, the suggestion has been that small businesses should avoid price competition because by definition they lack economies of scale (Reid et al., 1993; Stearns et al., 1995). There are caveats to this. One is that there exist fragmented industries without dominant producers that exploit economies of scale. In the US, the most fragmented industries are those such as new car dealerships, florists and machine shops (Katz and Green, 2007). Hence, the smaller and/or newer business can successfully compete on price, such as a low cost outlet that has a high level of throughput ('pile them high and sell 'em cheap'). Alternatively, another traditional response has been through the payment of poorer wages off-set by a 'better' environment for the employee (Marlow, 2000).

The second generic strategy is differentiation. By this we mean fitting the product or service more closely to the requirements of the consumer than is available from competitors. The business may do this through different opening hours, better marketing, or personal service. Businesses can differentiate themselves from the competition on just one aspect, what can be termed 'imitation plus one' (Katz and Green, 2007). There is evidence that, for small business, differentiation is an effective strategy. Reid et al. (1993) showed that small business prospered when they managed the product profile, improved the product range and improved the quality of their products.

Focus is the last of the three generic strategies. The idea behind focus is that the business concentrates on a particular segment of the market. Here a distinction is made between a price focus and a differentiation focus, where businesses either offer lower prices to a particular group, or offer a service tailored to the requirements of a particular group. Markets often have cut-price segments, aimed at more price-sensitive customers, whose primary motivation is perhaps to have cheaper imitations of what is currently 'fashionable'. Another market segment might be customers seeking branded 'fashionable' goods. Focus can be particularly effective when there are dominant producers who decide not to serve a particular group. Carroll and Hannan (2000) argued that because dominant producers concentrate their attention on offering 'general' products to satisfy the mass market, they leave gaps in the market for those buyers who crave more variety. As consumers' taste preferences diversify then there is more room in the market for specialist providers with a strategy based on focus (Peli and Nooteboom, 1999). Focus strategies concentrate on particular types of customers so that we might expect businesses that are closer to the customer to be those operating a focus strategy.

## Resource-based view

The generic strategies approach places the prime emphasis on market characteristics. The characteristics of customers (mainstream or niche) and the choices made on how to satisfy them (price or differentiation) are the dominant strategic considerations.

An alternative perspective is to focus on the internal aspects of the business and how these resources generate competitive advantage for the business (Rumelt, 1991). This has come to be called the resource-based view. It seeks to understand the ability of some businesses to sustain their performance above and beyond the industry norms. This ability to sustain super-normal profits seemed incompatible with standard economic theory which argued that excess profits would generate entry which, in turn, would erode high profits. Surely competitors would copy those factors that lead to the success of the high profit businesses?

However, the resource-based view was that the key to the competitive advantage of an individual business lay within the processes and procedures of that business, but were those not easily identified or mimicked by competitors. Grant (1991) distinguished between business resources and capabilities, where resources refer to the business's inputs, capital equipment, individual skills and brand names. The capabilities referred to 'the capacity for a team of resources to perform some task and activity' (1991: 119). The resource-based view has been extensively used in strategy research yielding insights into the internationalisation in small business, and business advice amongst others (Westhead et al., 2001; Chrisman and McMullan, 2004).

## The Stinchcombe view

From the above it might be expected that in a 'high' entrepreneurship area such as Buckinghamshire, businesses would have better performance than middling Shropshire or 'poor' Teesside on the grounds that there would be more businesses with better strategic orientation or greater internal resources. This is a question discussed more formally in Chapter 9. However, for the moment, it is sufficient to note that the source of competitive advantage in smaller and newer businesses is not always clear cut. Stinchcombe (1990) argues that there are fundamental differences between the "routinised" behaviour of large firms and the more informal, flexible decisions potentially available to the newer or smaller businesses.

In many respects, this mirrors the existing debate about 'training' in small businesses (Storey, 2004). The policy orthodoxy on training and skills is that there is a training deficit in small businesses (Tregaskis and Brewster, 1998) because entrepreneurs lack the time, money or inclination to undertake training (Pettigrew et al., 1989). In so doing, they harm the performance of both their own business and the skill set of their employees. The alternative argument is that this criticism of entrepreneurs fails to understand the nature of competition they face, their short time horizons and the nature of the enterprise that they own.

## Strategic orientations of new businesses

We now examine how new entrepreneurs viewed their business in comparison with their competitors across a number of dimensions. Table 5.1 clearly shows entrepreneurs typically regarded their business as superior to the competition in every dimension, but particularly in some areas. For example, 61.1 per cent thought they were *much better* in terms of understanding the customer; 56.6 per cent thought their workforce had *much better* skills than their competitors; and 44.6 per cent thought

*Table 5.1*   Factors underlying competitive advantage

|  | Much worse | Slightly worse | About the same | Slightly better | Much better |
|---|---|---|---|---|---|
| Understanding the customer | 0.2 | 0.0 | 12.2 | 26.5 | 61.1 |
| Lower prices | 3.3 | 13.6 | 41.8 | 19.2 | 22.1 |
| Novelty of product/service | 2.4 | 3.7 | 43.9 | 20.5 | 29.4 |
| Low cost base | 4.2 | 12.1 | 34.7 | 23.7 | 25.3 |
| Skills of our workforce | 0.2 | 0.7 | 12.3 | 30.3 | 56.6 |
| Owners managerial skills | 0.8 | 3.3 | 22.7 | 28.6 | 44.6 |
| Better admin | 1.8 | 7.9 | 35.7 | 23.4 | 31.1 |
| Locational advantages | 5.2 | 9.6 | 36.1 | 19.1 | 29.9 |

*Table 5.2*   The two most important factors for competition

|  | First factor | Second factor |
|---|---|---|
| Understanding the customer | 59.6 | 12.3 |
| Lower prices | 10.6 | 14.4 |
| Novelty of product/service | 4.8 | 13.3 |
| Low cost base | 2.4 | 5.0 |
| Skills of our workforce | 13.6 | 37.2 |
| Owner's managerial skills | 2.9 | 6.3 |
| Owner's administrative skills | 1.0 | 3.0 |
| Locational advantages | 3.8 | 6.7 |

their owner's managerial skills were *much better* than their competitors.

The pre-eminence of understanding the customer and the skills of the workforce were also regarded as the two most important factors underlying competitive advantage. In Table 5.2, nearly three out of five businesses cited this as being their principal source of competitive advantage. This dwarfed the second most important factor (in terms of the first factor) – skills of the workforce. Overall, then, it might be thought that these two factors alone may be responsible for the underlying competitive advantage of the business.

Nonetheless, much of the source of competitive advantage underlying the business could be due to other factors or combinations of factors. The *actual* choices available to the entrepreneur may be in terms of lower prices, novelty of the product/service or its cost basis. These factors, in turn, may work in combination. To control for this, therefore, a data reduction technique such as factor analysis allows for the grouping of data into a number of underlying factors that account for the bulk of the differences between business' strategies. The eight items were subjected to a principal component factor analysis using the varimax method of factor rotation, which is standard practice for an exploratory factor analysis (Girden, 2001). The location item had a very low communality (.300) which suggested that only 30.0 per cent of the explanation was based on the location. This item was excluded. The resulting three factor solution (eigenvalues above 1) explained 61.75 per cent of the variance in the remaining seven items.

The factor analysis resulted in three principal components. This is shown in Table 5.3. The first of these is labelled 'skills' which has three factors associated with it (above 0.5): workforce skills, owner's managerial skills and better administration. The second component has been termed 'cost' in that it is a combination of both lower prices and having a low cost base. The final component has been termed 'quality' in that it combines both understanding the customer and the novelty of product/service.

Factors two and three are to be expected since they relate to price competition and differentiation, respectively. Factor one is more surprising and the 'skills' component may be one that applies more to imitative businesses. (An alternative factor analysis was tried which excluded the use of workforce skills. In terms of subsequent univariate and multivariate analyses, this exclusion made little qualititative difference.)

*Table 5.3* Rotated component matrix sources of competitive advantage

|  | Component | | |
|---|---|---|---|
|  | Skills | Cost | Quality |
| Understanding the customer | 0.380 | −0.037 | 0.578 |
| Lower prices | 0.201 | 0.804 | −0.131 |
| Novelty of product/service | −0.074 | 0.102 | 0.805 |
| Low cost base | −0.110 | 0.768 | 0.240 |
| Workforce skills | 0.557 | 0.049 | 0.417 |
| Owners managerial skills | 0.850 | 0.010 | 0.050 |
| Better administration | 0.774 | 0.065 | 0.002 |
| Eigenvalue | 2.07 | 1.24 | 1.01 |
| % explained | 29.56 | 17.71 | 14.48 |
| Kaiser-Meyer-Olkin measure of sampling adequacy |  |  | 0.651 |
| Bartlett's test of sphericity | Chi-square |  | 389.15 |
|  | Degrees of freedom |  | 21 |
|  | Sig. |  | 0.000 |

Extraction method: principal component analysis; rotation method: Varimax with Kaiser normalization; rotation converged in 5 iterations.

## Teasing out the basis of the three strategies

To more fully understand the basis of these three strategic orientations by new businesses, tests for an association between the three components (skills, cost and quality) and a profile of determinants are conducted. This begins by examining if individual factors are positively (+) or negatively (–) statistically associated with skills, cost or quality (at the 5 per cent level). Subsequently, each of the three components was placed within a multivariate regression to further interrogate differences in the profile of each component. Finally, an assessment of the impact of each component on performance is conducted.

Table 5.4 provides a summary of all determinants that are either positively or negatively associated with an emphasis on skills either in terms of chi-square or t-tests (determinants that were insignificant were excluded from Table 5.4 – a full list of such factors is included in the subsequent multivariate analysis).

Table 5.4 shows the determinants associated with the skill component appear much more likely to be positively associated with entrepreneurs who were born and bred in their local area (indigenous) and who were full-time in the business. They are also more likely to make use of local customers and suppliers. Moreover, given the interest in sectoral choices (Chapter 4), there is further evidence here that the skill component is linked with the Motors and Beauty and Distribution sectors. Finally, businesses located in Teesside are more positively associated with this component.

On the negative side, those with other businesses or with some post-compulsory education (A Level/HND) were less likely to be profiled in

*Table 5.4*　Univariate profile of 'skill' component

| Positive factors | Negative factors |
| --- | --- |
| Indigenous, full time | Portfolio entrepreneur, A level/HND |
| Local supplier, local customer | Limited company |
| Motors and beauty and distribution sectors | Used pre start support |
| Teesside | Demand and finance problems in the 1st year |
| | Use email, have a website |
| | National customer |
| | Professional service sector |
| | Buckinghamshire, Shropshire |

the skill component. So, too, were limited companies and those that had used pre start-up support. Interestingly, they were also less likely to experience demand or financial problems in their first year of operations. Such individuals were less likely to use email or have a website, or to have national customers or operate in the professional service sector. Equally, they were less likely to be associated with either the high enterprise area of Buckinghamshire or Shropshire. The clear overall picture emerging from this profile is that businesses that tend to see themselves as 'skill-based' tend to be primarily imitative.

A further analysis of the determinants of the 'cost' component was also undertaken. Again, as with Table 5.4, Table 5.5 provides a summary of the results of chi-square and t-tests, grouped into those determinants that were either positively or negatively associated (at the 5 per cent level) with a cost based strategic orientation.

The first noticeable feature of Table 5.5 is that there were fewer determinants that were significant. In terms of the positive factors, the only human capital feature evident was that entrepreneurs with this strategic orientation were more likely to have been previously unemployed. A second feature was that their business records were more likely to be kept by themselves than using an internal or an external accountant/bookkeeper. Table 5.5 also shows that those with this strategic orientation were also more likely to make use of friends and family as a source of finance at start-up. Finally, such an orientation was seemingly more prevalent in the low enterprise area of Teesside. By contrast, a Buckinghamshire location was the only determinant that was negatively associated with this orientation.

In essence, therefore, a cost strategic orientation seems to be a proxy for poorer quality businesses for the following reasons. First, individuals that were previously unemployed might be regarded as being more likely to have lower human capital than individuals in employment; and the self-recording of business records might also hint at a limited

*Table 5.5*  Univariate profile of 'cost' component

| Positive factors | Negative factors |
| --- | --- |
| Previously unemployed | Buckinghamshire |
| Self-recorded business records | |
| Used friends and family and public authorities as sources of finance at start-up | |
| Teesside | |

managerial competency. Equally, although it might be anticipated that entrepreneurs would use family and friends as a source of start-up support (Chapter 7), the evidence that they are more reliant on public financial support may again signal that this strategic orientation is more associated with lower quality businesses.

The final component 'quality' was also examined. Following the pattern of the two previous Tables, Table 5.6 reports a summary of the statistically significant results from chi-square and t-tests (at the 5 per cent level) of the association between quality and individual determinants.

Table 5.6 shows a positive association between this form of strategic orientation and having a totally new product or service and, as well, conducting research and development (R&D). This is perhaps unsurprising since central to this orientation was the importance of having a novel product/service as a source of competitive advantage. Equally compatible, is the association between this orientation and manufacturing. The final positive factor is Buckinghamshire, which is the only time Buckinghamshire appears in the positive column.

In the negative column, is the use of a finance company for post start-up finance support. Table 5.6 also shows that this orientation is less likely to be associated with those that were more reliant on local customers. This orientation was also less likely to be found amongst businesses in the 'motors and beauty' sector and in Teesside.

*Table 5.6*   Univariate profile of 'quality' component

| Positive factors | Negative factors |
| --- | --- |
| Totally new product or service, R&D Manufacturing Buckinghamshire | Used finance company for post start-up finance Local customer Motor Repairs and Beauty Teesside |

## A multivariate examination of skills, cost and quality

From Tables 5.4 to 5.6, what emerged were groups of factors for each of the components of the factor analysis. The first of these, clearly related to skills (entrepreneur, worker and administration skills), suggested a profile of businesses that appeared more likely to be imitative in their strategic orientation. The second component, suggested that cost orientated businesses were more likely to be lower quality businesses. The third component was a focus on a strategic orientation that sought to differentiate the business from its competitors. What also emerged was a strong sense of regional differences. New businesses in the high enterprise area of Buckinghamshire were more likely to have a strategic orientation towards quality rather than skills or cost. In contrast, the profile of Teesside businesses was orientated much more towards being imitative (skills), being cheaper (cost) rather than seeking strategic differentiation (quality).

However, profiles derived from univariate associations risk being potentially misleading since a range of other potential determinants that may influence the profile are not held constant. To probe this issue further, regression analysis was conducted on each of the three factors using robust standard errors, with the findings displayed in Table 5.7. Here 58 potential determinants are used to determine the likely profile of each of the three strategic orientations. These cover the human capital of the individual entrepreneur (including education), business level characteristics (e.g. start-up size, limited company), use of support, problems in the first year, use of finance, geographic reach (e.g. local, regional or inter/national supplier) sector and geographic location.

Dealing first with the orientation towards skills, Table 5.7 shows that the only significant human capital determinant is having experience in the same sector (sectoral experience). There are no other internal factors to the business that are either positively or negatively significant (at the 5 per cent level). Instead, Table 5.7 demonstrates that, of vastly greater importance is sector and geographic location. New businesses in the manufacturing, construction and professional services were all less likely to have a skills orientation. This is also true for businesses in Buckinghamshire and Shropshire. Relative to the 'poor' enterprise area of Teesside, the high and medium enterprise areas were much less likely to have businesses with a strategic orientation.

One of the few factors associated with the cost orientation is the age of the business. It seems that this orientation is more likely to be found amongst older businesses, perhaps implying that businesses without this characteristic cease to trade early in their lifespan. This, however, tails away with increasing age (age of business squared). It also appears that the cost orientation is more characteristic of those using mortgage finance at start-up. Nevertheless, the central finding is that Buckinghamshire businesses, even after controlling for a range of determinants, still emerge as being statistically less likely than Teesside businesses to be found with this strategic orientation.

In terms of the quality-orientation, it is noticeable that Buckinghamshire has a positive sign, even if this is insignificant. However, geographic location is often strongly correlated with sector – most

*Table 5.7*   Factor regressions for skills, cost and quality

| | Skills | | Cost | | Quality | |
|---|---|---|---|---|---|---|
| | Coef. | t.stat | Coef. | t.stat | Coef. | t.stat |
| **Entrepreneur characteristics** | | | | | | |
| Age | −0.019 | −0.49 | −0.050 | −1.2 | −0.064 | −1.68 |
| Age$^2$ | 0.000 | 0.79 | 0.001 | 1.35 | 0.001 | 1.8 |
| Male | −0.185 | −1.58 | 0.111 | 0.84 | −0.005 | −0.04 |
| Prior entrepreneur experience | 0.031 | 0.29 | 0.038 | 0.33 | 0.015 | 0.13 |
| Portfolio entrepreneur | −0.098 | −0.75 | −0.014 | −0.1 | −0.188 | −1.44 |
| Managerial experience | −0.069 | −0.7 | −0.092 | −0.81 | 0.213 | 1.87 |
| Sectoral experience | 0.240 | 2.18** | 0.091 | 0.79 | 0.092 | 0.8 |
| Previously unemployed | −0.062 | −0.52 | 0.249 | 1.93 | 0.075 | 0.61 |
| Full time in business | 0.305 | 1.49 | 0.196 | 0.94 | −0.182 | −1 |
| Indigenous | 0.004 | 0.04 | −0.071 | −0.61 | −0.001 | −0.01 |
| **Education** | | | | | | |
| Degree | 0.080 | 0.54 | 0.173 | 1.04 | 0.029 | 0.17 |
| A level/HND qualification | −0.133 | −0.88 | −0.292 | −1.67 | −0.111 | −0.7 |
| Vocational qualification | −0.143 | −1.06 | −0.028 | −0.18 | −0.128 | −0.85 |
| Professional qualification | 0.041 | 0.23 | −0.091 | −0.48 | −0.053 | −0.29 |
| **Business level characteristics** | | | | | | |
| Age of business | −0.061 | −0.28 | 0.498 | 2.37** | 0.033 | 0.15 |
| Age of business$^2$ | 0.006 | 0.38 | −0.040 | −2.67* | −0.001 | −0.08 |
| Limited company | 0.093 | 0.86 | −0.069 | −0.57 | −0.136 | −1.09 |
| Employment size in 2001 | −0.008 | −0.68 | −0.014 | −1.03 | −0.020 | −1.64 |
| **Use of support** | | | | | | |
| Pre start support | −0.072 | −0.48 | 0.190 | 1.22 | 0.055 | 0.38 |
| Post start support | −0.081 | −0.76 | 0.116 | 0.99 | −0.009 | −0.08 |
| **Problems in the first year** | | | | | | |
| Supplies | 0.018 | 0.1 | −0.146 | −0.65 | −0.051 | −0.28 |
| Skilled labour | 0.083 | 0.78 | −0.109 | −0.84 | 0.093 | 0.78 |
| Labour turnover | 0.053 | 0.23 | −0.299 | −1.17 | 0.034 | 0.14 |
| Wages | 0.112 | 0.83 | −0.129 | −0.82 | 0.073 | 0.52 |
| Demand | −0.085 | −0.72 | −0.042 | −0.32 | 0.000 | 0 |
| Finance | 0.045 | 0.14 | −0.496 | −1.93 | −0.769 | −1.94 |
| **Strategy** | | | | | | |
| Totally new product or service | −0.207 | −1.27 | 0.165 | 0.9 | 0.404 | 2.52** |

Continued

*Table 5.7* (Continued)

| | Skills | | Cost | | Quality | |
|---|---|---|---|---|---|---|
| | Coef. | t.stat | Coef. | t.stat | Coef. | t.stat |
| Research & development | 0.102 | 0.99 | −0.181 | −1.59 | 0.336 | 2.81* |
| Self-records | 0.024 | 0.21 | 0.092 | 0.73 | −0.005 | −0.05 |
| Internal records | 0.259 | 1.92 | −0.032 | −0.22 | 0.023 | 0.17 |
| Computer | 0.176 | 1.52 | −0.008 | −0.06 | −0.147 | −1.15 |
| Used pre start business plan | −0.130 | −1.19 | −0.101 | −0.84 | 0.010 | 0.08 |
| Use post start business plan | 0.049 | 0.42 | 0.024 | 0.19 | 0.020 | 0.16 |
| Use email | −0.202 | −1.44 | −0.053 | −0.36 | −0.147 | −0.89 |
| Have a website | −0.001 | −0.01 | 0.060 | 0.48 | −0.031 | −0.23 |
| Use of finance | | | | | | |
| *Pre start-up* | | | | | | |
| Savings | 0.112 | 0.83 | −0.187 | −1.35 | 0.076 | 0.6 |
| Mortgage | 0.130 | 0.39 | −0.860 | −2.46** | −0.241 | −0.61 |
| Bank | −0.125 | −0.74 | −0.088 | −0.51 | 0.095 | 0.55 |
| Finance company | 0.720 | 1.56 | 0.024 | 0.07 | 0.153 | 0.53 |
| Public authorities | 0.287 | 1.29 | 0.193 | 0.83 | 0.234 | 1.02 |
| *Post start-up* | | | | | | |
| Savings | 0.271 | 1.29 | −0.146 | −0.61 | −0.302 | −1.23 |
| Profits | 0.260 | 1.57 | −0.226 | −1.33 | −0.108 | −0.69 |
| Bank | 0.185 | 0.97 | −0.288 | −1.49 | 0.022 | 0.12 |
| Finance company | 0.527 | 1.86 | −0.723 | −1.45 | −0.498 | −1.42 |
| Public authorities | 0.131 | 0.24 | −0.455 | −1.2 | −0.397 | −1.21 |
| Geographic reach | | | | | | |
| Regional supplier | 0.000 | 0.09 | 0.000 | −0.19 | 0.001 | 0.24 |
| Inter/national supplier | 0.001 | 0.44 | −0.001 | −0.78 | 0.003 | 1.75 |
| Regional customer | 0.002 | 1.01 | −0.002 | −0.75 | −0.002 | −1.03 |
| National customer | −0.002 | −1.29 | 0.001 | 0.59 | −0.002 | −1.01 |
| Sector | | | | | | |
| Motors and beauty | −0.276 | −1.63 | −0.037 | −0.19 | −0.400 | −2.24** |
| Manufacturer | −0.297 | −1.99** | 0.338 | 1.7 | 0.219 | 1.19 |
| Construction | −0.447 | −2.59** | 0.040 | 0.2 | 0.169 | 0.8 |
| Professional services | −0.456 | −3.06* | 0.074 | 0.4 | 0.159 | 0.88 |
| Other | −0.449 | −2.9* | 0.109 | 0.58 | 0.093 | 0.53 |
| County | | | | | | |
| Buckinghamshire | −0.696 | −5.11* | −0.371 | −2.15** | 0.214 | 1.41 |
| Shropshire | −0.714 | −4.69* | −0.245 | −1.56 | 0.044 | 0.26 |
| Constant | 0.475 | 0.45 | −0.297 | −0.28 | 1.157 | 1.04 |
| N. | 422 | | 422 | | 422 | |
| F. Stat | 3.34 | | 2 | | 1.71 | |
| Sig. | 0 | | 0.0001 | | 0.002 | |
| $R^2$ | 0.2663 | | 0.1727 | | 0.1554 | |

*Table 5.8*   Strategic orientation and performance outcomes

|                              | Skills         | Costs           | Quality         |
| ---------------------------- | -------------- | --------------- | --------------- |
| Survival                     | 0.404 (0.687)  | 2.049 (0.017)   | –1.210 (0.228)  |
| Relative employment growth   | 0.033 (0.454)  | –0.041 (0.345)  | 0.028 (0.519)   |
| Annualised employment growth | 0.009 (0.843)  | –0.079 (0.068)  | 0.058 (0.184)   |

notably in this case with the importance of the 'motors and beauty' sector. Table 5.7 also points to two other plausible determinants of a quality-orientation: having a totally new product/service and conducting R&D. These are the only factors in any of the three regressions that may be remotely thought to be more akin to 'strategy' determinants.

## The impact of strategic orientation

One of the key questions underlying each of the three strategic orientations is the extent to which they influence business performance. To explore this, we identify three performance outcomes. The first of these is survival. Here the interest is in whether a new business survived until 2004. The two other measures are relative and annualised employment growth. Table 5.8, therefore, shows two types of results. The first is a t-test (t.stat and p. value) for differences between business survival and each of the three strategic orientations. For the two employment growth measures, correlations are provided (pearson correlation statistic and p. value).

Only one statistically significant association at the 5 per cent level emerges. Businesses with a cost-orientation strategy are less likely to survive. Since survival is perhaps the basic measure of a business performance, owner-managers who chose to compete on low price and cost do seem to perform significantly worse than others. This is in line with other findings (Reid et al., 1993; Stearns et al., 1995; Saridakis et al., 2008).

## Summary

This chapter has examined the strategic orientation of entrepreneurs and any evidence that links this to the subsequent performance of their enterprise. In making this link, there remains the criticism that important cognitive biases are likely to be ignored. Likely sources of such bias include a willingness to take risks or adopt over-optimistic approaches to strategy (Fairlie, 2002; de Meza, 2002).

The view here, though, is that there are important advantages of looking at the strategic orientation of the new entrepreneur because the interest is in new businesses that are tiny and, if strategy is important, then its impact should be identifiable in these fledgling businesses.

Isolating the impact of strategy is, of course, problematic. The chapter began by recognising that such businesses had three (largely reactive) strategic choices available to them. The first was to compete on price. The second was to differentiate and the third was to 'focus' on a particular environment. Of these three strategies prior work suggested that one based on low cost and price competition was the least likely to be effective.

The alternative theoretical approach that we discussed was one that placed much more weight on the internal competencies of the business. This is the resource-based view of the firm. Here, the competitive advantage of the business is seen in terms of its access to superior resources or knowledge that may lever it a sustainable competitive advantage over others in the marketplace.

Empirically, this chapter has sought to investigate such issues in terms of the strategic orientation of the entrepreneur. The findings were that entrepreneurs, when asked about the most important source of competitive advantage, were most likely to emphasise understanding the customer and the skills of the workforce. This is in keeping with a resource-based view of the business that competitive advantage accrues from the internal competencies of the business.

To investigate this more fully, a factor analysis was conducted. This identified three factors which we have called 'skills', 'cost' and quality. The first emphasised the skills of the entrepreneur, administrative skills and the skills of the workforce. The argument here was that this factor would be more likely to be found in imitative businesses. The second component comprised lower prices and a lower cost base. Based on prior research this was also expected be a sub-optimal choice by the entrepreneur. Finally, the third component called quality, and characterised by differentiation, was linked closely to understanding the customer and the novelty of the product/service provided.

Some very interesting results emerge from subsequent analysis of these three strategic orientations. Our key result was the presence of stark regional differences between the 'high' entrepreneurial region of Buckinghamshire and the 'low' region of Teesside. It seemed that Teesside businesses were more likely to be focussed towards either a cost or a skill strategy, whilst Buckinghamshire businesses were much more focussed on a quality strategic orientation.

One reason for the greater likelihood of the adoption of these strategic orientations in a low enterprise area such as Teesside is that it may simply reflect differences in the value placed on skills. For businesses adopting a price competition strategy, one central element is a low cost base achieved by the payment of low wages. As was shown in Chapter 3, Teesside does have more than its fair share of individuals with low skills and such skills rarely attract a high premium. Of course, some skills may be more intangible or informal (Podsakoff et al., 1997; Keep and Mayhew, 1999) so that the imitative entrepreneurs may require and recognise (but perhaps not reward) a set of skills that give them some intangible advantage.

The stronger impression, however, is that the strategic profile of a new business is much more strongly influenced by the environment in which it operates rather than its ability to marshal particular skills and intangible resources. In essence, what matters is *where* not how. Indeed, the only evidence to support the resource-based view is found amongst the Buckinghamshire businesses. The implication is that the areas of high entrepreneurship are also areas where there are more likely to be new businesses that start with novel products and services and conduct R&D (Keeble and Wilkinson, 2000; Kalantaridis and Bika, 2006). In this sense, then, it might be possible to talk about the value of a resource-based view in explaining strategy.

However, two other patterns are evident. First, none of the education or human capital variables was associated with a quality strategy. This might be considered significant since, apart from R&D and innovation, there was little that linked closely with internal competitive advantage. Second, there was no discernable effect of following a high technology path in terms of employment or survival outcomes – in other words such businesses were not more likely to outperform the other new businesses.

For Teesside, however, there was a far greater likelihood of following an imitative or low cost strategic approach. This suggests, above all, either the lack of alternative choices or the constrained nature of choices available to the Teesside entrepreneur. The sense is that they are following a 'me-too' strategy which, at least in terms of subsequent survival outcomes, does little to enhance business performance.

The above is broadly consistent with the entrepreneurs replicating the industrial structure year upon year (see Chapter 4). Buckinghamshire's new businesses are more likely to be the 'seed' beds of innovation whereas those founding new businesses in Teesside till less fertile soil. The implication of such a finding is that just having greater numbers of new businesses looks ineffective from a policy perspective, since the new businesses simply replace but do not seem to enhance the quality of the business stock.

# 6
# Business Advice and the New Business

## Introduction

The decision to start a business often necessitates the support of others. Pivotal here is the entrepreneur's family and friends. Archer (2003), for example, reports on an entrepreneur that gave up a successful business because he believed his new family situation was better served by the safety of stable earnings from employment. For those just starting out, there is perhaps also a need to seek out support from banks, accountants, lawyers, consultants, potential customers, other business owners and publicly funded organisations.

This chapter examines the nature of business advice both prior to start-up and in the early years of a business's life. Whilst recognising the important role of all sources of advice, the focus is on formal public advice. As in the other chapters, this turns around support in Teesside over the 1970s, 1980s and the 1990s and also a spatial comparison between Teesside, Shropshire and Buckinghamshire for the 1990s.

Two main questions drive the discussion. First, are publicly supported advice services improving? Second, what is the impact of support? To examine these questions more fully, the chapter will examine pre and post start-up across the three decades and the use of private and public sector support across the three regions.

The chapter starts with a discussion of the theory of advice, including the choices available to policy makers. Subsequently, the empirical data, both temporal and spatial, is presented. The chapter concludes with a discussion of the implications of these findings.

## The theory of business advice

For ease of exposition, the chapter assumes there are two main theoretical frameworks that seek to offer insight into the subject of business advice. The first is the resource-based view which sees external advisers as a potential resource for a fledgling business (Chrisman and McMullan, 2004). The second is the rational choice perspective that privileges information. This views information and advice as the service offered to those imperfectly informed individuals either starting or in the early stages of running a business. From this perspective, the case for public intervention – the public provision of such services using taxpayers' funds – rests upon the existence of market failure. The rational choice perspective also deals with the potential for opportunism, using an agency theory approach (Mole, 2002) or linking with a wider debate concerning trust (Bennett and Robson, 2004).

### Advice as a resource

Chrisman and McMullan (2004) approach business advice from a resource-based view of the business. In their view, business advice provides knowledge to potential entrepreneurs. However, the circumstances surrounding this knowledge are highly contextual: knowledge is created or transferred through the interaction between the adviser and the potential entrepreneur. The implications of this are two-fold. First, this means that there is an element of tacit (not coded) knowledge acquired by the potential entrepreneur. Since this knowledge is not coded but based on experience, it is not easily acquired or available to others – it is not lying around in books. Therefore, this type of knowledge can be valuable and may sustain competitive advantage under the resource-based view (Barney, 1991, 1997). Second, this means that outside assistance yields different knowledge with different combinations of advisers and entrepreneurs. In essence, no two sessions of outside assistance will be the same and the quality of the advice may be a function of the quality of the adviser (Bennett and Robson, 2003).

Chrisman and McMullan (2000) argue that the role of advisers is that of a counsellor rather than a consultant. This is because the role of the adviser is to enable the client to perform the tasks themselves, rather than doing it for them. Hence, the trained adviser provides an opportunity for entrepreneurs to enhance their knowledge. Chrisman and McMullan (2000) believe that this counselling role and process results in a better transfer and a gain of both tacit and explicit knowledge that is relevant to a specific opportunity.

The view of advice, therefore, suggests a causal mechanism between the transfer of combinations of knowledge through a learning-by-doing process to those who face an acknowledged 'knowledge gap'. The concern is to understand how business support can lead to better outcomes for individual businesses. Whether this is a role for the public sector or should be a supported by the public purse is not a great concern of this perspective. That issue is the focus of the rational choice perspective.

## Rational choice

Within rational choice, intervention is justified only when there is evidence of market failure. There are three main elements of market failure that justify intervention: externalities, incomplete markets and asymmetric information. This leads to three central questions:

(1) Does publicly provided business advice have spillover effects (externalities) that make it a public good?
(2) Does public advice have incomplete markets?
(3) Is business advice exposed to information asymmetries?

Externalities are (unpriced) impacts on those who are not directly involved in the production, or consumption of a good. The classic example of this is the provision of public goods such as defence: if a defence force makes an area safe then it protects all the inhabitants of that area, not simply those that pay directly for the benefit. Externalities are impacts that cannot be confined to the businesses. They may impact others negatively (such as pollution), or positively (such as research and development).

The first argument for public intervention then is that business advice produces externalities. For instance, if advice is provided it may, much like R&D, have spillover effects on to other businesses. These social aspects are not taken into account when decisions are taken by an individual business. Failure to take into account these spillovers would mean a less than socially optimal amount of business advice would be taken by the individual businesses.

Second, markets may be incomplete. This may seem strange as virtually all businesses need someone at least to store (bank) and count (accountants) their money. However, business advice is neither uniform nor homogeneous. Private sector professionals tend to give specialist advice, whereas there may also be a need for more generic advice. This generic advice is where markets might be incomplete. In particular, there may be little incentive for private sector advisers to provide free impartial diagnosis or to tell people their advice is not needed (Hjalmarsson and Johansson, 2003; Turok and Raco, 2000). It is the absence of a market for impartial diagnosis that provides the rationale for intervention.

The third argument is based on asymmetric information (Stiglitz, 2000). Because advice is referred to as an 'experience good' (Nelson, 1970) its real value is difficult to assess prior to purchase. The costs and benefits of advice are potentially uncertain (Lambrecht and Pirney, 2005; Storey, 2003). Hence, if the entrepreneur is unable to assess the quality of advice, it generally leads them to underestimate its benefits and purchase a less than optimal amount of business advice. In seeking to solve such asymmetry, public support seeks to overcome these difficulties.

In summary, the theory on business advice emphasises that it has the potential to transfer tacit knowledge and add to the sustainable competitive advantage of the business. Policy makers have justified public involvement in the market for business advice using three forms of market failure arguments. What is interesting is that policy makers in different countries, and in the same countries in different time periods, have used different market failure arguments to justify their policies (Storey, 2003; Mole and Bramley, 2006). In theory, business advice can lead to improvements at the business level and in economic welfare. Whether this actually happens is another matter and, in part, this depends on implementation issues.

Implementation is important because there exists a wide range of policy options available to policy providers. Building on Turok and Raco (2000), Mole and Bramley (2006) provide a five point menu of key policy choices in the area of business advice:

1. Who delivers ... public, private or quasi?
2. What 'type' ... generic, standards, tailored, regulated, face-to-face, e-based?
3. How is it rationed ... time, sector, price, market segmentation?
4. How is it integrated ... into other economic and social programmes?
5. How is it funded ... by charges, by donations, directly from public funds?

Mole and Bramley (2006) use this choice framework to historically compare two very different but well established business advice programmes that operated in the UK (the Enterprise Initiative and Business Link) and go on to show that the type of business support available has changed over time. Their central point is that policy makers do have a wide choice of options on the delivery of business support and that the outcomes and impact of the support is likely to vary considerably depending on the choices made. Implicitly, Mole and Bramley imply that policy makers are often unaware of this range of choice and, therefore, perhaps make sub-optimal decisions in this area.

## The data on business support

Ideally, for us to assess this range of implementation issues, as well as differences in terms of public and private advice, a whole range of data would be required. Table 6.1 shows the initial 1970s survey collected information on the use and helpfulness of business advice services. This is an important measure of value since, all else equal, if public agencies were of no help whatsoever to business, then client numbers would be expected to fall. One simple measure of whether matters have improved over time, therefore, is the use of such services.

A second test of whether the publicly funded business advisory services are improving is to measure their perceived quality – as reflected in the response of those that used them. In practice, data has become more wide-ranging over time: for the 1970s–1990s there is a measure of helpfulness; whilst for 1980s–1990s there is a second measure which is 'use again'. Since repeat business is recognised as an indicator of quality or at least of contentment with the service, it is used to supplement the 'helpful' question. Finally, in the 1990s, we have a measure of satisfaction from 1–7 (1 denotes that the assistance was vital and 7 denotes that the assistance was no help at all).

The next issue is to identify both the major sources of business advice used in each of the three decades and whether these sources changed. There have been two debates of note concerning the type of advice. The first has been a controversy over targeting and the second has been whether minority groups have access to support.

*Table 6.1* The information collected on use of advisory services

| Year | Timing | | Type | | Quality indicators | | |
|------|--------|--------|--------|--------|--------|--------|--------|
| | Pre start | Post start | Private | Public | Helpful | Use again | Satisfaction |
| 1970s | ✓ | | | ✓ | ✓ | | |
| 1980s | ✓ | ✓ | | ✓ | ✓ | ✓ | |
| 1990s | ✓ | ✓ | ✓ | ✓ | ✓ | ✓ | ✓ |

The targeting debate concerns the merits of focusing support only on certain 'types' of business on the presumption that either they have highly specific problems or exceptional potential to benefit from such advice. As well as targeting towards those business sectors where there are particular negatives to counteract or where positive externalities are likely to be high, targeting has also been on individuals – particularly those from minorities thought to experience some form of disadvantage such as the unemployed or young people.

This chapter interprets this supplementary targeting debate by assessing how the type and usage of advice differs between the pre start advice and advice given to the established businesses. Equally important is how the profiles of those who take pre start-up advice differ from those who take post start-up advice.

In summary, we have data for pre start advice for the 1970s, 1980s and 1990s, and post start advice for the 1980s and 1990s. The types of advice columns show that data are available for public advice in the 1970s and 1980s; in the 1990s it is also available for private sector suppliers. The indicators of quality columns show that data are available for 'helpful' for all three decades, data are presented for 'use again' for the 1980s and 1990s; data for satisfaction ratings are restricted to the 1990s. As in the rest of the book, the comparisons between Teesside, Shropshire and Buckinghamshire are restricted to the 1990s.

## Change over time Teesside 1970s–1990s

In this part of the chapter, our aim is to explore business advice within the major historical changes in the Teesside area over three decades. It begins by looking at pre start business advice (usage, quality, suppliers of support and users of advice) and then considers post start-up support.

In terms of usage, Table 6.2 shows the percentage of new businesses that used public support before they began in business. It also shows

Table 6.2  Use of pre start business support, 1970s–1990s

| Decade | Usage % | Quality | |
|---|---|---|---|
| | | Helpful % | Use again % |
| 1970s | 35.7 | 46.4 | |
| 1980s | 44.4 | 73.7 | 76.8 |
| 1990s | 53.0 | 88.4 | 76.1 |

the two measures of quality: helpfulness and 'use again'. What Table 6.2 shows is that, in the 1970s, just over 1-in-3 businesses (36 per cent) took advice from the public sector prior to starting their business. In the 1980s, when enterprise policy effectively began, this rose to 44 per cent and in the 1990s it rose again to 53 per cent. In essence, there has been a steady rise in the proportion of new businesses that sought advice from the public sector prior to start-up. The increase in the take-up implies a policy impact.

Table 6.2 also shows that, in the 1970s, fewer than half of the businesses that took advice thought that the advice they received was helpful. Since only one-third took advice anyway, only 1-in-5 businesses were in receipt of helpful advice from the public sector. In contrast, by the 1980s, 74 per cent of those who sought advice found it helpful. By the 1990s, 88 per cent of advice received was regarded as helpful – an improvement of 14 per cent compared with the previous decade. However, in terms of the 'use again' measure, the picture was static: in the 1990s in 76 per cent said they would use the source again – identical to the 1980s. Overall, on one of the quality measures, it seems that again the performance of Teesside business support is improving over time. On the other the improvement is less clear.

The public agencies that provided business advice in the 1970s were the local authorities, both county and district councils, the Department of Trade and Industry, Small Businesses Information Centre and English Industrial Estates Corporation (Storey and Strange, 1992). By the 1980s both the suppliers and the nature of the advice given to small businesses had changed. Storey (1982) shows that, in the 1970s, new businesses contacted agencies primarily for information on finance and grants or for premises. Only 9 per cent of contacts were for 'advice on business', but by the 1980s this had risen to 33 per cent.

Table 6.3 shows the most popular sources of pre start business advice in the 1980s and 1990s in terms of usage. It also shows, for users, the percentage of those who found the advice helpful and the percentage that would use the advice again. Table 6.3 shows that over half of businesses seeking public sector advice obtained it from Enterprise Agencies, over one-third from national government (which included the DTI and the Manpower Services Commission). Similarly, more than four-in-five found national government agencies helpful, over 71 per cent found the Enterprise Agencies helpful and 70 per cent found the councils helpful. This was a big improvement on the picture for those taking pre start advice in the 1970s (see Storey and Strange, 1992). Indeed, Enterprise Agencies alone were providing helpful advice

*Table 6.3*   Agencies providing pre start advice in the 1980s and 1990s

| | 1980s | | | 1990s | | |
|---|---|---|---|---|---|---|
| Agency | Usage | Helpful | Use again | Usage | Helpful | Use again |
| Enterprise agencies | 55.8 | 71.7 | 67.9 | 44.7 | 92.2 | 78.1 |
| National government | 34.7 | 81.8 | 81.8 | | | |
| Councils | 31.6 | 70.0 | 73.3 | 14.7 | 71.4 | 71.4 |
| Walker Hall | | | | 32.1 | 89.1 | 71.7 |
| Teesside TEC | | | | 17.5 | 88.0 | 80.0 |
| Start Right/InBiz | | | | 39.1 | 85.7 | 76.8 |

to more start-up businesses in the 1980s than were all of the 1970s agencies put together.

In the 1990s, the pre start advice was delivered by a greater variety of agencies. Enterprise Agencies continued to be the most frequently used source, although by the end of the decade their role had declined as Business Link became established. Within Teesside, local institutions had evolved to aid new business owners. The programme, 'Start Right in Business' (InBiz) and the agency Walker Hall ran programmes on behalf of the public sector. These programmes proved popular with a high proportion of respondents indicating they would use them again. Overall, the clear impression is that by the 1990s business advice to individuals starting a business in Teesside was vastly better on all dimensions than 20 or even 10 years previously. It was used by more new businesses and it was valued by those that used it.

### Factors influencing usage

In the 1970s, Storey and Strange (1992) reported that larger new businesses were more likely to be in receipt of advice than smaller new businesses, primarily because advice was focussed upon the manufacturing sector where new businesses were generally larger. To examine this, and the influence of other factors, Table 6.4 presents three logistic regression models to determine usage (1 = use of public support, 0 = otherwise) for each of the three decades. What is expressed in columns 2,4 and 6 is the odds ratio (ExpB) for a particular variable, For instance, the 1970s model shows that males were only about one-third (0.346 or 34.6 per cent) as likely as females to take pre-start advice. Equally, those with vocational qualifications were about half (0.466 or 46.6 per cent) as likely to take advice as those without such qualifications. The key factor, however, was manufacturing sector which is significantly and positively associated with usage in the 1970s.

*Table 6.4*  Logistic regression of usage, 1970s–1990s

| | 1970s | | 1980s | | 1990s | |
|---|---|---|---|---|---|---|
| | Exp(B) | Wald | Exp(B) | Wald | Exp(B) | Wald |
| Males | .346 | 3.904** | .718 | .830 | .497 | 5.518** |
| Limited company | | | 7.359 | 11.105* | | |
| Found age | 1.010 | .206 | .970 | 2.588 | .982 | 1.655 |
| Degree | .954 | .003 | | | | |
| HND/A Level | 2.083 | 1.227 | | | | |
| Time-served | .466 | 2.803* | | | | |
| Unemployed | | | 2.099 | 4.517** | 1.505 | 1.566 |
| Serial entrepreneur | | | .726 | .435 | .413 | 9.058* |
| Portfolio entrepreneur | | | 3.626 | 2.865*** | | |
| Start-up finance | | | | | | |
| Savings | | | .517 | 2.722*** | .580 | 2.450 |
| Mortgage | .341 | .966 | 2.280 | 1.494 | | |
| Bank finance | | | .900 | .091 | | |
| Finance company | 2.748 | 1.163 | | | 4.203 | 2.567 |
| Manufacturing | 3.401 | 6.829* | 3.511 | 10.264* | 2.199 | 3.451* |
| Professional services | | | 3.053 | 2.574 | | |
| Constant | .822 | .065 | .166 | 1.633 | 23.819 | 8.536* |
| N. | 156 | | 200 | | 264 | |
| log likelihood | 184.1 | | 234.4 | | 335.9 | |
| R² | | .153 | | .245 | | .141 |
| % correct | 69.9 | | 71.5 | | 63.3 | |
| X² | 18.396 | | 40.418 | | 29.523 | |
| Sig. | | .018 | | .000 | | .000 |

*** denotes significant at the 10 per cent level; ** denotes significant at the 5 per cent level; * denotes significant at the 1 per cent level.

Table 6.4 then shows the results for the 1980s. Gender was no longer significant, but being a limited company was a highly significant factor influencing the take-up of pre start advice. The finding that the unemployed were more likely to use advice could perhaps be attributed to the large numbers starting under the Enterprise Allowance Scheme in the 1980s where advice was compulsorily supplied along with the public financial support. Amongst the other influences, portfolio entrepreneurs were (weakly) more likely to seek pre start advice. Those with their own savings were about half as likely (weakly significant) to take advice from the public sector. Manufacturers were three and a half times more likely to seek pre start advice (highly significantly) from the public sector. In summary, in the 1980s, the key users of business support were manufacturers, the unemployed and those starting limited companies.

By the 1990s matters changed again. The significant influences on use of business support were gender (a factor that was significant in the 1970s), serial entrepreneurship, those using personal savings, and being in manufacturing. One other interesting finding is that serial entrepreneurs were substantially less likely to seek advice prior to start-up.

Overall, the pattern over the three decades shows there are factors that influence the seeking of advice. Women are fairly consistently more likely to seek advice than men. Those starting a manufacturing business are consistently more likely to seek advice. Other factors vary between the decades. For example, in the 1980s limited company status and being unemployed was significant but not in other decades.

### Factors influencing helpfulness

Table 6.5 reports three further logistic regressions models. This time our interest is in the factors influencing helpfulness (1 = helpful, 0 = otherwise) amongst those using public support. Again, we use odds ratio (ExpB). The results are weak for the 1970s: the model itself is only just significant and the only significant variable is manufacturing. The 1980s model is more statistically robust. It shows that businesses that

*Table 6.5*   Logistic regression of helpfulness, 1970s–1990s

|  | 1970s | | 1980s | | 1990s | |
|---|---|---|---|---|---|---|
|  | Exp(B) | Wald | Exp(B) | Wald | Exp(B) | Wald |
| Age | .952 | 2.298 | 1.632 | 2.916*** | 1.070 | *2.907 |
| Age$^2$ |  |  | .994 | 3.040*** |  |  |
| Manager |  |  | 3.661 | 3.942** |  |  |
| Same trade |  |  | 3.412 | 3.615* |  |  |
| Serial entrepreneur |  |  |  |  | .418 | 1.593 |
| Use of pre start bank finance |  |  | .280 | 4.195** |  |  |
| Use of pre start public finance |  |  |  |  | 5.619 | 4.487** |
| Manufacturing | 4.506 | 4.691** | 2.218 | 1.381 |  |  |
| Constant | 4.581 | 1.771 | .000 | 2.549 |  |  |
| N. | 55 |  | 84 |  | 138 |  |
| Log likelihood | 69.364 |  | 76.857 |  | 72.528 |  |
| R$^2$ | .147 |  | .280 |  | .142 |  |
| % correct | 60.0 |  | 78.6 |  | 91.3 |  |
| X$^2$ | 6.427 |  | 17.615 |  | 9.013 |  |
| Sig. | .040 |  | .007 |  | .029 |  |

*** denotes significant at the 10 per cent level; ** denotes significant at the 5 per cent level; * denotes significant at the 1 per cent level.

were started by those who had been managers in their previous job were more likely to report finding advice helpful. Somewhat surprisingly, those using bank finance at start-up were less likely to find advice helpful. It also shows that those who had started their business in the same trade were positive about advice. Manufacturing was now insignificant. The age variables imply that older entrepreneurs are less likely to regard advice as helpful. In the 1990s, though, one issue dominates. Those who gained financial support from the public sector were more than five times as likely to say the advice was helpful than those that did not.

### Post start-up advice

Besides pre start-up support, further evidence was collected for the 1980s and the 1990s on post start-up support. Table 6.6 shows that almost one-quarter of the businesses used some post start support in the 1980s. The support was found to be helpful by 77 per cent and a similar proportion reported they would use such support again. The big difference between pre start and post start, therefore, is that those taking post start-up advice are only about half those who take advice before start-up. Table 6.6 also shows for the 1990s that the usage of public post start support had increased, as had the two measures of quality: helpfulness and 'use again'.

Table 6.7 identifies specific sources of post start business advice. For each source it shows usage and then two quality measures: helpful and use again. Comparing these findings with those on pre start advice in Table 6.3 shows both sources are equally highly valued. As with pre start advice, Enterprise Agencies were the most likely to provide helpful advice, but the national government agencies and councils were more appreciated by existing than by pre start businesses. Indeed, in the 1980s, national government agencies were more likely to provide helpful advice to existing businesses than Enterprise Agencies who were mostly concerned with pre start-up support. So, the quality and quantity of public sector advice continued to improve in the 1990s compared with the previous decade.

*Table 6.6* Use of post start business support over time: Teesside

| Decade | Usage % | Quality | |
|---|---|---|---|
| | | Helpful % | Use again % |
| 1980s | 24.8 | 77.4 | 73.6 |
| 1990s | 35.9 | 81.5 | 82.9 |

*Table 6.7* Agencies providing post start advice in the 1980s and 1990s

| Agency | 1980s | | | 1990s | | |
|---|---|---|---|---|---|---|
| | Usage | Helpful | Use again | Usage | Helpful | Use again |
| Enterprise agencies | 50.9 | 65.4 | 65.4 | 26.8 | 69.2 | 84.6 |
| National government | 43.4 | 95.7 | 82.6 | | | |
| Councils | 28.3 | 80.0 | 86.7 | 16.5 | 81.2 | 81.2 |
| Teesside TEC | | | | 31.0 | 83.3 | 80.0 |
| Start Right/InBiz | | | | 41.3 | 92.5 | 90.0 |

*Table 6.8* Logistic regression of usage of post start-up public support, 1980s–1990s

| | 1980s | | 1990s | |
|---|---|---|---|---|
| | Exp(B) | Wald | Exp(B) | Wald |
| Males | | | .704 | 1.335 |
| Age | 1.124 | .352 | 1.253 | 3.062*** |
| Age$^2$ | .998 | .378 | .997 | 3.142*** |
| Degree | 8.145 | 5.667** | | |
| HND/A Levels | 13.062 | 18.549* | 2.340 | 6.830* |
| Sectoral experience | .370 | 5.623** | | |
| Unemployed | 2.402 | 4.647** | | |
| Serial entrepreneur | 2.304 | 2.441 | .566 | 3.285* |
| Business plan at start | | | 3.548 | 18.079* |
| Manufacturing | 1.541 | .844 | | |
| Construction | .192 | 1.282 | | |
| Professional services | .346 | 1.477 | | |
| First year problems | | | | |
| Supply shortage | 3.187 | 3.242*** | 5.219 | 3.147* |
| Skilled labour shortage | 5.420 | 9.858* | | |
| Constant | .017 | 1.115 | .004 | 4.484 |
| N. | 181 | | 264 | |
| log likelihood | 159.811 | | 290.924 | |
| R$^2$ | .370 | | .194 | |
| % correct | 80.1 | | 72.1 | |
| $X^2$ | 53.541 | | 39.336 | |
| Sig. | .000 | | .000 | |

*** denotes significant at the 10 per cent level; ** denotes significant at the 5 per cent level; * denotes significant at the 1 per cent level.

## Factors influencing usage of post start-up advice

As with the earlier logistic regression analysis, Table 6.8 reports three models of usage of post start-up support for the available data on the 1980s and 1990s. What this shows for the 1980s is that educated entrepreneurs – those with a degree or A Level/HND – were significantly more likely to use post start advice. Individuals that were previously unemployed were also more likely to use post start advice – which may reflect the fact that such advice was provided to those that had previously participated in the Enterprise Allowance Scheme. In contrast with pre start advice, manufacturing was no longer significant. Finally, those businesses reporting a shortage of skilled labour in their first year of operations were also more likely to use post start advice. Several of these influences continue into the 1990s. For example, owners with an A Level/HND (although not a degree) were more likely to use post start advice. It is also the case that, perhaps unsurprisingly, businesses reporting problems in their first year of operation were more likely to use advice (Keogh and Mole, 2005). However, the most influential factor is whether the business had a business plan when it began.

In terms of helpfulness, Table 6.9 again reports the odds ratios and significance in terms of whether or not respondents reported the advice to be helpful. For the 1980s, we see that businesses owned by males, rather than females, were more likely to report advice was helpful. However, businesses owned by an individual with A Level/HND Levels were less likely to find the public sector provided advice helpful. Businesses reporting demand shortages were likely to view advice as helpful. By the 1990s, many more businesses reported receiving post start advice and 82 per cent found it helpful. Given the overall success of business advice the 1990s results are best interpreted by asking: for whom was advice unhelpful? The clear answer is those businesses operated by individuals who were born and bred in Teesside.

This suggests that, overall, public sector provided business support has improved over time both for pre and post start businesses. Perhaps because it has a higher opportunity cost, fewer businesses make use of post, than pre start, advice, but it is now the case that the providers of pre start support are also relied on to provide post start support (such as InBiz). The providers of post start support have also changed over the period. National government and its agencies now play a much more modest role.

There are also both changes and similarities in the types of businesses that use advice. The changes reflect a reduced policy focus upon the manufacturing sector and more emphasis in the 1990s on businesses with potential to grow. The similarities imply that educated

*Table 6.9*  Logistic regression of helpfulness of post start-up public support, 1980s–1990s

|  | 1980s | | 1990s | |
| --- | --- | --- | --- | --- |
|  | Exp(B) | Wald | Exp(B) | Wald |
| Males | 8.125 | 6.399** | | |
| Age | 1.063 | 1.556 | 1.002 | .005 |
| HND/A Levels | .173 | 3.492* | | |
| Indigenous | | | .151 | 3.114** |
| Finance at start-up | | | | |
| Family and friends | | | .415 | 2.226 |
| First year problems | | | | |
| Demand shortage | 10.427 | 2.757* | | |
| Constant | .101 | 1.179 | 29.308 | 3.333** |
| N. | 53 | | 102 | |
| log likelihood | 42.427 | | 83.975 | |
| R² | .359 | | .126 | |
| % correct | 79.2 | | 83.3 | |
| X² | 14.273 | | 7.939 | |
| Sig. | .006 | | .047 | |

*** denotes significant at the 10 per cent level; ** denotes significant at the 5 per cent level and * denotes significant at the 1 per cent level.

individuals are more likely to use and appreciate advisory services – more, for example, than individuals born and bred in the locality. One of the more intriguing aspects is the impact of gender, where our results seem to imply that women are more likely to use business advice, whereas men are more likely to report it was helpful to them.

So, whilst according to most dimensions, public sector provided business advice was improving over time on Teesside, the anticipation is still that most business advice is delivered by the private sector. For this reason, differences between private and public advice is now examined. In making this comparison, the available data are only for the 1990s.

## Business advice across the three regions

This part of the chapter compares the three regions to highlight differences in the use of pre start and post start-up support. Because the data are richer (e.g. private sector support, measure of satisfaction), we are also able to investigate more closely the value of such support in terms of three performance outcomes: survival, relative employment growth and annualised employment growth. However, prior to this, pre start-up business support is examined.

## Pre start-up support in the three regions

In the 1990s there were marked differences in terms of the use of business support across the three regions. Pre start-up support, in general, was most likely to be used in Shropshire (96 per cent) and in Buckinghamshire (94.7 per cent) rather than Teesside (81.3 per cent). These differences were statistically significant ($X^2$: 29.7, p. value: 0.000). However, very different results are obtained if only public sources of advice are included: in both Teesside and Shropshire just over half of new businesses took business advice from public sector sources (53 per cent and 51 per cent, respectively). In Buckinghamshire, the proportion was only 27 per cent. This, again, was statistically significant ($X^2$: 29.3, p. value: 0.000).

The obvious explanation is the extensive availability of public support in Teesside, compared with Buckinghamshire, but this does not explain why the public sector advice sources are so important in Shropshire. One possibility is the presence of a threshold, beyond which extra (public) supply has no impact on take-up. The evidence here might lead to the conclusion that the around about 50 per cent mark is a 'natural limit' for public sector business support.

Table 6.10 shows data on three measures of service quality: helpfulness, use again and a third measure that of satisfaction with a particular source of business support (1 was vital, 7 of no help at all). The most vital sources of advice were from family and friends, business contacts or potential customers. Yet, in terms of being helpful, the advice provided by DHP Enterprises (Teesside) and by business contacts and by family and friends scored highest. This emphasises the heterogeneity of business support and suggests that more than one 'satisfaction' measure is appropriate.

Even so, some patterns do emerge. First, several public sector sources of advice rated weakly. However, providers of advice are in more than one 'marketplace' and it may be that providers play more than one role. Councils, for example, have regulatory as well as advisory responsibilities. Similarly, banks are opening accounts or granting loans as well as providing advice. So, even if they receive useful business advice from a council or from a bank, the entrepreneur may be more strongly influenced in their judgement of that organisation by whether the council turned down a planning application or the bank rejected their loan application. A second difficulty of interpreting Table 6.10 is that those thinking of starting a business may take a package of advice from more than one source of support, implying that there are combinations of support that are used by potential entrepreneurs.

Earlier on, it was shown that gender, sector and previous experience were all factors that influenced the take-up of business advice in

*Table 6.10* Satisfaction scores from pre start business support (%)

| Adviser | Vital | 2 | 3 | 4 | 5 | 6 | No help | Helpful | Use again |
|---|---|---|---|---|---|---|---|---|---|
| Accountant | 36.1 | 21.3 | 21.8 | 5.6 | 5.1 | 3.2 | 6.9 | 90.3 | 88.9 |
| Bank | 28.6 | 17.4 | 21.1 | 11.8 | 3.6 | 5.6 | 11.8 | 83.2 | 85.5 |
| Business contacts | 51.7 | 17.2 | 18.4 | 6.3 | 2.3 | 2.3 | 1.7 | 98.9 | 93.7 |
| Customers | 58.4 | 18.2 | 8.8 | 5.8 | .7 | 2.2 | 5.8 | 95.6 | 97.1 |
| Family and friends | 68.2 | 13.4 | 10.6 | 0.9 | 2.3 | 2.3 | 2.3 | 97.7 | 97.7 |
| Property consultants | 34.4 | 21.9 | 18.8 | 0.0 | 6.3 | 6.3 | 12.5 | 87.5 | 90.6 |
| Solicitors | 35.7 | 26.4 | 14.0 | 6.2 | 7.0 | 2.3 | 8.5 | 91.5 | 90.7 |
| Suppliers | 39.7 | 19.8 | 22.1 | 6.1 | 7.6 | 2.3 | 2.3 | 95.4 | 95.4 |
| Trade association | 30.6 | 13.9 | 19.4 | 2.8 | 11.1 | 13.9 | 8.3 | 72.2 | 77.8 |
| Walker Hall | 28.3 | 21.7 | 10.9 | 13.0 | 13.0 | 8.7 | 4.3 | 89.1 | 71.7 |
| Tees Valley TEC | 20.2 | 14.3 | 16.7 | 8.3 | 9.5 | 6.0 | 25.0 | 69.0 | 61.9 |
| Council | 20.0 | 15.4 | 15.4 | 13.8 | 4.6 | 6.2 | 24.6 | 66.2 | 63.1 |
| Start Right/InBiz | 39.0 | 15.3 | 16.9 | 11.9 | 0.0 | 10.2 | 6.8 | 84.7 | 78.0 |
| Prince's Trust | 45.5 | 0.0 | 27.3 | 0.0 | 9.1 | 9.1 | 9.1 | 81.8 | 63.6 |
| Enterprise agency | 21.2 | 23.5 | 11.8 | 15.3 | 10.6 | 8.2 | 9.4 | 87.1 | 74.1 |
| DHP enterprises | 11.8 | 29.4 | 17.6 | 17.6 | 11.8 | 11.8 | 0.0 | 100.0 | 94.1 |
| Darlington business venture | 13.6 | 22.7 | 9.1 | 18.2 | 4.5 | 4.5 | 27.3 | 72.7 | 63.6 |
| Public support in Buckinghamshire | 14.0 | 23.3 | 16.3 | 18.6 | 4.7 | 7.0 | 16.3 | 69.8 | 69.8 |

Teesside. In terms of the three regions, Table 6.11 compares the users of public sector provided business advice. It shows that Teesside and Shropshire businesses were more likely to take advice than those in Buckinghamshire. It also shows that those individuals least likely to use public sector advice were serial entrepreneurs. Most of the other variables are, at best, only weakly significant with, for example, gender now dropping out of the equation. Overall, the most significant impact is from the geographical area in which the business starts.

In terms of reported helpfulness, Table 6.11 shows that those most likely to report receiving helpful advice were those that obtained finance and those located on Teesside. There were also some negative reactions from those who used finance company funds to help start-up their business – perhaps a reaction to a negative financing decision.

## Post start-up advice across the three regions

The expectation from the earlier evidence on the three decades is that the usage of support will fall away once the business has begun operations.

*Table 6.11* Logistic regressions of usage and helpfulness of pre start-up support across the three regions

|  | Gets advice | | Helpful | |
|---|---|---|---|---|
|  | Exp(B) | Wald | Exp(B) | Wald |
| Males | .790 | 1.154 | 1.156 | .147 |
| Limited company | 1.018 | .008 |  |  |
| Age | .993 | .493 | 1.022 | 1.414 |
| Degree | 1.175 | .417 |  |  |
| HND/A Levels | 1.540 | 3.397*** |  |  |
| Managerial experience | 1.034 | .030 |  |  |
| Sectoral experience | .829 | .965 |  |  |
| Indigenous | 1.335 | 2.092 |  |  |
| Unemployed | 1.510 | 3.634*** |  |  |
| Serial entrepreneur | .613 | 6.486** |  |  |
| Start-up finance |  |  |  |  |
| Bank finance | 1.272 | 1.424 |  |  |
| Finance company |  |  | .265 | 3.912** |
| Public authority finance |  |  | 5.565 | 7.330* |
| Teesside | 2.215 | 10.227* | 2.416 | 6.284* |
| Shropshire | 2.457 | 11.240* |  |  |
| Constant | 1.225 | .083 | .814 | .053 |
| N. | 566 |  | 287 |  |
| log likelihood | 729.399 |  | 248.05 |  |
| $R^2$ | .116 |  | .158 |  |
| % correct | 63.1% |  | 82.2% |  |
| $X^2$ | 51.5 |  | 29.5 |  |
| Sig. | .000 |  | .000 |  |

\*\*\* denotes significant at the 10 per cent level; \*\* denotes significant at the 5 per cent level; \* denotes significant at the 1 per cent level.

Overall, this was also evident for the three regions: the percentage of businesses using advice post start-up was lower at 67 per cent than the 88 per cent that used pre start-up support. In terms of the regions, the earlier differences between Shropshire, Buckinghamshire and Teesside disappear with 67 per cent of Teesside, 70 per cent of Buckinghamshire and 66 per cent of Shropshire businesses making some use of post start-up support. These small differences were not statistically significantly different between the three areas ($X^2$: 0.73; p. value: 0.694).

Nonetheless, there were differences in the use of private support (private support consists of the professions, contacts, suppliers and trade associations). Two-thirds (66 per cent) of the Buckinghamshire businesses used these sources compared with just under half of the businesses in Teesside and Shropshire (47 per cent and 50 per cent, respectively). This was a significant difference ($X^2$: 15.509; p. value: 0.000). Likewise, post start-up, Teesside and Shropshire businesses were more likely to use public support (36 per cent and 31 per cent, respectively) than Buckinghamshire businesses (13 per cent). This was statistically significant ($X^2$: 24.194; p. value: 0.000).

The factors influencing the use of post start-up public support are shown in Table 6.12. Again, from the logistic regression for use of support, a key positive influence is having a business plan at start-up. A second factor is the education of the founder, so that those with HND/A Levels were twice as likely to take advice than those without. The third key influence is geography, with businesses in Teesside and Shropshire being much more likely to use public sector advice than those in Buckinghamshire. Some, much weaker, gender and age effects are also identified.

*Table 6.12*   Logistic regressions of usage and helpfulness of post start-up support across the three regions

|  | Gets advice | | Helpful | |
| --- | --- | --- | --- | --- |
|  | Exp(B) | Wald | Exp(B) | Wald |
| Gender | .666 | 2.848*** | 1.464 | .712 |
| Age | 1.213 | 4.344** | 1.008 | .097 |
| Age² | .998 | 4.871** |  |  |
| Limited company |  |  | 1.698 | 1.159 |
| HND/A Levels | 2.053 | 7.933* |  |  |
| Business plan at start-up | 2.464 | 16.491* |  |  |
| Business size at start-up | 1.065 | 3.230*** |  |  |
| Problems with supplies |  |  | 1.777 | .486 |
| Problems with labour turnover |  |  | 9.619 | 3.482*** |
| Start-up finance |  |  |  |  |
| Family and friends |  |  | .413 | 3.021*** |
| Public finance |  |  | 3.026 | 4.369** |
| Teesside | 2.732 | 11.5658 | 60.119 | 20.925* |
| Shropshire | 2.417 | 7.2108 | 39.458 | 17.471* |
| Constant | .003 | 8.664* | .033 | 4.968** |
| N. | 482 |  | 180 |  |
| log likelihood | 532.225 |  | 153.468 |  |
| R² | .163 |  | .375 |  |
| % correct | 73.9% |  | 82.8 |  |
| X² | 59.002 |  | 53.250 |  |
| Sig. | .000 |  | .000 |  |

\*\*\* denotes significant at the 10 per cent level; \*\* denotes significant at the 5 per cent level; \* denotes significant at the 1 per cent level.

*Table 6.13*   Satisfaction scores from post start business support

| Adviser | Vital | 2 | 3 | 4 | 5 | 6 | No help | Helpful | Use again |
|---|---|---|---|---|---|---|---|---|---|
| Accountant | 48.8 | 20.1 | 17.1 | 5.5 | 1.2 | 3.0 | 4.3 | 95.2 | 91.5 |
| Bank | 35.7 | 21.6 | 16.8 | 7.0 | 2.7 | 7.0 | 9.2 | 90.3 | 90.8 |
| Business contacts | 50.9 | 15.8 | 19.3 | 8.8 | 0.0 | 1.8 | 3.5 | 96.5 | 98.2 |
| Customers | 76.6 | 14.1 | 6.3 | 1.6 | 1.6 | 0.0 | 0.0 | 98.4 | 96.9 |
| Family and friends | 70.6 | 15.3 | 9.4 | 1.2 | 1.2 | 0.0 | 2.4 | 100.0 | 100.0 |
| Property consultants | 25.0 | 37.5 | 25.0 | 12.5 | 0.0 | 0.0 | 0.0 | 100.0 | 100.0 |
| Solicitors | 38.2 | 32.7 | 12.7 | 5.5 | 3.6 | 3.6 | 3.6 | 98.2 | 96.4 |
| Suppliers | 44.4 | 15.9 | 22.2 | 9.5 | 4.8 | 1.6 | 1.6 | 95.2 | 96.8 |
| Trade association | 23.1 | 34.6 | 7.7 | 19.2 | 0.0 | 7.7 | 7.7 | 92.3 | 84.6 |
| TEC | 23.0 | 16.4 | 16.4 | 8.2 | 8.2 | 6.6 | 21.3 | 78.7 | 68.9 |
| Council | 38.2 | 23.5 | 11.8 | 0.0 | 0.0 | 2.9 | 23.5 | 63.6 | 69.7 |
| Start Right/InBiz | 47.5 | 15.0 | 22.5 | 0.0 | 5.0 | 10.0 | 0.0 | 92.5 | 90.0 |
| Enterprise agency | 37.8 | 16.2 | 18.9 | 2.7 | 8.1 | 5.4 | 10.8 | 72.7 | 87.9 |
| Public support in Buckinghamshire | 14.3 | 19.0 | 14.3 | 9.5 | 19.0 | 0.0 | 0.0 | 76.2 | 71.4 |

Unlike usage, however, helpfulness is less influenced by the human capital of the owner (e.g. age and gender) and more related to whether the business experienced problems in its first year, gaining finance from the public sector and, in Buckinghamshire, not using the public sector sources prior to start-up. The significance of having problems in the first year reinforces the earlier finding that appreciation of post start advice depends on that advice overcoming a specific problem. Finally, those starting with finance from family and friends were less likely to report finding public sector business advice to be helpful.

This is perhaps also evident in the satisfaction with particular sources of support. Table 6.13 shows that most vital sources of post start-up business support came from family and friends, customers, and business contacts. This mirrors the sentiments found in terms of pre start-up support. It is also interesting that in term of satisfaction, Start Right/InBiz is seen as being vital to nearly half of the people who used the programme. This puts it on a par with accountants and above that of the bank and the solicitor.

## Assessing the value of support

The pattern that emerges thus far is one of a marked increase in the usage of public sector support across the three decades. Equally, there has been a general increase in satisfaction with such support. In the 1990s, the evidence suggested that there were clear differences between the three regions: greater intensity of usage in the high and modest entrepreneurial regions of Buckinghamshire and Shropshire but more concentrated use of the public sector outside of Buckinghamshire.

One further test of the value of such support is to examine any links between the use of business advice and the performance of the business. After all, it may be thought, from a rational choice perspective, that the real value of public support is its ability to shape either the longevity or the growth of the business. Equally, from the resource-based view, the value of support may also be thought to be in terms of enhancing the performance of the business.

To examine this, Table 6.14 presents a summary of simple univariate tests of the relationship between a particular source of pre start-up support and one of three outcomes: if the business survived; what its relative employment performance was; and what was its annualised employment growth. In addition, further tests were conducted to see if there were any performance differences in terms of use of prestart-up support, use of private or public support and in terms of the number of sources of support.

Table 6.14 points to only five associations (at the 5 per cent level). Businesses that used council support and TEC (Training and Enterprise Council) support were more likely to survive. Those that used property consultants were also more likely to see relative and annualised employment growth outcomes. Finally, using business contacts as a source of support at start-up saw superior relative employment growth outcomes.

What is perhaps more interesting about Table 6.14 is that there are only five such associations. For instance, it does not seem to matter whether a fledgling business made use of pre start-up support or if this support was confined just to the private or public sector. Similarly, it does not appear that new businesses that make greater use of support, again either in total or disaggregated in terms of private or public sources of pre start-up support, achieve observable performance benefits. Support at the pre start-up stage does not, therefore, seem to make an identifiable impact on performance.

Table 6.15 points to similarly weak links with performance for the provision of post start support. Nonetheless, what is interesting about Table 6.15 is that there does some to be some evidence of the impact of some informal sources of support. Both business contacts and customers' support is positively and significantly associated with relative and annualised employment growth outcomes (at the 5 per cent level).

*Table 6.14*  Summary of univariate tests between sources of pre start-up support and performance

|  | Survival | Relative employment | Annualised employment |
|---|---|---|---|
| Accountant[1,2] |  |  |  |
| Bank[1,2] |  |  |  |
| Business contacts[1,2] |  | + |  |
| Customers[1,2] |  |  |  |
| Family and friends[1,2] |  |  |  |
| Property consultants[1,2] |  | + | + |
| Solicitors[1,2] |  |  |  |
| Suppliers[1,2] |  |  |  |
| Trade association[1,2] |  |  |  |
| TEC[1,2] | + |  |  |
| Council[1,2] | + |  |  |
| Start Right/InBiz[1,2] |  |  |  |
| Enterprise agency[1,2] |  |  |  |
| Public support in Buckinghamshire[1,2] |  |  |  |
| Used support in the 1990s[1,2] |  |  |  |
| Only used public support[1,2] |  |  |  |
| Only used private support[1,2] |  |  |  |
| Number of sources of support[3,4] |  |  |  |
| Number of public sources of support[3,4] |  |  |  |
| Number of private sources of support[3,4] |  |  |  |

1: Chi-square tests between factor and survival; 2: t-test between factor and employment growth outcome; 3: t-test between factor and survival; 4: correlation between factor and employment growth outcome.

There is also evidence that use of family and friends is supportive of relative employment growth.

Presented in this simple way, the link between the provision of business support and business performance is difficult to discern. In part, this may be because any relationship is more complex than is implied by Table 6.15. For example, it may be that the more able new entrepreneurs are less likely to seek business advice so, even if business advice does enhance the performance of low performing businesses, it only raises their performance to that of the businesses that did not seek such advice. In practice, taking account of such arguments is very difficult, and better data than are available to us would be required for such work. Even so, we believe that this lack of association does point to the difficulty of linking business advice to enhanced business performance since this

*Table 6.15*   Summary of univariate tests between sources of post start-up support and performance

|  | Survival | Relative employment | Annualised employment |
|---|---|---|---|
| Accountant[1,2] |  |  |  |
| Bank[1,2] |  |  |  |
| Business contacts[1,2] |  | + | + |
| Customers[1,2] |  | + | + |
| Family and friends[1,2] |  | + |  |
| Property consultants[1,2] |  |  |  |
| Solicitors[1,2] |  |  |  |
| Suppliers[1,2] |  |  |  |
| Trade association[1,2] |  |  |  |
| TEC[1,2] |  |  |  |
| Council[1,2] |  |  |  |
| Start Right/InBiz[1,2] |  |  |  |
| Enterprise agency[1,2] |  |  |  |
| Public support in Buckinghamshire[1,2] |  |  |  |
| Used support in the 1990s[1,2] |  |  |  |
| Only used public support[1,2] |  |  |  |
| Only used private support[1,2] |  |  |  |
| Number of sources of support[3,4] |  |  |  |
| Number of public sources of support[3,4] |  |  |  |
| Number of private sources of support[3,4] |  |  |  |

1: Chi-square tests between factor and survival; 2: t-test between factor and employment growth outcome; 3: t-test between factor and survival; 4: correlation between factor and employment growth outcome.

result also emerges from other, much larger scale and econometrically sophisticated research, on this matter (Wren and Storey, 2002; Mole et al., 2007).

## Summary

This chapter began by examining whether publicly provided business advice has improved over three decades. The measures used were 'take-up' and 'satisfaction'. The evidence is that there has been a marked improvement according to both measures. First, take-up has increased. In the 1970s, it was found that 38 per cent of businesses took business advice from the public sector before they began to trade. By the 1980s, this had risen to 44 per cent and on to 53 per cent in the 1990s. Second, there has been a sharp rise in the proportion reporting this advice to be helpful. In the 1970s it was 17 per cent, rising to 33 per cent in the 1980s and 37 per cent in the 1990s.

Other indicators also point to improvement. The number of sources of advice has increased over the three decades. Potential entrepreneurs have become more likely to seek advice and there are more choices available to them.

The businesses using advice have also changed over the period. In the 1970s, the most significant distinguishing characteristic of those receiving pre start business advice were that they were manufacturers, who reported high satisfaction with public agencies. By the 1980s, manufacturers continued to use advice services, but they were joined by those who intended to run limited companies. However, manufacturers were less likely than before to regard it as helpful. Those regarding these services as helpful were the more 'capable managers' judged by their previous experience and their choice of legal form-limited companies. However, it is noticeable that, in the 1980s, males running businesses that have sales problems are also likely to regard public sector advice as helpful. This ties in with Bennett (2006) who found that men were significantly more likely to take advice from consultants.

By the 1990s, manufacturers continued to be important users of public advice services, as were women and novice entrepreneurs. Those least likely to regard the advice as helpful were business owners indigenous to the area. Those taking advice once their business had started tended to be novice entrepreneurs responding to specific problems.

These differences in the patterns of usage and satisfaction potentially mirror wider policy differences. As we saw in Chapter 3, there have been key changes in enterprise policy brought about by very real economic changes in the shape and structure of the UK economy over the three decades. These problems have roots in the 1970s when the economic problems of poorer enterprise areas were often regarded as a manufacturing problem (Blackaby, 1979). By the 1980s, matters had changed, with unemployment the dominant issue. The evidence here suggests that the unemployed individual considering starting a business was much more likely – either willingly or because they had to – to take business advice. Indeed, perhaps because it was imposed on many of them, the unemployed did not tend to find pre start advice helpful.

The evidence also suggests that women do not seem to be reluctant to take business advice. This is at odds with Shaw et al. (2001) who have suggested that women entrepreneurs faced particular barriers to enterprise, including networks, and access to resources and, based on this, women may be less likely use advice agencies (reported in Deakins and Freel, 2003). Our evidence instead, points to no significant gender differences in seeking advice. The only significant finding is that males in the 1980s were more likely to report that advice was helpful – perhaps because women were less likely to get helpful advice at that time.

In terms of the three regions, the evidence is that, in general, clients tend to value advice provided by the private sector more highly than that from the public sector. This is particularly the case in Buckinghamshire but the same is true in Teesside even though public advice is extensively accessed and has clearly improved over time. A second finding was that there were distinctive regional differences in the take-up and delivery of business advice. In Buckinghamshire, there were fewer public sector advisory services available and a lower take-up of public sector advice. Even so, in all three locations there was an expectation that public advice should be focussed on businesses with growth potential.

The 1990s data also allowed a comparison to be made between public and private sector support. Overall, informal and private sector sources were regarded more highly by their users than were the services provided by public organisations. However, the types of advice that each source provided was often very specific. The highest rated advisers were the informal contacts with customers, business contacts, friends and family. Next were private sector advisers such as accountants, bankers and solicitors. Even so, some public sector advisory services were deemed vital before the entrepreneur started their business: Start Right in Business in Teesside was particularly noteworthy in this respect. Nonetheless, we were unable to show that advisory support, provided either by the public or private sector, clearly enhanced new business performance. Instead, what seemed to matter more was informal post start-up support from business contacts and customers.

Overall, there does seem a modicum of support for resource-based view of business support (Chrisman and McMullan, 2004) since more experienced business owners were less likely to use public advisory services. This is in keeping with seeing business support as addressing a 'knowledge-gap' (Chrisman and McMullan, 2004). Nonetheless, the considerably greater use of support in a 'low' enterprise area such as Teesside implies the presence of a resource, rather than a knowledge, gap.

Our most disconcerting finding is that, whilst recognising the simplicity of the analytical approach, there remain few clear links between advisory services and business performance. So, whilst there has been a clear increase in take-up, and marked increases in the satisfaction with the service provided, the economic impact remains an open question.

Finally, looking back at Mole and Bramley's (2006) checklist, what this chapter shows is that over the 30-year period the choice of who delivers has changed from primarily national to primarily regional bodies. The role of the public sector in delivery has ebbed and flowed with, for the most part, the private sector as deliverer. The 1980s saw tailored consultancy overlaid on top of schemes such as the Enterprise Allowance Scheme or the development of the Enterprise Agencies. Rationing has also been altered with a failed attempt to ration through price in the early days of Business Link. The role of grants has been downgraded from its heyday in the 1970s when manufacturers demanded and felt entitled to grants. The 1980s saw a move towards subsidised advice and on in the 1990s to the 'nationalised' advice of Business Link. So, what comes through quite strikingly from these results and surveys is the key part that the business support plays within other policy priorities.

# 7

# Finance for New Businesses

## Introduction

It is frequently argued that a lack of finance blocks people starting their business and limits the subsequent growth of the business (Beck and Demirguc-Kunt, 2006). In other words, if there was more finance available, then it is likely that we would get stronger business growth and, therefore, healthier economies.

One task of this chapter is to examine this issue carefully. For all the theory on the rationing of credit to new businesses (e.g. Stiglitz and Weiss, 1981; Evans and Jovanovic, 1989), is it really self-evident that new businesses struggle unnecessarily? Parker (2004) suggests that the struggle is not as dismal as it appears and, if anything, entrepreneurs either tend get as much finance as they are generally worth or, according to De Meza (2002), too much finance is available, particularly to weaker entrepreneurs. Moreover, even if there is a grain of truth in any access to finance problems, does this mean that there is a need to design and deliver public responses to attempt to correct perceived deficiencies?

To examine these issues, the chapter begins by providing a review of the general concerns that motivate some of the discussions of new small business finance. From this what emerges is that, if entrepreneurs are financially constrained, this is largely because of informational problems and that they typically make use of their own rather than other's money in setting up their business. Empirically, the chapter goes on to consider how the use and importance of particular forms of finance have evolved over time. A comparison is also made between those that sought finance but were rejected in the 1980s and the 1990s to tease out if there were further temporal differences.

The chapter then considers regional variations by empirically exploring the use and importance of finance. We review the scale of enterprise
support provided by the public sector in the 'low' enterprise region of
Teesside. Finally, we examine the size of this intervention (measured by
the use of pre start-up finance amongst entrepreneurs) and investigate
the value of such support.

## The access to finance problem for small businesses

There is a fundamental reason why small businesses struggle to attract
finance. Compared with larger businesses, small (new) businesses suffer 'informational opacity' (Berger and Udell, 1998: 616). This stems
from a number of sources. At a mundane level, existing small businesses are often exempt from having to provide financial information
to external groups. Equally, unlike existing business, new businesses
lack a track record to enable potential financiers to judge their prospects. This potentially makes it difficult for those interested in buying
a share of the business (equity finance) or those who could provide a
loan (debt finance) to invest in the business.

Equity and debt providers may also be suspicious of new businesses
because they are unsure of the quality or talent of the entrepreneur.
Although some individuals do own or manage more than a single business at any one time, the bulk only own a single business. This isrisky
because having all their assets in one place may mean that the entrepreneur might be tempted to oversell the business potential to finance
providers. Suppose, for example, an entrepreneur knows their business
is struggling, they might be tempted (in their darker moments) to try
to hide this information from investors. Genuinely, the entrepreneur
may be worried that by telling them, the investors might want their
money back, even though the entrepreneur knows or believes the business is just about to become successful. This option is more likely to be
available when information is opaque than when it is in the public
domain.

Alternatively, some entrepreneurs are so optimistically pre-disposed
that they are unaware even of current problems and even if they were,
they are so confident about the future that they do not consider inform-
ing their financial providers.

It is not just the entrepreneur's motives that can be difficult to discern. New businesses, even if they are run by people with entrepreneurial talent, have a high risk of closure. First, because they are new,

they suffer because they have to overcome the understandable conservatism of customers and suppliers. Even if they overcome this 'liability of newness' (Stinchcombe, 1965), most professional financiers have built up pools of knowledge and experience which demonstrates that smaller and newer businesses are less likely to survive than older and larger businesses. Equally, they also know that the performance of new businesses is highly variable. This means that the experienced provider of finance has more – but still imperfect – knowledge of the likely success of the new business than the owner of that business. So, in addition to the market for new business finance being informationlly opaque, it is also asymmetric.

For these reasons it is difficult to tell who is likely to be a high or a low risk so that any financier might make an incorrect choice from a pool of available entrepreneurs. Indeed, this task is made more difficult and costly. A judgement has to be made whether it is worthwhile to devote resources monitoring what may be (for them) relatively small amounts of finance.

In an opaque market place two types of lending errors are made. The first is that some businesses only obtain a smaller quantity of finance, even though they look the same as entrepreneurs who are fully funded (*Type I credit rationing*). A second is that businesses are rejected for finance, even though, again, they look like those that obtained funding in full (*Type II credit rationing*).

Type II errors mean that some that some "good" businesses may be rejected for funding, regardless of the repayment terms (interest rate). This is sometimes referred to as *redlining*, in which providers of finance refuse to provide funds to certain types of business presumably because their prior experience with such businesses has been poor. This may also have damaging economic consequences for both the individual business and society as a whole if some of the 'redlined' businesses are suitable for funding.

In short, because the market for new businesses finance is opaque, some businesses that would benefit society are not funded. For example, there may be an under-investment of support to high technology businesses because banks cannot judge if they are good propositions. Equity financiers such as venture capitalists or business angels may also struggle, first to find such businesses and, second, even if they can agree terms, there is the potential that there may be divergent interests at play. For instance, venture capitalists may be interested in selling shares in the business on a stock exchange within a six to seven year time horizon to maximise their capital gains and re-cycle their funds. This may not correspond with the time horizon of the business owner.

The above reasons explain why there has been a long history of concern about the finances of small businesses beginning in the UK with the Macmillan Committee (1931) but followed in later decades by several government investigations (Bolton, 1971; Wilson, 2004; Graham, 2004) and numerous policy initiatives (see Chapter 3).

The UK is not unique in this respect. For example, the US created the Reconstruction Finance Corporation in the early 1930s to, *inter alia*, support smaller businesses. Such support has continued with the legal identification of the need to support US small businesses through the creation of the Small Business Administration in 1953.

## Accessing finance

We prefix our discussion about access to finance by reflecting on the role that windfalls play in entrepreneurship. This is important because windfalls, either from redundancy money, lottery winnings or inheritance money, represent 'free' money. The question is whether this free money increases the likelihood that individuals start a business compared with otherwise similar individuals who did not benefit from such a windfall? The basic answer to this is yes, but generally only up to a certain point (Holtz-Eakin et al., 1994a; Lindh and Ohlsson, 1996; Blanchflower and Oswald, 1998). In essence, having free money is helpful since it overcomes a wealth constraint, but that does not of course mean that all wealthy people start businesses or that they derived their wealth from business-related activities.

A second fairly robust empirical result is that entrepreneurs do not place equal value on the source of their funding. Instead of being indifferent to whether it is a bank or a business angel that funds their business, the evidence is that there exists a quite clear hierarchy or pecking order (Myers and Maljuf, 1984). The pecking order is based upon the assumption that the business owner favours those sources of finance over which he or she has the greatest control or discretion. So, the most common, and highly favoured, source of start-up finance is personal savings and 'inside' sources of finance, whether this is from family (Basu and Parker, 2001) or friends (Shaffer and Pulver, 1985; Van Auken and Carter, 1989; Carter and Van Auken, 1990). Second in the pecking order is debt (bank) finance. The business owner may already be 'fully borrowed' from their family or friends but needs to supplement this by seeking from the bank some form of repayable finance, usually over the short to medium term. Least attractive, and hence coming at the bottom of the pecking order, is outside equity, typically obtained either from a business angel or from a venture capitalist.

Equity finance provided by angels or venture capitalists, is a subject of considerable interest, perhaps because it is seen as being at the forefront of dynamic entrepreneurship. However, it is a very atypical source of finance for new businesses. Berger and Udell (1998) show that it plays a negligible role in financing new businesses in the United States – a country in which venture capital is more significant than anywhere in the world. In the UK, Hughes (1997b) estimated that in 1992, venture capitalists provided 2.9 per cent of the *additional* sources of funding for *existing* small business. Fraser (2005) looked specifically at start-up finance. He found that the 0.3 per cent of UK start-ups made some use of venture capitalists. Amongst start-ups, meanwhile, 20.4 per cent made use of a bank loan, a rate 6,800 times greater than the use of venture capital. Similarly, personal savings predominate at 69.4 per cent, making it 23,331 times more prevalent than venture capital.

The situation is much the same in the US. The US Census Bureau (2007) estimated that 2.7 per cent of start-up funding for US businesses comes from 'outside investors'. Bygrave and Hunt (2007), meanwhile, estimated that there were some 3 million new businesses created in the US in 2004. Of these, entrepreneurs put in $200 billion and family and friends a further $70 billion. The contribution of business angels was much more modest. Bygrave suggests that such support was made available to 50,000 businesses and offered $30 billion. This equates to 1.67 per cent of the 3 million businesses and 11.1 per cent of the $270 billion finance. Venture capital support was, however, almost a complete irrelevance. In 2004, 799 businesses were supported (0.26 per cent) – strikingly similar to the Fraser (2005) results for the UK - to the tune of $4.4 billion (1.63 per cent).

Overall, the picture is one of internal sources of finance being preeminent partly because of the information opacity of new businesses and partly because of the preferences of the entrepreneur. We now turn to our question of whether there are finance "gaps" and whether government can play a key role in reducing their scale and significance and so enhance economic welfare.

Our broad position is that currently in the UK such gaps are modest and that most individuals would be able to access the necessary funding required to start a 'typical' new business. The median average spent in the UK on starting up a business was £15,000 (Fraser, 2005). Although it may be higher in other countries in terms of the time and costs of business regulation and compliance (Djankov et al., 2002), the resources required are modest. These costs are unlikely to have changed much over time: Berger and Udell (1998) estimated that in the US in 1993 the average was around $5,000.

The argument, however, might be that banks or the television and internet-based finance companies offering 'cheap' loans with 'easy' repayment terms still typically require home ownership as security or collateral and so, whilst funding is, in principle, available, it can only be accessed at a high cost. The reply is that banks have become vastly more sophisticated since the early 1990s in processing data about their clients and using this to make more informed judgements about lending applications without having to resort to collateral-based lending (Bank of England, 2004). Indeed, whilst in the past collateralisation was endemic (Berger and Udell, 1990; Cressy, 1993), the argument is that banks have increasingly focussed upon cashflow and moved away from short term overdraft financing to more fixed term finance (Bank of England, 2004). So, decisions on loans are made on the basis of credit scoring, which reflects either the past performance of the applicant or the past performance of individuals with the applicant's characteristics. Hence, whilst the relationship with the loan manager may be still important (Berger and Udell, 2002), more pertinent nowadays is the credit history of an individual. In effect, loan decisions are largely automated for small amounts.

Banks also have changed from just relying on asset-based lending (collateral) but now may look at financial statement lending (cashflow) or by encouraging businesses to use factoring, invoice discounting, leasing, hire purchase and trade credit to support the needs of the businesses. Many of these may not appear available to the new start-up because they do not have a track record to gain credit from trade suppliers. However, personal individual finance has also changed: besides personal savings, and any available house mortgage, new entrepreneurs have at their disposal personal forms of cash either through overdrafts or credit cards. Indeed, overall, the most likely source of finance used by existing small businesses is a credit card. Whilst interest rates on credit cards are very high on balances they provide effectively free finance for short periods. Business owners, certainly in the UK, have therefore become extremely skilled in minimising their interest charges on borrowed funds (Fraser, 2005).

The negotiating skills of the entrepreneur have also improved in recent years, along with the greater competition amongst suppliers in this marketplace. As Hughes (1997b) argues, if entrepreneurs have real confidence in their ability and the likely success of their product or service, their urge is either to 'play the market' to obtain the best possible deal from a loan supplier or to retain the highest possible share in a deal over equity. To emphasise both these points Fraser (2005) finds, for instance, that those with financial management skills were much more likely to gain a bank loan than those without. To reflect the 'playing of the market' he finds nearly 60 per cent of business owners turned down for a bank loan find the money from someone else (Fraser, 2005).

Of course matters are very different during a credit crunch (Bank of England, 1994), but in more economically benign times, access to finance almost disappears as a problem for new businesses. Fraser (2005) finds that only one in 10 of new entrepreneurs suggest that finance is an issue. A much more common problem is finding customers. Similar findings were also found by finance providers (e.g. NatWest/SBRT, 2003), the government (SBS, 2001/2002) and other studies of external finance (e.g. Cosh and Hughes, 2003).

Thus far we have only reported on research that uses loan rejections as a measure of market imperfection. However, another dimension may be those individuals that are discouraged from accessing finance (Kon and Storey, 2003) on the grounds that they might be rejected. Levenson and Willard (2000), looking at the US in the late 1980s, argued that the rejection rate was very modest (2.14 per cent) but that nearly double this number (4.22 per cent) did not apply because they feared rejection. Other empirical evidence, more focused upon existing businesses rather than start-ups, suggests that the rate, at least in the UK, ranges from 11 per cent (Cosh and Hughes, 2003) to 15 per cent (Wilson, 2004). Fraser (2005), though, finds that the rejection rate for new start-ups is around 4 per cent and that, overall, for small businesses the discouragement rate was again 4 per cent. What is clear is that, if there are imperfections in the market for small/new business finance, they are significantly underestimated by simply quantifying those businesses that are rejected for loans.

Our view chimes with those of Parker's (2004) who urges the need to be sceptical over the existence of widespread credit constraints in a modern economy with a benign macro environment.. Indeed, if de Meza (2002) is correct, the main problem in finance is not the undersupply of finance but its *oversupply*. Because finance is readily available, de Meza argues that it tempts into entrepreneurship those who are ill-suited to it and that this leads ultimately to a loss for society as these more marginal entrepreneurs fail to prosper. If anything, de Meza (2002) counsels, there is a need for tax breaks for employment rather than for new start-ups as this would balance the current taxation inequities enjoyed by the self-employed but not by the employed. Making entrepreneurship less financially viable to lower quality entrepreneurs will also have a virtuous impact in that only higher quality businesses would be more likely to be created and, because these are less risky, the average cost of finance would, in turn, fall.

The final difficulty with access to finance is the design and delivery of government support programmes. Even if there were evidence that people were being ill-served or under-served by the existing range of finance providers because of direct discrimination against particular groups in society; or because finance providers like the banks were either anti-competitive; managerially incompetent or socially irresponsible; or because the range of finance on offer was wrong because it was the wrong type, wrong amount or came at the wrong time, the case has still to be made that government intervention would improve matters significantly.

Public sector attempts to provide such funding have experienced major difficulties. A classic vignette of this is provided by Mason and Harrison (2003). In response to the UK government's attempts to provide regional venture capital funds, they caustically suggest that governments have a poor record of employing appropriate people to manage such funds; that the funds themselves are too small; and that they are unable to specify the appropriate equity gap. Parker (2004) also finds loan guarantee schemes to be, at best, ineffective: 'while they do not do much obvious harm, they do not appear to do very much good either.' (p. 241). Publicly designed programmes also carry the risks that giving money to one business impairs another (displacement effect) and potentially ignores the fact that the business could have got the money from somewhere else (deadweight effect). All in all, even if there are credit constraints, there is no surety that public finance providers are able to design and deliver effective support.

To conclude this section, we recognise that markets do not always work perfectly and that there are powerful, information-based, reasons why the market for small business finance means that some suitable people will either be denied finance or fear that they would be denied.

What is more open to question is that because there are cases when some people, or types of people or business complain that they were unable to obtain finance on the scale and at the cost they required, this means there is something *generally* wrong with the provision of finance for new businesses.

## The three decades

Aside from the work of Fraser (2005) and Cosh and Hughes (2003) there is surprisingly little empirical UK evidence that charts in detail the characteristics of the market for new business finance. There is even less evidence on how this has changed over time.

So, in this section, we report on how finance was used by new businesses across the three decades. In charting this pattern, what is clear is the availability of new finance sources. So, whilst in the 1990s, credit cards were hugely important, they were largely unheard of in the 1970s. Equally, there were no real sources of public finance assistance in the 1970s nor was there much recognition of trade credit or more currently prevalent sources such as leasing or factoring.

### The stability of a finance hierarchy

Pecking order theory implies that if entrepreneurs are going to use finance to start a business, this is likely to be their own resources or their immediate family's rather than drawing upon other sources. There appears to be no reason why that ordering should change over time.

Table 7.1 bears this out. It first compares the five most frequently used sources of pre start-up finance for the financing of new businesses on Teesside. It compares the sources used in the 1970s with that for the 1980s and 1990s. Although there seems to be some movement, particularly in terms of the use of personal savings and friends and family being more popular, the overall ranking suggests a static picture. Personal savings remain ranked first across all three decades. The next most used source is bank finance which consistently remains second. In fact, all five sources do not change their position at all over the time period.

There are some minor changes in the importance of particular sources of finance over the three decades. For instance, the use of a house mortgage was seen as being the least likely important source of the five in the 1970s, yet ranked the third most important in the 1980s. The only major difference is that in the 1970s bank finance was the single most important source of funds – greater even than personal savings.

*Table 7.1* Finance sources used at start-up and their importance

|  | 1970s | Rank | 1980s | Rank | 1990s | Rank | $X^2$ stat |
|---|---|---|---|---|---|---|---|
| **Finance sources used at start-up** | | | | | | | |
| Personal savings | 59.3 | 1 | 79.4 | 1 | 82.0 | 1 | 29.81* |
| House mortgage | 5.3 | 4 | 6.2 | 3 | 4.4 | 4 | 0.766 |
| Bank | 34.0 | 2 | 35.6 | 2 | 31.5 | 2 | 0.898 |
| Finance company | 4.7 | 5 | 2.1 | 4 | 2.7 | 5 | 2.116 |
| Friends and family | 7.3 | 3 | 6.2 | 3 | 21.4 | 3 | 29.39* |
| **Important finance sources used at start-up** | | | | | | | |
| Personal savings | 32.4 | 2 | 45.8 | 1 | 58.0 | 1 | 163.4* |
| House mortgage | 2.9 | 5 | 11.9 | 3 | 1.7 | 4 | 4.129 |
| Bank | 44.1 | 1 | 37.3 | 2 | 16.6 | 2 | 4.845 |
| Finance company | 5.9 | 4 | 5.1 | 4 | 1.7 | 4 | 0.094 |
| Friends and family | 14.7 | 3 | 0.0 | 5 | 10.5 | 3 | 37.922* |

* significant at 1 per cent level.

Post start up, the expectation is that internal sources of finance would dominate. This is confirmed in Table 7.2. Central to the finance of a new business is the use and importance of profits from the business to fund the business. In other words, there seems a stated preference, which is time invariant, for using the business's own money to support the business. The second most likely source and the second most important source, at least for the 1980s and the 1990s, is bank finance. Below this, the general pecking order of personal savings, finance company and friends and family seems fairly stable.

Two things, however, stand out from Table 7.2. First, personal savings were much more important in the 1970s. Second, the importance of profits from businesses is significantly lower in the 1980s than during either the 1970s or the 1990s. Profits from business were the most common and important source of post start-up finance support. This may reflect both the lower levels of human capital of those starting businesses in the 1980s (Chapter 4) and the more difficult trading conditions of the time.

Two other issues emerge from this review. First, there has clearly been an increase in the number of financial sources available to entrepreneurs over time. In the 1970s, the mean average number of sources of pre start-up finance used was 1.1 sources. Typically, therefore, entrepreneurs tended to use personal savings and bank finance to start their business. In the 1980s this increased to 1.29 and by the 1990s, it increased again to 1.77. These differences from 1.1 to 1.77 are statistically significant (1 per cent level) and indicate that over the three decades that

*Table 7.2*  Finance sources used post start-up and their importance

|  | 1970s | Rank | 1980s | Rank | 1990s | Rank | $X^2$ stat |
|---|---|---|---|---|---|---|---|
| **Finance sources used post start-up** | | | | | | | |
| Profits from business | 66.0 | 1 | 66.5 | 1 | 82.4 | 1 | 10.962* |
| Bank | 44.0 | 2 | 34.0 | 2 | 34.6 | 2 | 2.321 |
| Personal savings | 16.7 | 3 | 20.3 | 3 | 17.6 | 3 | 0.442 |
| Finance company | 7.3 | 4 | 6.6 | 4 | 6.1 | 4 | 0.124 |
| Friends and family | 1.3 | 5 | 3.6 | 5 | 5.8 | 5 | 2.609 |
| **Most important finance sources used post start-up** | | | | | | | |
| Personal savings | 16.8 | 2 | 7.3 | 3 | 7.4 | 3 | 11.333* |
| Profits from business | 65.0 | 1 | 47.3 | 1 | 70.2 | 1 | 97.409* |
| Bank | 14.6 | 3 | 38.2 | 2 | 16.1 | 2 | 1.262 |
| Finance company | 0.7 | 4 | 3.6 | 4 | 1.8 | 5 | 0.490 |
| Friends and family | 0.0 | 5 | 0.0 | 5 | 2.8 | 4 | |

* significant at 1 per cent level.

entrepreneurs found themselves making use of a greater range and portfolio of start-up finance options.

A similar picture is evident when the number of post start-up finance options is considered. Here, the number rose from 1.25 in the 1970s to 1.52 in the 1990s. Such differences are statistically significant (1 per cent level). Of more interest, though, is that the number of post start-up finance sources used in the 1980s dipped. Entrepreneurs in this decade used 1.18 sources of finance which is lower than both the other two decades.

## Rejection in the 1980s and 1990s

One other marked difference between the decades is in terms of the rejection rates. Although not asked in the 1970s, there were big differences between the 1980s and the 1990s: in the 1980s the rejection rate was 9.9 per cent whilst in the 1990s the rate had nearly doubled to 18.2 per cent. Leaving aside (for the moment) the 1990s, what is relevant about the 1980s rate is that it is relatively low. It may, therefore, be thought that there were relatively fewer barriers to accessing finance faced by entrepreneurs in the 1980s.

To test this, three probit models were estimated to find out why people were rejected in the 1980s. The first included only the human capital of the individual. The expectation here is that some forms of human capital (e.g. age, sex, qualifications or unemployed) may increase the probability of an individual being rejected whilst others such as prior entrepreneurship experience, being full time in the business or having a degree may lower this probability. Banks, for example, may be impressed by businesses that seek to become limited companies if prior experience shows these businesses are more likely to grow and survive.

Lending or rejection decisions may also be influenced by the sector in which the business trades. The second model then sought to investigate these impacts. Finally, although the actual amount of finance available is unknown from the data, the third model sought to supplement the two earlier models by including whether the use of other finance sources (personal savings, house mortgage) and the use of pre start-up support influence the rejection decision.

None of the three models were significant. In other words, the human capital attributes identified were unrelated to the rejection decision (model 1: LR $chi^2(13)$ = 19.18.85, sig. 0.118); also unrelated were legal form (limited company) or trading in any of the identified sectors (model 2: LR $chi^2(19)$ = 24.85, sig. 0.165). Finally, current finance sources were also not relevant (model 3: LR $chi^2(22)$ = 30.14, 0.115) implying either that during the 1980s rejection was random or that it was influenced by factors other than ones for which we have data (it must still be remembered that our data are non-random in the sense that we do not have data on those who, as a result of rejection, chose not to start a business –our data only covers businesses that actually began).

By way of contrast, an identical set of probit models were estimated to see if these helped explain the reasons why people were rejected in the 1990s. Again, as before, three models were run: one included human capital; a second looked at limited company and sector; and the third considered finance and support. There was, however, one difference between these models and those for the 1980s. To control for regional effects, Buckinghamshire and Shropshire were contrasted with Teesside for models two and three (these estimations were run without these regional effects with no qualitative differences in the results).

Table 7.3 shows three models were significant. Model 1, like the other two models, shows that a significant determinant of rejection is portfolio entrepreneurship. In other words, once sector, region and pre start-up finance and support is controlled for, it still remains likely that those with other concurrent businesses are more likely to face rejection. Models 2 and 3 also suggest that individuals without formal qualifications were more likely to be rejected for funding.

Table 7.4 turns to look at the other side of the coin – the discouraged borrower. It shows the marginal effects of a probit analysis on discouraged borrowers and human capital attributes. In the 1990s – the only time discouragement was investigated – there were identifiable human

*Table 7.3*  Probit marginal effects for rejection (1 = rejected, 0 = otherwise) in the 1990s

|  | Model 1 dF/dx | Model 1 z | Model 2 dF/dx | Model 2 z | Model 3 dF/dx | Model 3 z |
|---|---|---|---|---|---|---|
| Male | −0.027 | −0.620 | −0.027 | −0.610 | −0.027 | −0.61 |
| Age | 0.007 | 0.470 | 0.006 | 0.370 | 0.004 | 0.24 |
| Age$^2$ | 0.000 | −0.810 | 0.000 | −0.710 | 0.000 | −0.56 |
| Indigenous | −0.027 | −0.730 | −0.034 | −0.880 | −0.040 | −1.03 |
| Degree | −0.006 | −0.110 | 0.016 | 0.290 | 0.016 | 0.31 |
| Vocational qualification | 0.058 | 1.220 | 0.049 | 1.020 | 0.055 | 1.14 |
| Professional qualification | −0.014 | −0.230 | −0.013 | −0.220 | −0.013 | −0.21 |
| No qualification | 0.112 | 1.690 | 0.145 | 2.070** | 0.160 | 2.23** |
| Previously unemployed | 0.076 | 1.790 | 0.081 | 1.870 | 0.079 | 1.86 |
| Prior entrepreneurial experience | −0.032 | −0.870 | −0.035 | −0.970 | −0.021 | −0.58 |
| Managerial experience | 0.041 | 1.12 | 0.029 | 0.820 | 0.030 | 0.83 |
| Sectoral experience | −0.019 | −0.52 | −0.012 | −0.330 | −0.017 | −0.46 |
| Portfolio entrepreneur | 0.110 | 2.32* | 0.122 | 2.570** | 0.116 | 2.45** |
| Full time | 0.117 | 1.94 | 0.123 | 2.140 | 0.117 | 2.04 |
| Ltd company |  |  | 0.043 | 1.110 | 0.041 | 1.05 |
| Motor repairs and beauty |  |  | 0.029 | 0.510 | 0.032 | 0.56 |
| Manufacturing |  |  | 0.120 | 1.94 | 0.120 | 1.95 |
| Construction |  |  | 0.085 | 1.14 | 0.092 | 1.23 |
| Professional services |  |  | −0.049 | −0.930 | −0.048 | −0.93 |
| Other |  |  | 0.093 | 1.770 | 0.086 | 1.66 |
| Buckinghamshire |  |  | 0.033 | 0.7 | 0.007 | 0.15 |
| Shropshire |  |  | −0.023 | −0.48 | −0.036 | −0.76 |
| Personal savings |  |  |  |  | −0.055 | −1.28 |
| House mortgage |  |  |  |  | 0.115 | 1.42 |
| Used pre start-up support |  |  |  |  | 0.084 | 1.67 |
| N. | 493 |  | 492 |  | 492 |  |
| LR chi$^2$ | 25.98 |  | 39.76 |  | 47.47 |  |
| Sig. | 0.026 |  | 0.012 |  | 0.004 |  |
| Pseudo R$^2$ | 0.0565 |  | 0.087 |  | 0.103 |  |

* significant at 1 per cent level; ** significant at 5 per cent level.

capital attributes associated with being discouraged. As with rejection, there is a greater likelihood of those with no qualifications and having some concurrent businesses (portfolio entrepreneurship) being more likely to be discouraged from seeking to borrow funds. Those who were previously unemployed were also more likely to be discouraged from seeking to borrow.

*Table 7.4* Probit marginal effects for discouraged borrowers (1 = discouraged, 0 = otherwise) in the 1990s

|  | dF/dx | z |
|---|---|---|
| Male | 0.003 | 0.08 |
| Age | 0.010 | 0.7 |
| Age$^2$ | 0.000 | −1.02 |
| Indigenous | −0.006 | −0.17 |
| Degree | −0.023 | −0.5 |
| Vocational qualification | 0.017 | 0.41 |
| Professional qualification | 0.000 | −0.01 |
| No qualification | 0.119 | 1.97** |
| Previously unemployed | 0.081 | 2.13** |
| Prior entrepreneurial Experience | 0.011 | 0.33 |
| Managerial experience | 0.022 | 0.7 |
| Sectoral experience | −0.004 | −0.11 |
| Portfolio entrepreneur | 0.091 | 2.18** |
| Full time | 0.070 | 1.29 |
| N. | 491 | |
| LR chi$^2$ | 22.92 | |
| Sig. | 0.062 | |
| Pseudo R$^2$ | 0.058 | |

* significant at 1 per cent level; ** significant at 5 per cent level.

Two interpretations of this are possible. The finding that there are identifiable characteristics of individuals who are discouraged might be taken as evidence that there is discrimination against such people in the credit market. A policy might be to design schemes to alleviate the discouragement and discrimination faced by the unemployed, those with no qualifications and those that are portfolio entrepreneurs.

The alternative interpretation is that the market became better at evaluating the likely risks involved in financing individuals. From a de Meza (2002) viewpoint, it does appear that virtually everyone had an equal chance of getting finance in the 1980s. This might sound ideal but the chances are that finance may have been *oversupplied* to individuals who might have been better off doing something else. MacDonald and Coffield (1991) argue, for instance, that individuals were encouraged into starting a business by a combination of the 'enterprise industry' and easy access to finance only to end up with substantial debts, trauma and permanently damaged self-confidence. The data here, although far from conclusive, does hint at such a suggestion. One indicator is that there were limited constraints in the 1980s on who was able finance a start-up

*Table 7.5*   Differences between rejected and discouraged borrowers in the use of bank finance

|  |  | Used bank finance | | Bank finance most important | |
|---|---|---|---|---|---|
|  |  | No | Yes | No | Yes |
| Rejected | No | 67.3 | 32.7 | 85.0 | 15.0 |
|  | Yes | 64.3 | 35.7 | 79.6 | 20.4 |
| $X^2$ |  | 0.320 |  | 1.724 |  |
| Discouraged | No | 67.2 | 32.8 | 85.2 | 14.8 |
|  | Yes | 64.6 | 35.4 | 78.5 | 21.5 |
| $X^2$ |  | 0.208 |  | 2.290 |  |

* significant at 1 per cent level; ** significant at 5 per cent level.

business but, once in business, a lower percentage were able to fund themselves from their retained profits.

The obverse is the case for the 1990s. More were rejected and the characteristics of those that were discouraged were clearer. However, once in business they were able to make ample use of retained profits. Indeed, although individuals were discouraged and rejected in their attempts to seek finance, there is also little evidence of them lacking resilience. For example, when the rejected and the discouraged are compared against those who were likely to use bank finance and who regarded bank finance as the most important, respectively, there was little evidence of any differences. This is shown in Table 7.5. This shows no statistical differences in the use of bank finance by either the discouraged or the rejected. It might, though, be thought that these two groups would be less likely to consider a bank as their most important source of finance, but this is not supported from Table 7.5.

Finally, we compared the performance of both the rejected and the discouraged borrowers with the businesses that successfully obtained funding. In terms of survival, there are no significant differences (rejected: $X^2$ 0.016, p. value of 0.496; discouraged: $X^2$ 0.594, p. value of 0.261) and both are just as likely to see employment growth regardless of controls for yearly variation (annualised employment growth) or just in terms of relative change. In short, the rejected are just as likely to have employment growth outcomes (t statistic for annualised growth: 0.378, p. value 0.705; t statistic for relative employment growth: 0.695, p. value 0.487) as the successful. The same is also true for the discouraged (t statistic for annualised growth: 1.362, p. value 0.174; t statistic for relative employment growth: 0.376, p. value 0.707). We find this somewhat surprising and suggest the need for further investigation of the topic.

## Access to finance in the regions

One of the other findings from the evidence on rejection in Table 7.3 was the unimportance of regional differences. Despite apparent differences between the entrepreneurship profiles of business owners in the three regions, rejection rates were very similar (Teesside 18.2 per cent; Shropshire 17.7 per cent; and Buckinghamshire 17.2 per cent). This was also the case in terms of discouragement. Here, the region with the highest rate was Buckinghamshire (15.6 per cent) but this was statistically indistinguishable from either Shropshire (15 per cent) or Teesside (13.8 per cent).

Table 7.6, as might be expected, shows that the sources of finance used in the three counties in the 1990s was very similar. The most commonly used source of pre start-up finance was personal savings and this was also the most important source. The bank was ranked second as the most commonly used source. Table 7.6 further suggests that there were no statistically significant differences (except in the use of 'other' finance) in terms of the importance of particular pre start finance forms.

What is different, though, is how common particular forms of finance are in the three regions. In the high entrepreneurship region of Buckinghamshire there is rather less reliance upon personal savings, bank

*Table 7.6*  Finance sources used at start-up and their importance

|  | Teesside |  | Shropshire |  | Buckinghamshire |  |  |
|---|---|---|---|---|---|---|---|
|  |  | Rank |  | Rank |  | Rank |  |
| Use of pre start finance |  |  |  |  |  |  |  |
| Personal savings | 82.0 | 1 | 80.8 | 1 | 71.5 | 1 | 3.15** |
| House mortgage | 4.4 | 6 | 4.6 | 5 | 8.5 | 5 | 1.55 |
| Bank | 31.5 | 2 | 21.5 | 2 | 20.8 | 2 | 3.84** |
| Finance company | 2.7 | 7 | 1.5 | 7 | 5.4 | 6 | 1.75 |
| Friends and family | 21.4 | 4 | 12.3 | 4 | 11.5 | 4 | 4.43** |
| Public authorities | 27.1 | 3 | 6.2 | 6 | 2.3 | 7 | 29.45* |
| Other | 7.8 | 5 | 13.1 | 3 | 20.8 | 2 | 7.38* |
| Importance of pre start finance |  |  |  |  |  |  |  |
| Personal savings | 58.8 | 1 | 61.2 | 1 | 58.6 | 1 | 0.11 |
| House mortgage | 1.7 | 6 | 3.3 | 5 | 5.4 | 5 | 2.01 |
| Bank | 16.8 | 2 | 14.9 | 2 | 9.0 | 3 | 1.96 |
| Finance company | 1.7 | 6 | 0.8 | 7 | 2.7 | 6 | 0.60 |
| Friends and family | 10.7 | 3 | 6.6 | 4 | 8.1 | 4 | 0.93 |
| Public authorities | 6.5 | 4 | 2.5 | 6 | 1.8 | 7 | 2.86 |
| Other | 3.1 | 5 | 9.9 | 3 | 14.4 | 2 | 9.06* |

* significant at 1 per cent level; ** significant at 5 per cent level.

finance, friends and family compared with Teesside. In part, this reflects a statistically greater use of pre start finance forms by businesses in Teesside who were made use of 1.77 forms of finance, compared to 1.4 in Shropshire and 1.41 in Buckinghamshire (F. statistic 14.55; p. value 0.000). In short, it would appear that the low enterprise area makes heavier use of banks, savings and friends and family support than a high enterprise area. This is perhaps a little odd because it may have been expected that the low enterprise area may be concomitantly poorer and, therefore, it may have been more difficult to access finance.

The biggest difference between the three areas shown in Table 7.6 is in the use of public financial support. 27.1 per cent of Teesside businesses accessed public finance support. To place this in context, this was almost the same number of businesses that accessed bank finance in Teesside (31.5 per cent) and was greater than the use of bank finance in either Shropshire (21.5 per cent) or Buckinghamshire (20.8 per cent). Finally, whereas public finance is ranked third in Teesside, it is ranked sixth and seventh, in Shropshire and Buckinghamshire, respectively.

The picture is more uniform when post start finance is considered (Table 7.7). There is little surprise that a hierarchy emerges with profits from business being the most common and most important source of post start-up finance. This then is followed by bank finance and personal savings. Another feature evident from Table 7.7 is the tiny percentages of businesses that make any use of equity finance through the sale of share capital. Use of this varies from the irrelevant in Teesside (0.3 per cent) to the negligible (1.5 per cent) in Buckinghamshire. Indeed, Table 7.7 clearly also shows that it was not ranked by any business as the most important source of capital post start-up.

A further interesting feature of Table 7.7 is that the use of public finance is no longer statistically skewed towards Teesside. Whilst not used at all in Buckinghamshire, only 4.1 per cent of businesses in Teesside make use of post start-up funding from the public sector. Teesside businesses were also much more likely to make use of profits from their own business than the other two areas. They were also more likely to make use of a greater number of post start-up sources (1.52) than either Shropshire (1.42) or Buckinghamshire (1.34) but these differences were not statistically significant.

Overall, the evidence in Tables 7.6 and 7.7 points to the inconsequential nature of equity support and the primary preference for using either personal savings or profits from the business to fund the business. In an environment where there is also no public support (Buckinghamshire) or limited public support (Shropshire) the evidence suggests that, pre-

*Table 7.7* Finance sources used post start-up and their importance

| | Teesside | | Shropshire | | Bucking-hamshire | | |
|---|---|---|---|---|---|---|---|
| | % | Rank | % | Rank | % | Rank | F stat.[1] |
| **Use of post start finance** | | | | | | | |
| Personal savings | 17.6 | 3 | 13.1 | 3 | 23.1 | 3 | 2.23 |
| Profits from business | 82.4 | 1 | 70.0 | 1 | 56.2 | 1 | 17.27* |
| Bank | 34.6 | 2 | 29.2 | 2 | 33.1 | 2 | 0.58 |
| Finance company | 6.1 | 4 | 10.0 | 4 | 6.2 | 5 | 1.15 |
| Friends and family | 5.8 | 5 | 6.2 | 5 | 3.8 | 6 | 0.42 |
| Public authorities | 4.1 | 6 | 2.3 | 6 | 0.0 | 8 | |
| Sale of share capital | 0.3 | 8 | 0.8 | 7 | 1.5 | 7 | |
| Other | 0.7 | 7 | 10.0 | 4 | 10.0 | 4 | 13.06* |
| **Importance of post start finance** | | | | | | | |
| Personal savings | 7.4 | 3 | 7.5 | 3 | 17.7 | 3 | 2.63 |
| Profits from business | 70.2 | 1 | 65.4 | 1 | 54.2 | 1 | 15.68* |
| Bank | 16.1 | 2 | 19.6 | 2 | 21.9 | 2 | 0.02 |
| Finance company | 1.8 | 5 | 2.8 | 4 | 2.1 | 5 | 0.13 |
| Friends and family | 2.8 | 4 | 2.8 | 4 | 4.2 | 4 | 0.07 |
| Public authorities | 1.4 | | 0.9 | 6 | | | |
| Sale of share capital | | | | | | | |
| Other | 0.4 | 6 | 0.9 | 6 | | | |

1: Numbers were too few to compute test. * significant at 1 per cent level; ** significant at 5 per cent level.

start-up, new entrepreneurs turn to banks for support. This is much less the case in Teesside. Here, a high proportion of new businesses draw upon public financial support to begin their business. The amounts paid to individual businesses seem modest and, in most cases, do not continue once the business is trading.

## Testing for the impact of public finance support

The conventional justification for using public funds to provide financial support to new businesses is either on the grounds of market imperfection or on social grounds. So, public finance support for new businesses in Teesside could be to address and overcome the high concentration in that area of individuals with low human capital whose businesses would not normally receive support from the bank. The risk with such a strategy is that the area becomes dependent upon such subsidies.

To examine this, a series of three probits – similar to those run earlier on rejection and discouragement – were run to see if there were differences in the profile of the users of pre start-up public support (1 = received public finance support; 0 = otherwise) in Teesside. As before, our focus is on exploring how human capital factors (i.e. age, gender, educational qualifications and entrepreneurial experience) influenced the use of public finance. Given also the interest in rejection and discouragement, these, too were included in the models. Further tests were also carried out, as before, on sector and use of other financial forms but none of these three models were significant. This is the case whether the focus was just on human capital (LR chi$^2$(16) = 19.72; p. value 0.2332), sectoral and limited company controls (LR chi$^2$(22) = 27.59; p. value 0.1897) or other sources of finance (LR chi$^2$(24) = 28.20; p. value 0.2082).

We are also unable to adequately explain whether it is the most 'deserving' cases that receive public funding. None of the three models are significant, suggesting that the human capital (LR chi$^2$(16) = 14.47; p. value 0.5640) or further controls (LR chi$^2$(22) = 16.93; p. value 0.7670; LR chi$^2$(24) = 22.73; p. value 0.4764) were important in explaining the importance of public finance.

Of course, perhaps it does not matter who gets the money in areas like Teesside because the area is so poor that it is important that public finance support is offered to assist individuals – any individuals – who develop the economy of the region. Even so, the taxpayer needs to be satisfied that these resources are being used effectively.

The evidence, is mixed. One indicator of the value of public funding might be a reduced likelihood of Teesside businesses reporting finance problems in their first year of operation (which was a question specifically asked in the 1990s). This, indeed, was the case: just over one-fifth of Teesside businesses (21 per cent) experienced finance problems in the first year, compared to 28.5 per cent in Buckinghamshire and 43.1 per cent in Shropshire. This difference was significant (X2: 21.84) and suggests that the provision of public assistance does limit the financial problems faced by businesses in the first year of operations. However, if public finance does reduce the likelihood of experiencing financial problems faced in the first year, it does not have a marked effect on survival. Business that make use of pre start-up or post start public finance were just as likely to survive as those who do not use such financial support (pre start *X2* 0.295; post start *X2* 0.711). Equally, businesses who regard the support as the most important at either stage are also just as likely to survive (pre start *X2* 1.228; post start *X2* 0.693).

Table 7.8 shows that businesses that were publicly supported at the post start-up stage were no more likely to grow – either in terms of

*Table 7.8* Annualised and relative employment growth outcomes for public finance support

| | | Annualised | | Relative | |
|---|---|---|---|---|---|
| | | Mean | t-stat. | Mean | t-stat. |
| Used at start-up | yes | 0.07 | | 0.96 | |
| | no | 0.14 | 2.499** | 1.80 | 1.043 |
| Important at start-up | yes | 0.05 | | 0.37 | |
| | no | 0.13 | 1.999 | 1.67 | 2.026** |
| Used post start-up | yes | 0.29 | | 1.94 | |
| | no | 0.12 | –1.331 | 1.56 | –0.311 |
| Important post start-up | yes | 0.47 | | 3.25 | |
| | no | 0.12 | –1.077 | 1.55 | –0.542 |

* significant at 1 per cent level; ** significant at 5 per cent level.

annualised employment growth or relatively – than those businesses in Teesside that did not use such support. It also suggests that, if anything, it is the businesses accessing public funds that have slower employment growth outcomes. Whilst not uniform, those who used pre start-up public support were likely to grow at half the mean rate of those that did not use this support. Similarly, although not apparent in terms of annualised growth, those that reported public support as the most important, experienced a mean relative employment growth of 1.3 fewer jobs than those where it was less important.

Even so, it is difficult to draw clear inferences from this finding. We do not have a clear control group so we are unable to identify the added value of public money. Indeed, our findings are compatible with an interpretation that those businesses receiving public funds were those likely to perform considerably worse than those not in receipt of such funds. It is, therefore, unsurprising that they perform less well in their early years – and that without such funding they would have performed even more poorly.

We cannot adequately test this interpretation, but our judgement is that it is less likely to be the case since the human capital characteristics of the owners of publicly funded businesses do not look markedly different from those that do not receive such subsidies.

## Summary

The evidence from this chapter is that new entrepreneurs adopt a structured approach to accessing finance. In simple terms, they prefer their 'near' money (savings, family and friends) or debt money from the bank. Equally, once in business their preference is to use retained profits rather than other sources. One of the contributions of this chapter has been to show that this is temporally and spatially invariant. Entrepreneurs across the three decades and across high, medium and low enterprise areas all ranked personal savings and retained profits as the most common and most important sources of finance.

Accessing finance, therefore, may be thought to be an issue of limited significance. In looking at an example of this, the chapter compared those new businesses that were rejected for loans in the 1980s with those in the 1990s. It found key human capital characteristics did not explain the 1980s rejections – prompting the interpretation that funding allocations were close to random in that decade. In the 1990s, however, matters were much clearer: founders who were portfolio entrepreneurs, and those with no qualifications were significantly more likely to be found amongst the rejected and the discouraged. This might suggest *prima facie* evidence of an unnecessary financial constraint faced by some types of entrepreneur in the 1990s. Nonetheless, an alternative interpretation is that finance was too easily acquired in the 1980s, particularly given the human capital attributes of individual entrepreneurs (Chapter 4) and the lower percentages of individuals that used retained profits in their business.

The other major issue addressed in this chapter has been the use of public financial support in the low enterprise area of Teesside. The central statistic here is that 27.1 per cent of new businesses made use of public support in Teesside, compared with 2.3 per cent in Buckinghamshire. Use of public funding in Teesside is higher than the use of bank finance in both Shropshire and Buckinghamshire.

Unfortunately, we are unable to reach clear conclusions about the impact of such funding. What is clear is that the new businesses that made some use of public funding at start-up exhibited significantly slower employment growth than those that did not. No such relationships were present when post start public funding was examined. What we are less confident about is whether the public funds improved the performance of the businesses.

In terms of the big picture of new business financing, our view remains that in developed countries in buoyant macro economic conditions access to finance is significantly less of a problem than was the case two decades ago. In part, this is because of greater competition amongst suppliers of finance and, in part, because those suppliers are better informed due to technological changes and the increased ease of processing customer information. Finally, it also supports our view that the entrepreneur is more financially 'savvy' than previously. This all leads to the conclusion that taxpayers' resources currently devoted to financing new start-up businesses – even in a low enterprise area such as Teesside – could be usefully redeployed elsewhere.

# 8
## The Impact of Teesside New Businesses in the 1970s, 1980s and 1990s

### Introduction

The evidence from previous chapters suggests that new businesses have not reinvigorated a low enterprise area such as Teesside over the last three decades. The human capital of the new entrepreneurs was modest, leading almost inevitably to enterprises being started in sectors where the opportunities for business growth are limited. Perhaps linked to the low human capital of the entrepreneurs we find new Teesside businesses are characterised by low levels of innovation and with an undue emphasis upon price-based strategies. Although both access to finance and business support has dramatically improved over the last 30 years, the evidence that it has actually strengthened new businesses in the Teesside economy is scant.

The above implies little improvement in the performance of Teesside new businesses over three decades. As was shown in Chapter 3, national and local policy towards new businesses has tended to vacillate between seeing new businesses as either a solution to endemic unemployment or as a source of innovation and competition. Both remain valid reasons for supporting new businesses. For example, notwithstanding some methodological issues (e.g. Davis et al., 1996), the weight of international evidence suggests that new businesses are net job generators (e.g. Davidsson et al., 1998; Picot and Dupuy, 1998; Kirchhoff and Greene, 1998; Wagner, 1995; Broersma and Gautier, 1997). As we shall argue later, however, the evidence is less clear that new businesses *always* lead to additional employment creation (Van Stel and Storey, 2004; Mueller et al., 2008). There is also research evidence that new businesses are the central mechanism by which new knowledge is commercialised (Acs and Armington, 2006). The third key role of new businesses is to provide a competitive threat to existing businesses. For all these reasons, new businesses provide not only the private benefits that accrue to the successful business (profits for the owner(s)), but also social benefits to the rest of society (e.g. taxes and employment).

Earlier chapters showed that in the 1980s the aim of policy makers was to increase the number of start-ups by creating an 'enterprise culture' in the UK so as to reduce unemployment. The evidence provided so far strongly suggested such policies were broadly ineffective – at least for Teesside. This chapter formally reviews this issue. It documents the historical performance patterns of new Teesside businesses to gauge their impact on the local economy. The experience of the 1980s is relevant today because policy makers in many countries are also seeking to make it easier for individuals to start businesses. Djankov et al's, (2002). Their research linked the height of regulatory barriers with poor economic outcomes such as low levels of wealth and high levels of corruption, and concluded that all measures of economic welfare would be enhanced by making the business creation process quicker and cheaper. Governments worldwide have responded to this evidence so that it is now both quicker and cheaper for individuals to set up their own business in almost all developed countries. For instance, the French government reduced the number of days required to start a new business from 53 days in 1999 to eight in 2004. The Spanish government reduced start-up time from 82 to 47 over the same time period, and the Italian government from 62 to 13.

It is, therefore, reasonable to examine whether such processes be actively encouraged. To some this may seem an almost heretical question: after all, new businesses represent the employment and innovatory flow in any economy. Our view is that this case is far from clear for reasons that we set out in detail in our concluding chapter. However, for current purposes, we focus upon examining the performance of new businesses, and particularly examining their performance in the 1980s – the decade when public policy could be categorised as 'pile them high and sell them cheap'.

To achieve this we have to identify the features of 'better' performing businesses. For instance, small business growth is not normally, or evenly, distributed. Instead it is highly concentrated amongst a small number of businesses (Birch et al., 1997; Hughes, 1997a), and it is these high growth businesses that are potentially central to economic development. Cognetics (2000) argued, for instance, that around 70 per cent of employment growth in the US was due to high growth businesses whilst Jovanovic (2001) suggested that it was such businesses that were associated with innovation.

Despite their potential economic significance our knowledge of high growth businesses is limited. Defining them presents a major challenge, partly because they are so rare (Storey, 1994a; Woods et al., 1993; Barringer et al., 2005). What is clear is that there is no definition of fast growth new businesses that is consistently used by researchers (Davidsson and Henrekson, 2002).

Given this lack of consistency, we view it as justifiable to use definitions that are appropriate for the sample of businesses available to us to investigate whether there are discernable features associated with new businesses that grow quickly. However, we do need to justify the use of our chosen measures by providing a short review of previous studies that have examined the performance of new and small businesses.

The chapter then turns to provide an understanding of the factors that influence new and small business performance. It sets out a new meta-analysis of 54 performance studies conducted over the period 1994–2006. All these studies make use of a multivariate framework to identify performance determinants, and are embedded within an international setting. The majority of the studies are from either North American or European countries, but we also include studies from Asian countries such as Japan and developing economies such as India, Cote D'Ivorie and Russia.

Following on from this review of performance determinants, the chapter uses these insights to document the performance of Teesside businesses across the three decades. Here our purpose is to identify the impact of new businesses on the local economy and the factors that influence business performance across the three decades. The situation of the three regions is considered in Chapter 9, so the current chapter only relates to Teesside.

## Methodological problems with performance

Understanding the historical performance of new Teesside businesses requires a review of the very real methodological difficulties that exist in defining business performance. The first difficulty is over the choice of performance measures (e.g. sales, employment, profits) and a second is using these measures for comparative purposes. We focus upon how performance measures have been used in previous meta-analytic studies.

Cooper (1993) suggested that available research on new and small businesses performance had tended to produce 'spotty and sometimes inconsistent findings to date' (p. 244). In part, he attributed this to the wide variety of indicators used to reflect performance, and the different measures of 'exceptional' performance that had been used.

The ideal economic measure of business performance is profits, but collecting reliable data is particularly problematic for new and small businesses for several reasons. The first is because some owner-managers of businesses have only a hazy grasp of accountancy, making it difficult for them to determine whether or not their business is profitable (Nayak and Greenfield, 1994). Even if this could be overcome, the reliability of a profit-based measure may be questionable (Dess and Robinson, 1984; Sapienza et al., 1988). It can be, for example, difficult to disentangle personal or household costs from those of the business. Third, most new businesses are likely to make trading losses in their early years, so even accurate profit and loss accounts may be no guide to longer term performance. Fourth, profit information is correctly viewed by the entrepreneur as highly sensitive: it is information that a rival might use to decide on whether to enter a market, and it is the basis of tax calculations by government. This makes it a closely guarded, even if imperfectly understood, secret by the entrepreneur and one that is difficult for external researchers to acquire.

Many of these considerations also make it difficult to rely upon 'efficiency' measures (e.g. return on assets), or liquidity measures (e.g. current ratio) since these are either likely to be unknown to the entrepreneur or reside in datasets that may either be out of date, inaccurate (Birley et al., 1995) or simply just focus on established surviving businesses. Similar limitations apply to measures such as 'market share' because one of the fundamental distinctions between small and large businesses is that the smaller businesses are likely to have much smaller shares of their market place (Bolton, 1971). For most new businesses such shares are likely to be microscopic.

The most obvious alternative quantitative performance measure is that of (annual) sales. The justifications for this are clear. Barkham et al. (1996) suggest that this is the measure most favoured by entrepreneurs themselves because it is a target which they both set and plan to achieve each year. Equally, it is largely insensitive to capital intensity and applies to virtually all businesses. However, a major problem with sales, from our perspective, is that price changes over time mean it is difficult to compare the absolute value of sales over three decades. Sales data is also closely guarded by the entrepreneur for reasons similar to the data on profitability.

Instead, researchers appear much more likely to use data on employment as a new business performance measure – even though superficially it appears inappropriate. This is because research has shown that very few new entrepreneurs have, as their primary motivation, the creation of employment in their business (Wiklund, 1998; Robson and Bennett, 2000a). Even so, European researchers in particular, favour employment as their chosen measure for several reasons. First, it is a simple, easy to answer, and relatively uncontroversial question to ask entrepreneurs. Fraser et al. (2007), for instance, showed that (small) business owners tend to be generally correct –and consistent- in gauging employment size. Employment also features within the resource-based view of the business as employees (including the entrepreneur) are a central resource of any business. Employment is also relevant because policy makers are often seeking ways of enhancing employability, particularly in poorer performing regions, and have seen new businesses as a useful mechanism for achieving this aim. Finally, where data on sales and employment are collected, it has been shown that the two are positively correlated – so employment can be used as a proxy for sales.

Other researchers have sought to place their emphasis upon the entrepreneurs' interpretations of the performance of their business. The logic here is that what really matters is the owner's perception of the performance of the business, rather than so-called objective measures of performance. Those favouring this approach argue that it is the interpretations of the entrepreneur which influence his or her decisions to continue in business or exit or to expand or contract. Hence, it is these interpretations that should be the focus of questioning. Gimeno et al. (1997) usefully employed this concept to investigate why some businesses continued to trade even though, the income the business generated was less than that which the individual might reasonably expect to earn as an employee. Central to the decision to continue as a business owner was the psychic energies invested in the businesses and the non-pecuniary benefits derived from business ownership by the entrepreneurs. Later work by Hamilton (2000), using a very different approach, also pointed towards the presence of such psychic benefits. Even so, our view is that, whilst seeking subjective performance measures may produce answers, it is difficult to separate respondents with a clear idea of the performance of their business from those that are subject to delusions. The latter may view the performance of their business as excellent, but a lack of sales will undermine their ability to survive even in the short term. Using satisfaction with business performance as a performance measure is not ideal given our current purposes.

The survival of the business is another measure of performance. After all, the primary objective of most businesses that start is continuation

– otherwise they would not have started in the first place. However, even this performance measure is open to question on several grounds. The first is that even if an individual starts a business, their circumstances may change. Their partner may become ill or die, they may be offered a highly paid job as an employee, or they may decide they are not suited to entrepreneurship. They may therefore quit the business even though the performance of their business was satisfactory. Second, identifying whether, and when, a business closes is not easy (Storey and Wynarczyk, 1996). It certainly cannot be assumed, for all the reasons given above, that businesses that exit are synonymous with those that 'fail' (Taylor, 1999; Headd, 2003).

In short, researchers have used several indicators of small business performance. None are ideal for all circumstances. However, for our purposes we favour the use of employment data on the grounds that it is a measure of size that is relatively unambiguous. We think that this, combined with the survival measure, is the best combination of performance indicators available to us.

## The use of performance measures

Table 8.1 shows five meta-analyses that have reviewed business performance in terms of growth. The meta-analyses are not directly comparable with each other given that they range across different time periods and have different interests. For example, the earliest study (Capon et al., 1990) looked at 320 studies published between 1921 and 1987, with a particular concentration on industrial economic factors. Later studies are more focussed on entrepreneurship growth (but not exit) performance: Murphy et al. (1996) looks at the period 1987–1993

*Table 8.1* Synopsis of meta-analytic studies

|  | Capon et al., 1990 | Murphy et al., 1996 | Weinzimmer et al., 1998 | Wiklund and Shepherd, 2005 | Janssen, 2006 |
|---|---|---|---|---|---|
| Sales | 77 (1) | 23 (3) | 18 (1) | 40 (1) | 12 (1) |
| Employees | 7 (4) | 5 (4) | 7 (2) | 11 (2) | 10 (2) |
| Profit | 0 (5) | 40 (1) | 0 (5) | 8 (3) | 2 (4) |
| Market share | 42 (2) | 2 (5) | 1 (4) | 0 (5) | 0 (5) |
| Equity/assets | 11 (3) | 40 (2) | 5 (3) | 5 (4) | 5 (3) |

drawing upon 51 studies; Weinzimmer et al. (1998) examined 35 studies between 1981 and 1992; Wiklund and Shepherd (2005) ranged across 147 articles during 1992–2003; and Janssen (2006) explored 21 studies during the period 1962–1999.

Table 8.1 reports five of the main measures of performance, both in terms of their number and their rank relative to the other four measures. It shows that in four out of the five meta-analyses, sales is the pre-eminent measure. After this, employment is the second most frequently used measure, with the three other measures being used less frequently.

Of course, simply because sales and employment win the "popularity contest", does not mean that they are suitable proxies for performance. Nevertheless, the finding of Storey et al. (1987) of a significant correlation between sales and employment growth is reassuring. The other performance measures are broadly uncorrelated with each other. This lack of association between the various measures is perhaps why multiple measures of business performance have become increasingly favoured by researchers in recent years (e.g. Brush and Chaganti, 1998; Reid and Smith, 2000; Nicholls-Nixon et al., 2001; Barringer et al., 2005).

Yet even this is not the full story. Other problems abound. There is the perennial issue of which metric is chosen: it might be thought that annualised measures would be more common in that they control for year-to-year variability but it appears that absolute and relative measures are much more prevalent (Delmar, 1997; Wiklund and Shepherd, 2005). The duration over which performance is measured also varies. Both Wiklund and Shepherd (2005) and Delmar (1997) argue that the most frequent period over which performance is measured is five years, but this does vary considerably. Some studies favour the use of panels –whereas others take a cross-section perspective. There is also the issue that there are likely to be differences between within-industry studies and studies that compare differing industries. Davidsson et al. (2004) point out that very few studies distinguish between sales growth which occurs through the acquisition of existing business and organic sales growth. Finally, researchers need to be aware that apparent performance differences may also reflect the use of different data sources – those based on primary information (largely postal, telephone or internet-based questionnaires) compared with those using secondary information (archived datasets, often collected by government) (Murphy et al., 1996) In essence, there is no ready, robust or universal guide to new/small business performance. Instead, as Penrose (1959) suggests, there continues to be a very catholic interpretation of performance: 'there is no way of measuring an amount of expansion, or even the size of a business, that is not open to serious conceptual objections' (p. 199).

Given such issues, it is perhaps unsurprising that it is difficult to identify the idiosyncrasies of new and small businesses that grow rapidly. As Storey et al. (1989) found in their comparison of fast growth and trundling businesses: 'In our examination of entrepreneurial backgrounds we were not able to clearly identify major differences between those establishing fast growth and those establishing 'match firms'' (Storey et al., 1989: 70).

More recent research tends to confirm this picture. Delmar et al. (2003) point to growth being heterogeneous, sensitive to growth metrics and time dependent. Parker et al. (2005) also point out that high growth is difficult to pin down given the heterogeneity of the external environment and internal developments within the business. This might be taken to imply that there is a strong chance, or stochastic, component to business growth, and that some entrepreneurs are simply luckier than others.

Acolytes of performance, however, reject the notion that growth is a stochastic process, dependent upon a lucky draw from the environment (Hannan and Carroll, 1992). They make the following case. First, there is evidence that very small and very young businesses grow quicker than older and larger businesses. Second, the very young and the very small businesses are also the ones most likely to cease trading.

It is argued that performance is a strategic choice (Child, 1972) available to the entrepreneur (Davidsson et al., 2004): the view here is that entrepreneurs just do not wake up one day to find that they are running a successful business. Instead, they have growth aspirations, tenacity, insight and their business has clear strategic plans and the ability to deliver them. Barringer et al. (2005) argue from their review of 106 growth studies that, instead of being highly fragmented, "the literature is rather rich and mature" (p. 666). In contrast, our view is that whilst the research literature may be very extensive and potentially rich, it does not explain a great deal of *why* it is that some businesses grow and others do not. There are three reasons for this. First, is that the explanatory power of models seeking to explain growth are very low. Second, very few of the independent variables that are used to explain growth consistently appear in different studies and, third, to raise the explanatory power of such models, researchers have created composite or clusters of variables, the true meaning of which is difficult to disentangle.

In summary, then, there may be grounds for hoping that fast growth businesses represent one essential element in developing regional prosperity. Prior evidence identified above suggests that they are likely to be the most fertile source of wealth and job creation. Set against this, there remain profound methodological issues in identifying growth businesses.

The next section begins by providing an overview of Storey's (1994a) earlier review of performance studies. This is complemented with 54 further multivariate studies (1994–2006). For reasons discussed above the review focuses upon only two measures of performance. The first is employment growth and the second is on exits. Unfortunately, survival data is available only for the 1990s cohort and so is covered in the next chapter.

## Identifying performance determinants

Storey's (1994a) overview of the available literature identified factors that had been used in empirical studies and shown to influence new and small business performance. Splitting his review into entrepreneurial characteristics (18 studies), business level characteristics (14 studies) and business strategy (12 studies), Storey (1994a) argued that the literature, largely from the 1980s, demonstrated the importance of the following to business growth:

- higher education;
- prior management experience;
- being older;
- team entrepreneurship;
- limited company;
- dispersed equity with external stakeholders;
- niche specialisation;
- product development; and
- the employment of non-equity owning managers.

In overall terms, the value of such evidence suggests that there are size and age effects apparent in determining the likely performance of a new business. In essence, what Storey (1994a) pointed to was the importance of experience, sharing risks/rewards (e.g. limited company, equity dispersion) and the exploitation of particular competitive advantage.

To complement these earlier findings, a fresh analysis of 54 international studies that examined the determinants of employment growth, business survival or some combination of the two was under-taken. These determinants are summarised in Table 8.2 (for a full delineation see Appendix 8.1). The first row of the table shows the factors that have been used. Rows two to four, grouped around growth, show if a particular variable has been shown to be positively associated with growth (+), less likely to be associated with growth (–) or is shown to have no statistically significant relationship (n.s.). This nomenclature is repeated for the exit studies.

### Growth determinants

Table 8.2 shows clearly that small, young, businesses are more likely to grow than are older and larger businesses. There is also evidence that older entrepreneurs, up to a certain point (age squared) are more likely to have businesses achieving faster employment growth. What is more interesting is that more highly educated business owners are likely to have faster growing businesses. Although this is also not a universal finding, Table 8.2 further suggests that having experience of working- as an employee – in the same sector as the business that they now own, and being male, either at best promotes growth or, at worst, has no significant relationship with growth.

Other human capital attributes are more equivocal. There is no real evidence that prior entrepreneurial experience (having previously owned a business), having management experience, being indigenous to a locality, team entrepreneurship or parental background play that much of a role in business growth.

Aside from being small and young, what is clear is that legal status has an important role in explaining growth. Limited companies appear to be more likely to show growth than businesses that choose other legal forms. There is also some evidence that being in a wider portfolio of businesses (multi-plant) and undertaking R&D also motivate growth. The sources of finance used within the business also seem to be associated with growth. There is some evidence that those who struggle to gain finance (access to finance) and those that make use of public assistance are likely to grow. What is more important, here, is having access to pools of capital/assets although, yet again, it is perhaps salient to remember Cressy's (1996) argument that the sources of finance merely reflect the human capital of the individual, and so should not be taken as an independent influence upon growth.

The evidence of links between business strategy and growth tends to be less clear. Whilst there are some studies that identify positive relationships (e.g. forward planning networking, customer numbers), the

*Table 8.2*   Review of international evidence

| | Growth | | | Survival | | |
|---|---|---|---|---|---|---|
| | + | – | n.s. | + | – | n.s. |
| **Human capital attributes** | | | | | | |
| Being older | 4 | 0 | 3 | 13 | 1 | 4 |
| Age squared | 0 | 2 | 1 | 0 | 4 | 2 |
| Coming from an ethnic minority | 1 | 0 | 1 | 1 | 3 | 4 |
| Having prior entrepreneurial experience | 1 | 1 | 4 | 5 | 0 | 4 |
| Previously unemployed | 0 | 1 | 0 | 0 | 1 | 4 |
| Being males | 3 | 0 | 1 | 7 | 0 | 7 |
| Education | 8 | 1 | 4 | 7 | 2 | 5 |
| Having children | 0 | 0 | 0 | 1 | 1 | 0 |
| Having a spouse | 0 | 0 | 0 | 1 | 0 | 2 |
| Prior sectoral experience | 5 | 0 | 4 | 4 | 1 | 1 |
| Prior managerial experience | 1 | 0 | 5 | 1 | 0 | 4 |
| Being disabled | 0 | 0 | 0 | 0 | 1 | 3 |
| Being indigenous to an area (born and bred) | 1 | 1 | 0 | 0 | 0 | 1 |
| Parental experience of entrepreneurship | 0 | 0 | 1 | 2 | 0 | 0 |
| Team entrepreneurship | 1 | 0 | 1 | 0 | 0 | 1 |
| **Business characteristics** | | | | | | |
| Smaller businesses | 6 | 0 | 2 | 5 | 17 | 0 |
| Younger businesses | 5 | 0 | 1 | 0 | 12 | 0 |
| Conducted research and development | 1 | 0 | 0 | 2 | 1 | 0 |
| Subcontracting business | 0 | 0 | 1 | 1 | 0 | 0 |
| Multi-plant business | 1 | 0 | 1 | 2 | 2 | 1 |
| Business has scale economies | | | | 1 | | |
| Limited company | 4 | 0 | 0 | 5 | 0 | 1 |
| Franchise business | 0 | 0 | 0 | 0 | 1 | 0 |
| Experienced change in ownership | 0 | 1 | 0 | 0 | 0 | 0 |
| **Industry** | | | | | | |
| Agriculture | 0 | 0 | 0 | 0 | 2 | 0 |
| Manufacture | 4 | 0 | 0 | 1 | 1 | 0 |
| Construction | 1 | 0 | 0 | 1 | 0 | 0 |
| Wholesale | 0 | 0 | 0 | 2 | 3 | 0 |
| Hotels | 0 | 0 | 0 | 0 | 2 | 0 |
| Transport | 0 | 0 | 0 | 1 | 2 | 0 |
| Financial | 1 | 0 | 0 | 0 | 1 | 0 |
| Business | 1 | 0 | 1 | 2 | 2 | 0 |
| Other | 0 | 0 | 0 | 0 | 1 | 0 |
| Industry's prior growth | 2 | 0 | 0 | 2 | 1 | 1 |
| Industry's level of R&D | 1 | 0 | 0 | 1 | 1 | 2 |
| Industry's capital/labour ratio | 0 | 0 | 0 | 4 | 1 | 0 |
| Industry's minimum efficient scale | 1 | 0 | 0 | 1 | 2 | 1 |
| Industry's demand for goods/services | 0 | 0 | 0 | 1 | 0 | 0 |
| **Strategy** | | | | | | |
| Business recognizes opportunities | 2 | 0 | 1 | 0 | 0 | 0 |

Continued

*Table 8.2* (Continued)

|  | Growth | | | Survival | | |
|---|---|---|---|---|---|---|
|  | + | – | n.s. | + | – | n.s. |
| Business has growth intention | 2 | 0 | 0 | 0 | 0 | 0 |
| Business conducts business planning/forward planning | 1 | 1 | 0 | 1 | 0 | 1 |
| Product range of business | 0 | 0 | 1 | 2 | 0 | 0 |
| Innovativeness | 1 | 1 | 0 | 3 | 1 | 0 |
| Use of email | 0 | 0 | 1 | 0 | 0 | 0 |
| Networking by businesses | 1 | 0 | 1 | 2 | 0 | 1 |
| Market adjustments conducted by business | 0 | 0 | 0 | 1 | 1 | 0 |
| Business Exports | 0 | 0 | 1 | 0 | 0 | 1 |
| Business changes location | 1 | 0 | 0 | 0 | 0 | 0 |
| Number of customers/competitors | 1 | 0 | 1 | 0 | 0 | 0 |
| Finance | | | | | | |
| Business has difficulty in accessing finance | 2 | 0 | 0 | 0 | 0 | 0 |
| Having assets/capital | 4 | 0 | 1 | 8 | 0 | 5 |
| Being a home owner | 0 | 0 | 0 | 0 | 0 | 1 |
| Cost of finance to business | 0 | 0 | 0 | 0 | 1 | 0 |
| Use of public assistance | 4 | 0 | 6 | 1 | 0 | 0 |
| Use of a bank loan | 0 | 0 | 0 | 0 | 0 | 1 |
| Demographics | | | | | | |
| Unemployment rate | 0 | 0 | 0 | 1 | 1 | 3 |
| Region | 1 | 0 | 0 | 3 | 0 | 3 |
| Employment growth | 0 | 0 | 0 | 2 | 0 | 0 |
| Entry rate of businesses | 1 | 0 | 0 | 0 | 3 | 0 |
| Population density/growth | 2 | 1 | 1 | 0 | 1 | 0 |
| Stock of existing businesses | 0 | 2 | 0 | 0 | 0 | 0 |

evidence here is weaker than what Storey (1994a) refers to as the pre- and at-start factors (This, of course, may be because the measures of strategy fail to capture the subtleties of the strategy).

In short, what the businesses do once they have begun to trade seems to exert a surprisingly modest influence upon their performance in terms of growth. If anything, growth seems to be more strongly influenced by choice of location and sector than by the strategy adopted by the business.

## Determinants of exit

The variable most commonly included in studies of business exit is business size. Table 8.2 shows that it appears in 22 studies. The age of the entrepreneur is used in 18 studies, the age of the business in

12 studies and the education of the entrepreneur in 14 studies. The results for each of these factors seem fairly robust. Although there is a touch of dissent about business size, the balance of evidence suggests that bigger businesses are more likely to persist when compared with their smaller counterparts. This finding is compatible with the Gamblers Ruin model (Cressy, 1996).

Age is also a strong proxy. The number of young people in entrepreneurship is very modest (Greene, 2002) and the evidence here suggests that older individuals have businesses with greater longevity (Cressy, 1993). That said, the age squared variable suggests, on balance, that an individual's age is only important up to a point. The age of the business itself is also important, with longer established businesses being more likely to persist than younger businesses.

Having higher levels of education also seems important. Amongst the other variables identified in Table 8.2, prior entrepreneurial experience, sectoral experience, having parents with a background in self-employment and being male all tend to have a positive influence on staying in business. Other attributes, however, remain more obscure. The evidence on ethnicity, disability, prior unemployment, prior management experience, having dependents or a spouse, being indigenous to the locality or being part of a team do not particularly emerge strongly as either positive or negative explanations.

Consistent with Storey (1994a), what emerges from the review of business characteristic features is the importance of legal status. Limited companies are more likely to survive when compared with other business ownership types (e.g. partnership). Hence, whilst there is some evidence that some other factors are important (e.g. R&D, subcontracting), what fundamentally emerges is that limited companies that are somewhat older and bigger are the most likely to stay the course. Industrial structure is shown in most studies to influence exiting behaviour and there is evidence that industry capital/labour, R&D and growth is more likely to support business persistence.

Table 8.2 also suggests that a number of business strategy factors such as being more innovative, indulging in networking and having a wider portfolio of products enhance business survival. These factors may seem either as further confirmation of the importance of size and age, or as reflecting the importance of having a business strategy appropriate for overcoming the constraints of an uncertain external environment.

Finance is another area that has been investigated. Here, besides the evidence of the importance of capital/assets, one other interesting finding – albeit from a single study – is that public assistance is seen as being important, whilst the cost of capital would seem to detract from exiting behaviour. Finally, the wider context is important. As with the studies on growth, Table 8.2 shows location can be important although, as with the industrial sector, it is difficult to identify general results from regional factors. Of clearer importance, is that regions with higher rates of entry and population density also have higher exit rates as greater competition in urban areas perhaps is responsible for punishing the more marginal businesses.

## Comparing survival and growth

A number of 'stylized' results emerge from Table 8.2 and these are abbreviated in Table 8.3. First, being small and young increases both the likelihood of exit and the likelihood of growth. However, it cannot be said from this that growth is independent of business size, once the very smallest businesses are excluded. Whilst the temptation may be to suggest that there is some relationship between very small and new businesses and growth, it has to be remembered that the review (although focussed solely on employment growth) does not focus on a particular business size category.

Alongside size issues, assets and capital play at least a supporting role in this process: having greater access to resources (wealth) provides a cushion for survival and perhaps a bed rock for future growth. Size and age effects are also mitigated by demographic influences. More difficult to pin down is which regions, or which sectors, have the best performing new and small businesses. There is evidence that a new entrant faces a tough time in buoyant regions and in competitive sectors. The consensus seems to be that, if they survive that difficult period, then their

*Table 8.3* Summary of recent empirical studies on performance

|  | Growth | Survival |
| --- | --- | --- |
| Older individuals | + | + |
| Age squared | – | – |
| Being male | + | +/n.s. |
| Education | + | + |
| Smaller businesses | + | – |
| Younger businesses | + | – |
| Limited company | + | + |
| Industry | +/– | +/– |
| Having assets/capital | + | + |
| Region | +/– | +/– |
| Entry rate | + | – |

longer term prospects for growth are considerably better than businesses in depressed regions and slow growing sectors.

A third result, common to both survival and growth, is that being a limited company enhances performance. In some senses this is an odd finding since is difficult to know precisely what is being captured in this choice of legal form. It may, for example, enhance performance because it adds legitimacy, helping the business to overcome the liability of newness (Stinchcombe, 1965) and, in terms of growth, further 'brands' the businesses positively in the eyes of outsiders such as customers, banks, suppliers and so on. Alternatively, being a limited company may mean that the business has access to a wider pool of resources compared with other business forms, or that it simply signals the growth intentions of the entrepreneur.

The fourth result, albeit somewhat equivocal, is the importance of human capital factors such as education and gender. Males are more likely to have growing businesses, but the impact of gender on survival appears ambiguous. Despite the burgeoning literature on female entrepreneurship (Cromie and Birley, 1992; Hundley, 2000; Cowling and Taylor, 2001; Westhead, 2003; Verheul et al., 2006; Marlow, 2006), it remains difficult to completely ascertain as to why such results should occur. Females earn less in the waged sector than men so this would be expected to make entrepreneurship more attractive. However, males are much more likely to start new businesses than females, indicating that there may be wider social and economic processes at work.

The strong positive finding for education is interesting. Lucas (1978) suggested that increases in educational attainment were likely to have an equivocal effect on entrepreneurship because, whilst it raised an individual's entrepreneurial capacity, it also made them more attractive to potential employers by effectively signalling the worth of that individual. Davidsson and Honig (2003), however, suggest that education may improve the ability of entrepreneurs to effectively spot and exploit entrepreneurial opportunities, and the implication of Table 8.3 is that this quality perhaps dominates the higher income that an educated individual can earn as an employee.

By way of concluding this section of the chapter, it is clear there remain profound and distinctive problems in measuring performance. Despite these problems, there are some factors that are associated with business performance, but whether they constitute a clear picture we leave to the reader to judge.

## Performance across the three decades in Teesside

This section begins by examining growth patterns of new businesses established in Teesside in the 1970s, 1980s and 1990s. Since the aim is to conduct a historical comparison across the three decades, the analysis is constrained by the availability of the performance measures collected in the 1970s. For the 1970s study, three types of variables were collected. First, there was information on sales turnover which was, however, only collected in turnover bands largely because collecting ranged information was thought to be more fruitful than asking for actual turnover sums.

This information does not readily lend itself to historical comparison for two reasons: first because individual respondents were on the whole loath to give even banded turnover information; and second because the effects of inflation may erode the reliability and robustness of any comparison made on turnover bands. To control for this, an alternative turnover measure is used from another original 1970s turnover question: entrepreneurs were asked if they had seen a rise, decline or stable level of turnover in the last year. Profitability is the second measure. Information here is even sparser, so that what is available is only whether the business made a profit or a loss. The third measure is employment. Actual numbers of employees were collected, both currently and during prior years.

For each of the three decades Table 8.4 shows the proportion of businesses reporting they were profitable. It also shows those reporting sales turnover and employment growth. In terms of the latter two measures, there are no clear differences between the three decades. Differences do exist between the sales turnover measures. Teesside businesses in the 1990s were much less likely to indicate, compared with earlier decades, that their sales had increased. The table also shows that around 40 per cent of businesses in each of the three decades displayed no growth in employment and about one-in-ten saw their employment fall. This was a fairly stable pattern across all three decades (Chi sq. 1.373; p. value 0.849).

## Performance: multivariate frameworks

This section examines the determinants of business growth using probit analysis (Table 8.5), ordered probit analysis (Tables 8.6 and 8.7) and tobit analysis (Table 8.8). These analyses pool the data from all three decades to draw appropriate temporal comparisons.

*Table 8.4*   Summary performance measures for the three decades

|  | 1970s | 1980s | 1990s | $X^2$ |
|---|---|---|---|---|
| Turnover |  |  |  |  |
| Increased | 78.87 | 76.73 | 58.6 |  |
| Remained the same | 15.49 | 15.84 | 30.57 |  |
| Declined | 5.63 | 7.43 | 10.83 | 28.217* |
| In Profit |  |  |  |  |
| No | 13.74 | 12.87 | 13.61 |  |
| Yes | 86.26 | 87.13 | 86.39 | 0.066 |
| Employment growth |  |  |  |  |
| Increased | 46.5 | 46.48 | 47.5 |  |
| Remained the same | 41.4 | 44.6 | 41.25 |  |
| Declined | 12.1 | 8.92 | 11.25 | 1.424 |

* significant at 1 per cent level; ** significant at 5 per cent level.

## Performance probits

We begin by using probit analysis. Three performance measures are examined: profitability, turnover and employment. Here our interest is in contrasting businesses that experienced turnover growth (= 1) with those that did not (= 0). A similar distinction was made between profitable and unprofitable businesses (1 = profitable, 0 = otherwise) and those that had seen employment growth and those that had not (1 = employment growth, 0 = otherwise). Finally, we created, a fourth performance measure which combined these measures (1 = growth in profitability, and turnover and employment, 0 = otherwise).

These four performance measures were subsequently tested against: human capital (e.g. age, age squared sex, educational attainment levels); business level characteristics (e.g. business age, business age squared, limited company); business problems in the first year (e.g. shortage of supplies, demand); finance (e.g. importance of a particular source of finance, number of financial providers used pre and post start); sector; and the three decades to examine how these influenced the likelihood of experiencing turnover, profitability, employment or the combined measure of growth.

There is little evidence of human capital factors being important influences on business performance judging from Table 8.5. The only statistically significant variables are: being born and bred in Teesside (indigenous), previously unemployed and being a serial entrepreneur. Each of these is negatively signed, indicating that people with such characteristics are less likely to have a new business that grows. Apart from these factors, there is also some sporadic evidence of the importance of human capital (A Level/HND – employment model), problems in the first year (demand – profitability model) and the value of pre start support (employment). Elsewhere, there is more general evidence of the utility of finance although these results are also far from uniform.

Clearer results emerge, however, in terms of the entry conditions faced by new businesses across the three decades. Limited companies are on the whole more likely to perform better, as were businesses in the professional services sector. More surprisingly is that it would appear that older businesses are more likely to grow even if this likelihood tails off with increased age (business age squared). Equally, the evidence from Table 8.5 suggests that the new businesses in the 1980s sample, at least in terms of employment and turnover growth, perform better than those in the 1990s sample. Indeed, one interpretation of these results is that it was the 1990s that generated the weakest performing new businesses.

However this result is not consistently found across all four performance parameters. When all performance parameters are reviewed the only consistent finding is that new businesses in professional services perform well and that new businesses in the 1970s and 1980s cohorts outperformed the 1990s cohort.

### Performance ordered probits

In Table 8.5 growth is defined as a binary variable: either the business was growing or it was not. To examine whether our results are sensitive to this formulation we now distinguish between those businesses that grew, those that stayed the same, and those that did not grow. These analyses were conducted only for turnover and employment measures, given that we did not have this type of measure for profitability in the 1970s.

Turning first to the results for turnover growth, Table 8.6 presents the marginal effects for a pooled ordered probit model (0 = decline; 1 = same; and 2 = grow). It shows that businesses established by entrepreneurs born and bred in Teesside experienced poorer sales turnover growth than businesses established by other entrepreneurs. This confirms our finding in Table 8.5. However, there is no evidence in Table 8.6 that being previously unemployed has a significant impact on growth outcomes. What is clear is that those with prior entrepreneurial experience are more likely to have stable sales turnover.

Table 8.5  Marginal effect probit estimations for performance measures, 1970s–1990s

| | Employment growth | | Turnover growth | | Profitability growth | | Combined performance | |
|---|---|---|---|---|---|---|---|---|
| | dF/dx | z | dF/dx | z | dF/dx | z | dF/dx | z |
| Entrepreneur characteristics | | | | | | | | |
| Age | 0.024 | 1.300 | -0.008 | -0.490 | 0.013 | 1.240 | 0.011 | 0.560 |
| Age² | 0.000 | -1.560 | 0.000 | 0.300 | 0.000 | -1.350 | 0.000 | -0.790 |
| Sex | 0.057 | 0.980 | 0.036 | 0.680 | -0.023 | -0.700 | 0.055 | 0.940 |
| Indigenous | -0.099 | -1.850 | -0.095 | -1.970** | -0.040 | -1.350 | -0.079 | -1.450 |
| Previously unemployed | 0.003 | 0.050 | -0.128 | -2.600* | -0.029 | -0.910 | -0.041 | -0.780 |
| Prior entrepreneurial experience | 0.024 | 0.430 | -0.112 | -2.220** | 0.038 | 1.230 | -0.037 | -0.670 |
| Full-time in business | -0.055 | -0.560 | 0.025 | 0.280 | 0.155 | 1.860 | 0.098 | 0.940 |
| Education | | | | | | | | |
| Degree | 0.079 | 0.840 | -0.087 | -0.980 | 0.036 | 0.740 | -0.015 | -0.160 |
| A level/HND | 0.179 | 2.340** | -0.005 | -0.070 | 0.060 | 1.600 | 0.144 | 1.860 |
| Vocational qualification | 0.035 | 0.590 | -0.026 | -0.490 | 0.014 | 0.400 | 0.010 | 0.170 |
| Professional qualification | 0.164 | 1.480 | 0.043 | 0.430 | 0.027 | 0.460 | 0.132 | 1.160 |
| Business characteristics | | | | | | | | |
| Business age | 0.210 | 3.480* | -0.083 | -1.580 | 0.064 | 1.640 | 0.152 | 2.140** |
| Business age² | -0.017 | -2.250** | 0.006 | 0.920 | -0.005 | -0.970 | -0.013 | -1.460 |
| Limited company | 0.198 | 3.290* | 0.070 | 1.260 | -0.028 | -0.830 | 0.121 | 2.030** |
| Business strategy | | | | | | | | |
| Problems in the first year | | | | | | | | |
| Supply shortage | 0.080 | 0.910 | 0.118 | 1.460 | 0.070 | 1.770 | 0.152 | 1.590 |
| Skilled labour | -0.016 | -0.260 | -0.073 | -1.260 | -0.014 | -0.380 | -0.076 | -1.280 |
| Labour turnover | 0.193 | 1.570 | 0.153 | 1.420 | -0.148 | -1.750 | 0.124 | 1.020 |
| Wage costs | 0.004 | 0.050 | -0.002 | -0.030 | -0.068 | -1.390 | -0.042 | -0.570 |
| Demand | -0.099 | -1.720 | -0.057 | -1.040 | -0.104 | -2.790* | -0.091 | -1.560 |
| Used pre start support | 0.137 | 2.580** | 0.018 | 0.360 | -0.030 | -0.950 | 0.083 | 1.540 |
| Regional suppliers | 0.000 | 0.010 | 0.001 | 1.130 | 0.000 | -0.380 | 0.000 | -0.260 |

| | | | | | | | | |
|---|---|---|---|---|---|---|---|---|
| Inter/national suppliers | 0.000 | 0.050 | 0.000 | 0.260 | 0.000 | -0.970 | -0.001 | -0.840 |
| Regional customers | 0.001 | 0.710 | 0.001 | 0.840 | 0.000 | 0.680 | 0.001 | 1.000 |
| Inter/national customers | -0.001 | -0.510 | 0.001 | 0.840 | 0.000 | 0.390 | 0.000 | -0.290 |
| **Finance** | | | | | | | | |
| *Pre start-up* | | | | | | | | |
| Savings | 0.114 | 1.790 | 0.010 | 0.180 | -0.004 | -0.100 | 0.021 | 0.330 |
| Mortgage | 0.293 | 1.820 | 0.049 | 0.320 | -0.321 | -2.410** | -0.033 | -0.200 |
| Bank | 0.098 | 1.290 | 0.021 | 0.300 | 0.060 | 1.590 | 0.195 | 2.490** |
| Finance company | 0.319 | 1.570 | 0.044 | 0.240 | 0.031 | 0.320 | 0.529 | 2.160** |
| *Post start-up* | | | | | | | | |
| Savings | 0.109 | 0.950 | -0.008 | -0.080 | -0.152 | -1.730 | -0.212 | -1.99** |
| Profits | 0.027 | 0.330 | 0.036 | 0.480 | 0.123 | 2.440** | -0.110 | -1.270 |
| Bank | -0.004 | -0.040 | 0.030 | 0.350 | -0.026 | -0.460 | -0.123 | -1.330 |
| Finance company | 0.055 | 0.260 | -0.218 | -1.100 | | | 0.161 | 0.660 |
| Number of sources of finance used pre start-up | 0.068 | 1.920 | 0.002 | 0.070 | 0.000 | 0.010 | 0.044 | 1.230 |
| Number of sources of finance used post start-up | 0.043 | 1.120 | 0.084 | 2.440** | -0.023 | -1.090 | 0.056 | 1.410 |
| **Sector** | | | | | | | | |
| Manufacturing | 0.098 | 1.200 | 0.054 | 0.750 | -0.066 | -1.320 | 0.107 | 1.260 |
| Construction | 0.043 | 0.440 | 0.039 | 0.450 | -0.009 | -0.150 | -0.033 | -0.350 |
| Professional services | 0.189 | 2.140** | 0.169 | 2.270** | 0.047 | 1.000 | 0.153 | 1.69 |
| Motor Repairs and Beauty | 0.041 | 0.520 | 0.033 | 0.480 | 0.006 | 0.140 | -0.053 | -0.650 |
| Other | 0.005 | 0.070 | 0.126 | 1.890 | 0.000 | 0.010 | 0.045 | 0.550 |
| **Decade** | | | | | | | | |
| 1980s | 0.217 | 2.710* | 0.204 | 2.980* | 0.075 | 1.920 | 0.093 | 1.100 |
| 1970s | 0.209 | 2.590* | 0.133 | 1.880 | 0.058 | 1.420 | 0.205 | 2.410** |
| N. | 569 | | 567 | | 490 | | 477 | |
| LR chi$^2$ | 125.44 | | 81.11 | | 77.61 | | 91.67 | |
| Prob chi$^2$ | 0.000 | | 0.000 | | 0.000 | | 0.000 | |
| Log likelihood | -330.2 | | -326.3 | | -156.7 | | -256.4 | |
| Pseudo R$^2$ | 0.160 | | 0.111 | | 0.199 | | 0.152 | |

** significant at the 5 per cent level; * significant at the 1 per cent level.

Table 8.6  Marginal effects for the turnover growth ordered probit

|  | Declining turnover | | Stable turnover | | Increasing turnover | |
|---|---|---|---|---|---|---|
|  | dy/dx | z | dy/dx | z | dy/dx | z |
| Entrepreneur characteristics |  |  |  |  |  |  |
| Age | -0.001 | -0.23 | -0.002 | -0.23 | 0.004 | 0.23 |
| Age$^2$ | 0.000 | 0.5 | 0.000 | 0.5 | 0.000 | -0.51 |
| Sex | -0.013 | -0.67 | -0.021 | -0.7 | 0.034 | 0.69 |
| Indigenous | 0.032 | 2.08** | 0.057 | 1.96 | -0.089 | -2.04** |
| Previously unemployed | 0.036 | 1.78 | 0.054 | 1.96 | -0.090 | -1.91 |
| Prior entrepreneurial experience | 0.037 | 1.77 | 0.056 | 1.98** | -0.093 | -1.91 |
| Full-time in business | -0.010 | -0.28 | -0.015 | -0.29 | 0.025 | 0.29 |
| Education |  |  |  |  |  |  |
| Degree | 0.023 | 0.65 | 0.035 | 0.73 | -0.058 | -0.7 |
| A level/HND | 0.010 | 0.37 | 0.016 | 0.38 | -0.025 | -0.38 |
| Vocational qualification | 0.009 | 0.47 | 0.015 | 0.48 | -0.024 | -0.48 |
| Professional qualification | -0.018 | -0.6 | -0.033 | -0.55 | 0.050 | 0.57 |
| Business characteristics |  |  |  |  |  |  |
| Business age | 0.039 | 1.97** | 0.065 | 1.96 | -0.104 | -1.99** |
| Business age$^2$ | -0.003 | -1.22 | -0.005 | -1.22 | 0.008 | 1.23 |
| Limited company | -0.011 | -0.62 | -0.020 | -0.6 | 0.031 | 0.6 |
| Business strategy |  |  |  |  |  |  |
| *Problems in the first year* |  |  |  |  |  |  |
| Supply shortage | -0.030 | -1.33 | -0.059 | -1.14 | 0.089 | 1.2 |
| Skilled labour | 0.039 | 1.52 | 0.057 | 1.75 | -0.096 | -1.66 |
| Labour turnover | -0.036 | -1.44 | -0.074 | -1.15 | 0.110 | 1.24 |
| Wage costs | -0.017 | -0.78 | -0.030 | -0.72 | 0.047 | 0.74 |

| | | | | | | |
|---|---|---|---|---|---|---|
| Demand | 0.022 | 1 | 0.034 | 1.08 | -0.056 | -1.05 |
| Used pre start support | -0.011 | -0.59 | -0.018 | -0.6 | 0.028 | 0.6 |
| Regional suppliers | 0.000 | -0.1 | 0.000 | -0.1 | 0.000 | 0.1 |
| Inter/national suppliers | 0.000 | 0.59 | 0.000 | 0.59 | 0.000 | -0.59 |
| Regional customers | 0.000 | -1.16 | -0.001 | 1.15 | 0.001 | 1.16 |
| Inter/national customers | 0.000 | -0.79 | 0.000 | -0.79 | 0.001 | 0.79 |
| **Finance** | | | | | | |
| *Importance of finance provider* | | | | | | |
| Pre start personal savings | -0.011 | -0.55 | -0.018 | -0.54 | 0.029 | 0.54 |
| Pre start mortgage | -0.056 | -2.87* | -0.144 | -1.85 | 0.200 | 2.09** |
| Pre start bank finance | -0.019 | -0.94 | -0.035 | -0.87 | 0.054 | 0.9 |
| Pre start finance company | -0.011 | -0.2 | -0.020 | -0.19 | 0.031 | 0.19 |
| Post start personal savings | 0.010 | 0.24 | 0.015 | 0.25 | -0.025 | -0.24 |
| Profits from business | -0.009 | -0.36 | -0.016 | -0.37 | 0.025 | 0.37 |
| Post start bank finance | 0.001 | 0.03 | 0.001 | 0.03 | -0.002 | -0.03 |
| Post start finance company | 0.119 | 0.94 | 0.114 | 1.76 | -0.233 | -1.23 |
| Number of sources of finance used pre start-up | 0.001 | 0.09 | 0.002 | 0.09 | -0.003 | -0.09 |
| Number of sources of finance used post start-up | -0.019 | -1.54 | -0.032 | -1.54 | 0.051 | 1.55 |
| **Sector** | | | | | | |
| Manufacturing | -0.004 | -0.17 | -0.007 | -0.16 | 0.011 | 0.17 |
| Construction | 0.006 | 0.21 | 0.011 | 0.21 | -0.017 | -0.21 |
| Professional services | -0.035 | -1.71 | -0.068 | -1.47 | 0.103 | 1.56 |
| Motor Repairs and Beauty | -0.009 | -0.4 | -0.016 | -0.39 | 0.025 | 0.4 |
| Other | -0.043 | -2.46** | -0.086 | -2.14** | 0.129 | 2.28** |
| **Decade** | | | | | | |
| 1980s | -0.065 | -3.33* | -0.124 | -3.12* | 0.189 | 3.31* |
| 1970s | -0.057 | -3.23* | -0.116 | -2.79* | 0.173 | 3.02* |

** significant at the 5 per cent level; * significant at the 1 per cent level.

*Table 8.7* Marginal effects for the employment growth ordered probit

| | Declining employment growth | | No employment growth | | Employment growth | |
|---|---|---|---|---|---|---|
| | dy/dx | z | dy/dx | z | dy/dx | z |
| **Entrepreneur characteristics** | | | | | | |
| Age | −0.010 | −1.51 | −0.015 | −1.51 | 0.024 | 1.52 |
| Age² | 0.000 | 1.75 | 0.000 | 1.74 | 0.000 | −1.76 |
| Sex | −0.028 | −1.27 | −0.038 | −1.41 | 0.065 | 1.35 |
| Indigenous | 0.040 | 2.44** | 0.068 | 2.19** | −0.108 | −2.32** |
| Previously unemployed | 0.005 | 0.28 | 0.008 | 0.29 | −0.013 | −0.29 |
| Prior entrepreneurial experience | −0.001 | −0.05 | −0.001 | −0.05 | 0.002 | 0.05 |
| Full-time in business | 0.012 | 0.4 | 0.020 | 0.37 | −0.033 | −0.38 |
| **Education** | | | | | | |
| Degree | −0.031 | −1.2 | −0.057 | −0.99 | 0.088 | 1.06 |
| A level/HND | −0.059 | −3.29* | −0.125 | −2.49** | 0.184 | 2.77* |
| Vocational qualification | −0.008 | −0.4 | −0.012 | −0.39 | 0.020 | 0.39 |
| Professional qualification | −0.052 | −2.28** | −0.117 | −1.58 | 0.169 | 1.77 |
| **Business characteristics** | | | | | | |
| Business age | −0.032 | −1.75 | −0.048 | −1.74 | 0.080 | 1.76 |
| Business age² | 0.002 | 0.72 | 0.003 | 0.72 | −0.004 | −0.72 |
| Limited company | −0.051 | −3.03* | −0.097 | −2.51** | 0.148 | 2.73* |
| **Business strategy** | | | | | | |
| *Problems in the first year* | | | | | | |
| Supply shortage | −0.010 | −0.36 | −0.017 | −0.34 | 0.027 | 0.35 |
| Skilled labour | 0.009 | 0.38 | 0.013 | 0.4 | −0.022 | −0.39 |
| Labour turnover | −0.020 | −0.55 | −0.035 | −0.48 | 0.055 | 0.5 |
| Wage costs | 0.041 | 1.22 | 0.049 | 1.55 | −0.090 | −1.39 |

| | | | | | | |
|---|---|---|---|---|---|---|
| Demand | 0.017 | 0.75 | 0.023 | 0.81 | -0.040 | -0.79 |
| Used pre start support | -0.053 | -2.51 | -0.072 | -2.76 | 0.125 | 2.72* |
| Regional suppliers | 0.000 | -0.48 | 0.000 | -0.48 | 0.000 | 0.49 |
| Inter/national suppliers | 0.000 | 0.39 | 0.000 | 0.39 | 0.000 | -0.39 |
| Regional customers | 0.000 | -0.95 | -0.001 | -0.95 | 0.001 | 0.95 |
| Inter/national customers | 0.000 | 1 | 0.001 | 1 | -0.001 | -1 |
| **Finance** | | | | | | |
| *Importance of finance provider* | | | | | | |
| Pre start personal savings | -0.037 | -1.82 | -0.061 | -1.69 | 0.098 | 1.76 |
| Pre start mortgage | -0.064 | -2.62* | -0.171 | -1.53 | 0.235 | 1.74 |
| Pre start bank finance | -0.026 | -1.17 | -0.045 | -1.02 | 0.071 | 1.07 |
| Pre start finance company | -0.078 | -4.3* | -0.265 | -2.01 | 0.343 | 2.34** |
| Post start personal savings | -0.011 | -0.3 | -0.018 | -0.28 | 0.028 | 0.28 |
| Profits from business | 0.009 | 0.32 | 0.014 | 0.32 | -0.023 | -0.32 |
| Post start bank finance | 0.065 | 1.44 | 0.070 | 2.08 | -0.135 | -1.73 |
| Post start finance company | 0.042 | 0.42 | 0.048 | 0.57 | -0.090 | -0.49 |
| Number of sources of finance used pre start-up | -0.017 | -1.39 | -0.026 | -1.38 | 0.043 | 1.39 |
| Number of sources of finance used post start-up | -0.014 | -1.09 | -0.022 | -1.09 | 0.036 | 1.1 |
| **Sector** | | | | | | |
| Manufacturing | -0.007 | -0.26 | -0.011 | -0.25 | 0.018 | 0.26 |
| Construction | -0.015 | -0.51 | -0.025 | -0.46 | 0.040 | 0.48 |
| Professional services | -0.046 | -2.07** | -0.092 | -1.61 | 0.138 | 1.76 |
| Motor Repairs and Beauty | -0.009 | -0.37 | -0.015 | -0.36 | 0.024 | 0.36 |
| Other | -0.008 | -0.34 | -0.013 | -0.32 | 0.022 | 0.33 |
| **Decade** | | | | | | |
| 1980s | -0.058 | -2.53** | -0.104 | -2.2** | 0.162 | 2.35** |
| 1970s | -0.061 | -3.02 | -0.121 | -2.39** | 0.182 | 2.63* |

** significant at the 5 per cent level; * significant at the 1 per cent level.

*Table 8.8* Tobit regressions for employment growth, 1970s–1990s

| | Annualised | | Relative | | Absolute | |
|---|---|---|---|---|---|---|
| | Coef. | T | Coef. | t | Coef. | t |
| *Entrepreneur characteristics* | | | | | | |
| Age | 0.022 | 1.330 | 0.039 | 1.140 | -0.006 | -0.590 |
| Age² | 0.000 | -1.380 | -0.001 | -1.260 | 0.000 | 0.720 |
| Sex | 0.072 | 1.410 | 0.162 | 1.500 | 0.051 | 1.450 |
| Indigenous | -0.037 | -0.810 | -0.087 | -0.900 | -0.033 | -1.070 |
| Previously unemployed | -0.027 | -0.580 | -0.023 | -0.240 | -0.038 | -1.190 |
| Prior entrepreneurial experience | -0.024 | -0.500 | -0.054 | -0.540 | -0.004 | -0.110 |
| Full-time in business | -0.042 | -0.490 | -0.079 | -0.430 | -0.028 | -0.470 |
| *Education* | | | | | | |
| Degree | 0.053 | 0.670 | 0.121 | 0.730 | 0.000 | 0.000 |
| A level/HND | 0.159 | 2.490** | 0.332 | 2.480** | 0.089 | 2.060** |
| Vocational qualification | 0.040 | 0.760 | 0.072 | 0.660 | 0.020 | 0.560 |
| Professional qualification | 0.081 | 0.870 | 0.217 | 1.110 | 0.035 | 0.550 |
| *Business characteristics* | | | | | | |
| Business age | 0.153 | 3.000* | 0.436 | 3.910* | 0.119 | 3.290* |
| Business age² | -0.016 | -2.430** | -0.037 | -2.670* | -0.009 | -2.030** |
| Limited company | 0.194 | 3.850* | 0.406 | 3.830* | 0.145 | 4.250* |
| *Business strategy* | | | | | | |
| *Problems in the first year* | | | | | | |
| Supply shortage | 0.036 | 0.480 | 0.105 | 0.660 | 0.004 | 0.070 |
| Skilled labour | -0.015 | -0.290 | -0.031 | -0.280 | -0.001 | -0.040 |
| Labour turnover | 0.160 | 1.690 | 0.284 | 1.430 | 0.212 | 3.370* |
| Wage costs | 0.046 | 0.710 | 0.103 | 0.760 | 0.054 | 1.260 |
| Demand | -0.069 | -1.360 | -0.131 | -1.240 | -0.067 | -1.930 |
| Used pre start support | 0.112 | 2.390** | 0.197 | 2.000** | 0.044 | 1.370 |
| Regional suppliers | 0.000 | 0.140 | 0.000 | 0.200 | 0.000 | -0.100 |

| | | | | | | |
|---|---|---|---|---|---|---|
| Inter/national suppliers | 0.000 | −0.500 | −0.001 | −0.610 | 0.000 | −0.470 |
| Regional customers | 0.001 | 0.920 | 0.002 | 1.000 | 0.000 | 0.260 |
| Inter/national customers | 0.001 | 0.610 | 0.001 | 0.470 | 0.000 | 0.360 |
| **Finance** | | | | | | |
| *Importance of finance provider* | | | | | | |
| Pre start personal savings | 0.075 | 1.400 | 0.164 | 1.450 | 0.027 | 0.750 |
| Pre start mortgage | 0.201 | 1.540 | 0.437 | 1.590 | 0.090 | 1.010 |
| Pre start bank finance | 0.068 | 1.070 | 0.165 | 1.240 | 0.054 | 1.250 |
| Pre start finance company | 0.358 | 2.230** | 0.657 | 1.940 | 0.258 | 2.390 |
| Post start personal savings | 0.069 | 0.720 | 0.069 | 0.340 | −0.033 | −0.500 |
| Profits from business | −0.041 | −0.590 | −0.114 | −0.780 | −0.087 | −1.830 |
| Post start bank finance | −0.072 | −0.870 | −0.160 | −0.920 | −0.087 | −1.550 |
| Post start finance company | 0.116 | 0.670 | 0.155 | 0.420 | 0.047 | 0.400 |
| Number of sources of finance used pre start-up | 0.059 | 1.980** | 0.109 | 1.740 | 0.051 | 2.530** |
| Number of sources of finance used post start-up | 0.041 | 1.270 | 0.111 | 1.640 | 0.060 | 2.750* |
| **Sector** | | | | | | |
| Manufacturing | 0.043 | 0.620 | 0.118 | 0.800 | 0.086 | 1.810 |
| Construction | 0.059 | 0.700 | 0.097 | 0.550 | 0.069 | 1.210 |
| Professional services | 0.174 | 2.320** | 0.322 | 2.050 | 0.115 | 2.270** |
| Motor Repairs and Beauty | 0.058 | 0.830 | 0.097 | 0.660 | 0.008 | 0.160 |
| Other | 0.046 | 0.670 | 0.065 | 0.450 | 0.027 | 0.590 |
| **Decade** | | | | | | |
| 1980s | 0.089 | 1.290 | 0.135 | 0.930 | 0.023 | 0.490 |
| 1970s | 0.146 | 2.120** | 0.283 | 1.960** | 0.092 | 1.960 |
| Constant | −1.182 | −3.300* | −2.555 | −3.360* | 2.387 | 9.780* |
| N. | 569 | | 569 | | 569 | |
| Uncensored N. | 264 | | 264 | | 264 | |
| LR chi² | 114.22 | | 138.72 | | 165.31 | |
| Prob. chi² | 0.000 | | 0.000 | | 0.000 | |
| Log likelihood | −302.3 | | −503.2 | | −177.8 | |
| Pseudo R² | 0.1589 | | 0.1211 | | 0.3174 | |

** significant at the 5 per cent level; *** significant at the 1 per cent level.

There is also more patchy evidence to suggest that entrepreneurs using mortgage finance, and those in 'other' sectors, are more likely to report sales growth. The business age effect is also interesting since it confirms the findings from other studies. Using this performance measure we now find that younger businesses are more likely to have higher turnover outcomes, but being a limited company is no longer significant. However, we continue to find that new businesses that were established in the 1970s and 1980s were more likely to report increased sales than businesses that began in the 1990s.

These results share some similarities with the marginal effect results for employment growth (Table 8.7). Here, again, being born and bred in Teesside does not improve growth but both unemployment and prior entrepreneurial experience have no significant impact. In contrast to the turnover results, however, what appears more likely to promote employment growth is having some education (A Level/HND) and a sense, if only for the growers, of the importance of pre start-up support. Another feature which distinguishes employment growth from turnover growth is that what promotes the former is being a limited company, rather than being a younger business. Again, though, there is consistent evidence to suggest that businesses in the 1990s sample experience poorer employment growth outcomes when compared to those started in the 1970s and the 1980s.

## Performance tobits

From the simple statistics presented earlier, it is clear that employment growth is highly skewed and that there are very many new businesses, in all three decades, that have zero employment growth.

Given the need to control for the large number of zeros – the so-called left censoring problem – we now present our results using a Tobit regression. Three employment based metrics will be used: absolute log employment growth (employment in latest year – employment in year 0); relative log employment growth (employment in latest year – employment in year 0/employment in year 0); and to control for inter-year variability, the favoured measure of annualised log employment growth ((employment in latest year – employment in year 0/employment in year 0)/age of business).

The results of these three tobit regressions are presented in Table 8.8. Each of the three models shows a number of consistent features. Chief of these is that those entrepreneurs with post-compulsory education (A Level/HND) are more likely to have businesses with better employment outcomes. There is also further evidence, although not uniformly across all measures, that professional service businesses have faster growth rates (annualised and absolute). We also find that new businesses using pre start-up support (annualised and relative growth) and those using more sources of post start-up finance (relative and absolute growth) grow faster.

Other effects are also evident. Again, what Table 8.8 illustrates is the importance of entry conditions and business characteristics. Unsurprisingly, businesses that are older are more likely than the youngest businesses to have had some employment growth, but the significant negative age squared term suggests that new businesses may increase and then decrease their employment size. Confirming our earlier results, Table 8.8 shows that limited companies are more likely to have employment growth. Finally, what is more surprising, given our earlier results, is that the new businesses in the 1980s sample are not statistically significantly different from those in the 1990s sample. Instead it seems that, relative to the 1990s, it is new businesses in the 1970s that had the strongest employment growth.

## Summary

This chapter has examined the performance, and the factors affecting the performance, of new businesses during three decades in the low enterprise area of Teesside. Our central performance result is that around 40 per cent of these businesses had no employment growth, and approximately 10 per cent saw employment fall over up to a five-year period. This finding is broadly true for new businesses started in the 1970s, the 1980s and the 1990s.

However, a key topic of interest to us is whether the picture was consistent over the three decades. Given that during the 1980s public policy was explicitly focussed upon creating new businesses in the expectation that this would lead to job creation we might have expected new businesses to have performed better – in terms of job creation – than in other decades. This is not, however, the reality. Table 8.9 examines the employment record of new businesses in Teesside over three decades. It shows that there were 1,082 jobs new jobs created by our sample of Teesside new businesses in the 1970s, 1,556 in the 1980s and 1,989 in the 1990s. Row 2 of the Table shows this is an arithmetic mean of about six to seven new jobs created by each new enterprise.

This scale of job creation has to be placed in the context of the evidence provided in Chapter 3. There it was shown that were some 97,291 jobs lost in the Teesside economy over the period 1971–2003. For new

*Table 8.9*   Job generation capabilities across the three decades

|  | 1970s | 1980s | 1990s |
|---|---|---|---|
| Total jobs | 1,082 | 1,556 | 1,989 |
| Mean | 6.89 | 7.31 | 6.22 |
| Std. Dev. | 7.36 | 20.28 | 10.68 |
| Median | 4 | 3 | 3 |
| Job contribution of top 10% businesses | 36.1% | 49.9% | 47.2% |
| Job contribution of top 5% businesses | 22.6% | 40.7% | 35.3% |

enterprises to replace these jobs, at seven jobs per new enterprise, would require 13,899 new enterprises. In 1995, the start-up rate of new businesses in Teesside was 17 new businesses per 10,000 of the adult population. In 2003, it peaked at 22 new businesses before falling back to 20 new businesses per 10,000 of the adult population in 2005 (see Chapter 1: Figure 1.2).

To create 13,899 new enterprises, this rate would have to increase to 643 new businesses per 10,000 adults. In the 1980s, Reynolds et al. (1994) established that the highest rate of new business formation was for Italian regions (144 new enterprises per 10,000 population). US data (Armington and Acs, 2002) also suggests that recent rates of new businesses formation in that country varied between 55 new enterprises per 10,000 population for Colorado and 29 for Pennsylvania. To create jobs on a scale that would replace those lost jobs, Teesside would have to move from having one of the lowest rates of new business formation in the UK to a rate of business formation that is unprecedented in any developed economy.

The question remains, however, whether new businesses make a greater employment contribution during the different decades. There is some evidence for optimism in Table 8.9. This is because the total number of jobs directly created by new businesses clearly increases in each decade. However, perhaps even more striking are two important consistencies. The first is that the median employment size of a new business is either 3 or 4 during each decade; the second is that the contribution to total employment made by a small proportion of businesses is considerable.

We are also able to examine the relative employment growth trajectories over time. Figure 8.1 tells a somewhat different story from Table 8.9. It shows that in the 1980s new enterprises created about 0.6 of a job one year after start-up. Amongst new businesses in the 1970s and the 1990s the comparable figure was 0.4 jobs. By year three, this

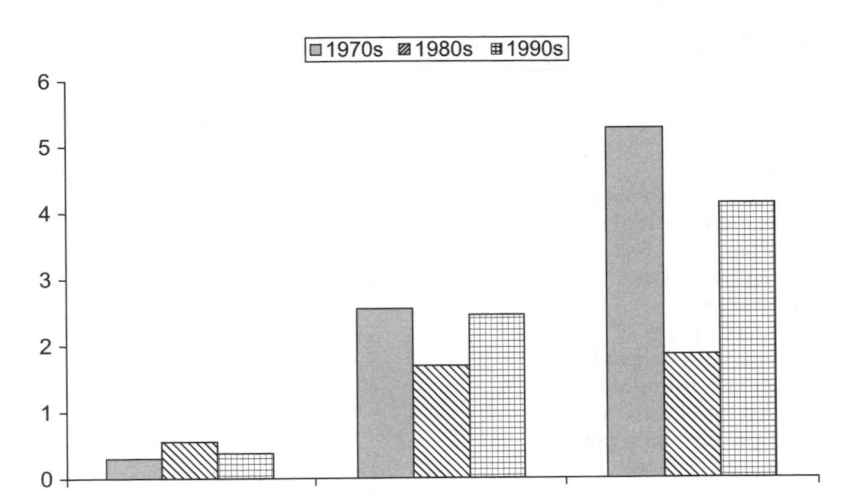

*Figure 8.1* Job generation by enterprises (absolute numbers).

situation had changed: 1970s and 1990s enterprises had created about 2.5 jobs compared with 1.7 jobs in the 1980s sample. This difference is even starker by year five: the 1970s enterprises created 5.3 jobs, the 1990s enterprises 4.1 jobs, but only a further 1.9 jobs were created by year five by the 1980s businesses. One possible explanation for this is the role played by the Enterprise Allowance Scheme where individuals starting a business were paid £40 per week over a two-year period to start a business. The EAS operated primarily during the 1980s and may have encouraged undue optimism amongst the new entrepreneurs of that time, reflected in premature expansion in terms of employment. Whilst we do not know which of our businesses attracted EAS support, it may subsequently have been that once the subsidy ended expansion was probably much lower.

This chapter has also examined the factors influencing the performance of new businesses, and how this has varied across the three decades. We considered a range of possible measures of performance (turnover, profitability, employment and 'combined' growth), differing techniques (probit, ordered probit and tobit) and three different metrics (annualised, relative and absolute) for the key measure of employment growth.

Table 8.10 provides a synopsis of these main findings from Tables 8.5 to 8.9. The synopsis was based on first identifying any factors which were found to be positively or negatively statistically significant in the

*Table 8.10*  Synopsis of employment growth performance

| | Prior studies | Probits | Ordered probits | Tobits |
|---|---|---|---|---|
| Indigenous | +/n.s. | − | − | |
| Previously unemployed | − | − | | |
| Prior entrepreneurial experience | n.s. | − | | |
| Education | + | + | + | + |
| Younger businesses | + | − | + | − |
| Businesses age$^2$ | − | + | | + |
| Limited company | + | + | + | + |
| Problems with demand | − | − | | |
| Used pre start support | + | + | | |
| Regional suppliers | | | | + |
| Use of pre start mortgage | ? | − | | |
| Use of pre start bank | ? | + | | |
| Use of pre start finance company | ? | + | + | + |
| Use of post start savings | ? | − | | |
| Use of post start profits | | + | | |
| Number of sources of finance used pre start-up | ? | | | + |
| Number of sources of finance used post start-up | ? | + | | + |
| Professional services | + | + | + | + |
| Other | ? | | + | |
| 1980s | ? | + | + | |
| 1970s | ? | + | + | + |

earlier tables. The first column of Table 8.10 summarises the findings derived from previous studies of employment growth reviewed in Table 8.2. Where the prior findings are broadly clear the impact is shown as either positive (+) or negative (−). Where the findings are more ambiguous these are denoted as '?' in Table 8.10. One such is finance. This, of course, is not to imply that finance has not been studied in relationship to new businesses. In fact, the opposite is true (e.g. Basu and Parker, 2001; Carter and van Auken, 1990; Cassar, 2004) but the issue is that no multivariate studies were found that explicitly looked at the issue of early stage finance and employment growth as a measure of performance. The two other unknowns from Table 8.10 relate to sector (Motor Repairs and Beauty and Other) and the three decades. Both of these may be thought to be unique, given that it is hard to think of another study that looks at enterprise in one area over a 30-year period.

Table 8.10 shows there is some evidence that the human capital of the new business founder is correlated with the performance of that business. Three factors were evident from the (turnover) probit and, to a certain extent, from the ordered probits. For example, businesses started by individuals that were born and bred in Teesside were less likely to grow. One interpretation of this is that if Teesside is to create more businesses that create jobs for others it needs to attract in-migrants from outside the area. We discuss this issue in the final chapter.

A second result from Table 8.10, at least in terms of the turnover probit, is that businesses started by individuals who were previously unemployed were also more likely to grow more slowly. Again this reflects the findings from previous research and signifies that, if unemployment is a good proxy for low human capital attributes, then those with limited human capital are less likely to own growth businesses. The third result from the turnover probit and the turnover ordered probit is that serial entrepreneurs – those who have been business owners previously – are more likely to have slower sales growth. To some this may be surprising since it appears difficult to reconcile this with the concept of entrepreneurial learning, given that prior business ownership experience would be expected to generate learning. The results contradict this. Our interpretation is that, despite the burgeoning literature on entrepreneurial learning (e.g. Minniti and Bygrave, 2001; Cope, 2005), most new entrepreneurs do not learn significantly from their previous experiences and, even if they do, they are unable or unwilling to apply it to their current business venture. Such a view accords with Parker (2006) who finds that the rate of entrepreneurial learning is extremely modest. Alternatively, however, such results may also point to a second possible explanation. Following on from Jovanovic (1982), it might be that entrepreneurs soon learn about their abilities. If these are limited, this may encourage them to be more risk averse and, hence, have slower growing businesses than novices. A third possible explanation is if they have failed in business previously – perhaps been declared bankrupt – they may find it more difficult to access funds for expansion. The key point here is that some, or perhaps all, of these reasons may explain our findings.

It is important to emphasise again that our findings are sensitive to how and what performance metrics are used. Even so, Table 8.10 does display some consistent findings. The first is that entrepreneurs that are educated or, more accurately, who have an education attainment level equivalent to post-secondary education (A Level/HND) are likely to have new businesses that are more likely to exhibit growth . This accords with findings from previous research – as shown in Column 1 of the Table. Nevertheless, this result surprised us because post-compulsory education, whilst it may have a vocational component or equip individuals with some generic skills and abilities provides only modest generic human capital attributes compared to that provided by a degree or a professional qualification. Our, clearly incorrect, expectation was that these 'intermediate' qualifications would provide insufficient vocational skills and also not enough specific entrepreneurial experience to form the basis for a growing new business.

A second puzzle is the positive association between business age and performance. Again this is a fairly resilient finding although there is evidence to suggest that it is non-linear and does tail off as the new business continues to age. Nonetheless, the earlier evidence (column 2, Table 8.10) suggested that it was younger businesses that were more likely to perform better. One reason for this finding may be that, in this research, stringent efforts were made to identify *de novo* businesses rather than those that appeared at first sight to be new. A potentially more important reason, though, is that the samples for Teesside businesses in the 1970s, 1980s and 1990s constitute surviving businesses. It may be that, in order for a business to grow, it has to first survive the earlier difficult transition towards legitimacy.

Legitimacy may also be important in explaining the third finding. As with the earlier evidence, Table 8.10 demonstrates a link between limited liability status and performance. Table 8.10 further demonstrates that businesses in professional services are more likely to experience positive growth outcomes compared with those in other sectors. The problem, evident in Chapter 4, is that there are insufficient entrepreneurs in Teesside entering this sector.

Finally we compare new business performance outcomes in the three decades. From both the probits and the ordered probits, it would appear that new businesses in the 1980s have better performance outcomes than new businesses in the 1990s. This is not, however, confirmed in the tobit analysis which looks specifically at employment growth. Using this metric it was the new businesses started in 1970s that outperformed new businesses in the other two decades across all three types of analysis. One further caveat on this, though, is that the macro-economic circumstances of the three decades were not identical. What is clear, however, is that each decade had its major recession year or years and Teesside has had high unemployment rates, certainly since the early 1980s (see Chapter ?).

In summary, what stands out from this analysis is the importance of experience rather than the optimism of youth; being a limited company; having some education; and being in the professional services sector. These results appear consistent and persistent across the three decades. However, equally uniform is that a sizeable minority of businesses displayed no growth whatsoever and are perhaps content largely to survive in the market place. We also observe that it would take a 30-fold increase in the rate of new business start-ups to even replace the jobs lost in the Teesside economy in recent decades.

Such results have two implications. First, unalloyed enthusiasm for new business start-ups is largely misplaced. A more sensible interpretation of our temporal data, is that they indicate that there has been little historical shift in the performance abilities of new businesses. Second, the tobit regressions, if anything, imply the performance of new businesses has declined over the three decades. Teesside was no better in the 1990s at producing growth businesses than it was 20 years previously.

## Appendix

*Appendix 8.1* Empirical studies of employment growth and survival

| | Survival | | | Employment growth | | |
|---|---|---|---|---|---|---|
| | (+) | (−) | n.s. | (+) | (−) | n.s. |
| **Human capital attributes** | | | | | | |
| Being older | 3, 4, 5, 15, 16, 25, 29, 32, 35, 43, 44, 45, 46 | 3 | 36, 40, 41, 42 | 17, 36, 39, 52 | | 28a, 40, 48 |
| Age squared | | 5, 25, 32, 46 | 35, 41 | | 51, 52 | 48 |
| Coming from an ethnic minority | 37 | 3, 32, 45 | 14, 16, 42,43 | 37 | | 14 |
| Having prior entrepreneurial experience | 18, 38, 41, 42, 43 | | 4, 14, 40, 44 | 39 | 50 | 14, 40, 49, 52 |
| Previously unemployed | | 4 | 42, 43, 45, 46 | | 52 | |
| Being males | 5, 9, 18, 32, 36, 40, 41 | | 14, 16, 37, 42, 43, 45, 46 | 14, 37, 40 | | 36 |

Continued

*Appendix 8.1*    (Continued)

| | Survival | | | Employment growth | | |
|---|---|---|---|---|---|---|
| | (+) | (−) | n.s. | (+) | (−) | n.s. |
| Education | 9, 14, 16, 32, 35, 37, 42 | 5, 29 | 36, 40, 41, 43, 44 | 36, 37, 47, 49, 50, 51, 52, 54b | 28b | 14, 39, 40, 48 |
| Having children | 9 | 5 | | | | |
| Having a spouse | 9 | | 16, 41 | | | |
| Prior sectoral experience | 14, 32, 35, 44 | 37 | 38 | 28b, 37, 39, 40, 52 | | 14, 48, 49, 50 |
| Prior managerial experience | 43 | | 14, 16, 35, 37 | 51 | | 14, 37, 48, 50, 52 |
| Being disabled | | 41 | 42, 43, 45 | | | |
| Being indigenous to an area (born and bred) | | | 29 | 33 | 52 | |
| Parental experience of entrepreneurship | 35, 37 | | | | | 37 |
| Team entrepreneurship | | | 37 | 52 | | 37 |
| **Business characteristics** | | | | | | |
| Smaller businesses | 1, 3, 7, 8, 11, 12, 14, 16, 20, 21, 22, 23, 25, 30, 31, 35, 42 | | 18, 36, 38, 45, 46 | | 1, 19, 30, 33, 34, 36 | 14, 17 |
| Younger businesses | 1, 11, 12, 18, 19, 22, 25, 29, 31, 38, 41, 42 | | | | 1, 2, 19, 28b, 33 | 28a |
| Conducted research and development | 1, 7 | 7 | | 1 | | |
| Subcontracting business | 1 | | | | | 1 |
| Multi-plant business | 3, 20 | 21, 24 | 30 | 30 | | 24 |
| Business has scale economies | 7 | | | | | |
| Limited company | 12, 15, 19, 30, 31 | | 38 | 30, 47, 48, 52 | | |
| Franchise business | | 16 | | | | |

*Appendix 8.1*  (Continued)

| | Survival | | | Employment growth | | |
|---|---|---|---|---|---|---|
| | (+) | (−) | n.s. | (+) | (−) | n.s. |
| Experienced change in ownership | | | | | 19 | |
| **Industry** | | | | | | |
| Agriculture | | 3, 4 | | | | |
| Manufacture | 12 | 41 | | 2, 28a, 34, 52 | | |
| Construction | 12 | | | 48 | | |
| Wholesale | 12, 32 | 3 | | | | |
| Hotels | | 3, 41 | | | | |
| Transport | 12 | 3, 41 | | | | |
| Financial | | 41 | | 51 | | |
| Business | 10, 12 | 3, 4 | | 48 | | 28b |
| Public | | | | | | |
| Other | | 3 | | | | |
| Industry's prior growth | 21, 24 | 25 | 38 | 17, 24 | | |
| Industry's level of R&D | 22 | 24 | 20, 25 | 24 | | |
| Industry's capital/labour ratio | 21, 22, 25, 31 | 20 | | | | |
| Industry's minimum efficient scale | 27 | 20, 24 | 25 | 24 | | |
| Industry's demand for goods/services | 23 | | | | | |
| **Strategy** | | | | | | |
| Business recognizes opportunities | | | | 2 | | 17 |
| Business has growth intention | | | | 2 | | |
| Business conducts business planning/ forward planning | 38 | | 13 | 6 | 6 | |
| Product range of business | 10, 22 | | | | | 6 |
| Innovativeness | 10, 12, 18 | 13 | | 52 | 6 | |
| Use of email | | | | | | 6 |
| Networking by businesses | 14, 40 | | 10 | 40 | | 14 |
| Market adjustments conducted by business | 12 | 10 | | | | |
| Business exports | | | 12 | | | 34 |
| Business changes location | | | | 19 | | |
| Number of customers/competitors | | | | 28a | | 28a |
| **Finance** | | | | | | |
| Business has difficulty in accessing finance | | | | 2 | | |

Continued

*Appendix 8.1*   (Continued)

| | Survival | | | Employment growth | | |
|---|---|---|---|---|---|---|
| | (+) | (−) | n.s. | (+) | (−) | n.s. |
| Having assets/capital | 5, 8, 14, 20, 26, 32, 35, 42 | | 4, 29, 31, 37, 41 | 14, 28b, 34, 37 | | 17 |
| Being a home owner | | | 4 | | | |
| Cost of finance to business | | 5 | | | | |
| Use of public assistance | 37 | | | 28a, 28b, 34, 54a | | 6 |
| Use of a bank loan | | | 13 | | | |
| **Demographics** | | | | | | |
| Unemployment rate | 43 | 45 | 4, 9, 44, | | | |
| Region | 8, 25, 36 | | 10, 12, 25 | 36 | | |
| Employment growth | 8, 27 | | | | | |
| Entry rate of businesses | | 21, 25, 27 | | 54a | | |
| Population density/ growth | | 27 | | 33, 33 | 54a | 54b |
| Stock of existing businesses | | | | | 54a, 54b | |

[1] Yasuda, 2005; [2] Saemundsson and Dahlstrand, 2005; [3] Persson, 2004; [4] van Praag, 2003; [5] Nziramasanga and Lee, 2002; [6] Reid and Smith, 2000; [7] Mahmood, 2000; [8] Fotopoulos and Louri, 2000; [9] Lin et al., 2000; [10] Littunen, 2000; [11] Wagner, 1999; [12] Brixy and Kohaut, 1999; [13] Reid, 1999; [14] Bruderl and Preisendorfer, 1998; [15] Cressy 1995; [16] Bates, 1995; [17] Brush and Chaganti, 1999; [18] Carter et al., 1997; [19] Davidsson et al., 2002; [20] Tsionas and Papadogonas, 2006; [21] Mata et al., 1995; [22] Doms et al., 1995; [23] Dunne et al., 2005; [24] Audretsch 1995; [25] Storey and Wynarczyk, 1996; [26] Audretsch et al., 2000; [27] Fritsch et al., 2006; [28a] Roper and Hewitt, 2001; [28b] Roper and Hewitt, 2001; [29] Nafziger and Terrell, 1996; [30] Harhoff et al., 1998; [31] Sleuwaegen and Goedhuys, 2002; [32] Bates, 2005; [33] Hoogstra and van Dijk, 2004; [34] Becchetti and Travato, 2002; [35] Gimeno et al., 1997; [36] Honjo 2004; [37] Cooper et al., 1994; [38] Delmar and Shane, 2004; [39] Box et al., 1994; [40] Bosma et al., 2004; [41] Taylor, 2001; [42] Meager et al., 2003; [43] Taylor, 1999; [44] van Praag, 1994; [45] Cowling and Hayward, 2000; [46] Pfeffer and Reize, 2000; [47] Almus and Nerlinger, 1999; [48] Shutjens and Wever, 2002; [49] Ramachandran and Shah, 1999; [50] Westhead, 1995; [51] Henley, 2005; [52] Storey, 1994b; [53] Bruton and Rubanik, 2002; [54a] Hart and McGuiness, 2003; and [54b] Hart and McGuiness, 2003.

# 9
# The Impact of New Businesses: Three Regions in the 1990s

## Introduction

This chapter compares the survival and growth of new businesses started at broadly the same time in a county with a high rate of enterprise creation (Buckinghamshire) with one with middling rates of enterprise creation (Shropshire), and with a third with very low rates (Teesside). Two contrasting expectations are possible. The first is that the low enterprise area of Teesside will have poorer performing businesses, both because of the low human capital of its entrepreneurs and because the businesses sell into depressed local markets. On these grounds, new Teesside businesses will have lower survival rates and slower growth rates than those in the middling county of Shropshire or the high county of Buckinghamshire.

The alternative hypothesis is that, because entry and exit are endogenous – the more entrants there are, the faster will be the revolving door churning businesses out (Love, 1996) – it is anticipated that the exit rate of new businesses in Buckinghamshire will be higher than Teesside or Shropshire since it has a higher rate of new starts. Counties with lower business formation rates such as Teesside or Shropshire may be anticipated to have much lower exit levels because competition in these marketplaces is less fierce.

The second aim of this chapter is to consider the growth performance of new businesses in the three counties. As with the previous chapter, we begin with a simple comparison between the counties in terms of the employment growth rates of new businesses. We then analyse the factors (e.g. human capital) that may be associated with survival and the growth of the new businesses.

Survival and growth are of course linked – since growth can only occur amongst surviving businesses. To investigate this link we use a Heckman procedure that examines if growth is contingent on survival. Because any such relationship can be modelled in many different ways, the subsequent analysis considers 19 differing Heckman models, but none show a significant statistical association between growth and survival. Survival and growth are then modelled independently to identify their determinants. For those uninterested in these more technical aspects, a concise table of findings is presented in the summary to this chapter.

### Comparing survival performance in the three regions

Table 9.1 presents basic statistics on new business survival in the three counties. It suggests there are strong similarities between the counties on this measure. The general pattern is that only a few businesses exit within one year (2002) but that this rises in the second and third years. Visually, it may seem as if Teesside compares poorly, certainly against Buckinghamshire, across this three-year period but the chi-square statistics suggests (at the 5 per cent level) that there are no statistically significant differences between the three counties.

We now turn to the factors influencing business survival. Table 8.2 in Chapter 8, provided a review of prior work on this topic isolating approximately 80 differing factors. For ease of presentation, Table 9.2 below shows – at the 5 per cent significance level –the factors that were either positively (+) or negatively (–) associated with new business survival for each of the three counties, and for three counties in aggregate.

Two human capital factors were found to be important, but not for all counties. New businesses in Shropshire were more likely to survive when the entrepreneur had been an employee in the same sector as the new business. For Teesside new businesses, prior entrepreneurial experience

*Table 9.1*   Exits 2002–2004

|  | 2002 | | 2003 | | 2004 | |
| --- | --- | --- | --- | --- | --- | --- |
|  | **Survivor** | **Exit** | **Survivor** | **Exit** | **Survivor** | **Exit** |
| Teesside | 94.7 | 5.3 | 80.0 | 20.0 | 74.2 | 25.8 |
| Buckinghamshire | 94.0 | 6.0 | 88.1 | 11.9 | 80.0 | 20.0 |
| Shropshire | 95.4 | 4.6 | 83.3 | 16.7 | 75.4 | 24.6 |
| $X^2$ & p. value | 0.264 | 0.876 | 4.740 | 0.093 | 1.675 | 0.437 |

*Table 9.2* Summary of Chi-square and t-tests of association with survival in 2004

|  | All | Teesside | Buckingham-shire | Shropshire |
|---|---|---|---|---|
| Sectoral experience |  |  |  | + |
| Prior entrepreneurial experience |  | – |  |  |
| A level/HND qualification | + |  |  |  |
| Limited company | + |  |  | + |
| Age of business | + |  |  | + |
| Use of post start support | + |  |  |  |
| Supply problems in 1st year | + |  |  |  |
| Business uses email |  | + |  |  |
| Pre start-up bank |  | + |  |  |
| Local supplier % | – |  |  |  |
| Regional supplier % | + |  |  |  |
| Regional customer % |  | + |  |  |
| Competitive advantage based on understanding competition |  |  |  | + |
| Competitive advantage based on lower prices | – |  |  | – |
| Competitive advantage based on owners managerial skills |  |  |  | + |
| Competitive advantage based on locational advantages |  |  | – |  |

was associated with lower business survival. This is compatible with the findings of Chapter 8 which indicated that prior entrepreneurial experience was associated with slower growth rates.

Entrepreneurs with A Level/HND as their highest educational qualification appear to be more likely to have businesses that survive, but other education-based differences are not significant. Much the same can be said of the finance variables. Although the use of several sources of finance were tested (i.e. personal savings, banks, friends and family, finance companies and the public sector), at both the pre and post start-up stages, the only significant result was that bank finance prior to start-up enhanced the performance of Teesside new businesses.

There also seems to be some evidence for the positive impact on new business survival of post start-up support (All), the use of email (Teesside) encountering and overcoming supply problems in the first year of operations (All) and the value of using regional suppliers (All) or customers (Teesside) rather than local suppliers (All).

Three other points emerge from Table 9.2. First, the value of the strategic orientation of the entrepreneur seems to vary. Entrepreneurs whose strategic orientation emphasised understanding their competitors and their own skills were more likely to survive in Shropshire. On the other hand, those who relied upon a strategy of lower prices (All and Shropshire) were less likely to survive.

A second feature is that none of the strategic orientation variables for Teesside businesses were found to be significant. The only significant difference found for Buckinghamshire's new businesses was that those reliant on location advantages were less likely to survive.

A third, wholly expected, feature is the importance of legal form and business age. Overall, businesses that were older and were limited companies were more likely to survive. Such a result also applies to Shropshire although it is noticeable that such effects are absent in Teesside and Buckinghamshire.

## Performance

We now provide simple measures of new business performance growth, such as employment, turnover and profitability. For new businesses in the three counties, Table 9.3 shows the arithmetic mean size of new businesses (as measured in 2001). Those in Buckinghamshire were approximately one employee smaller than those in the other two counties. The table also shows the median size of employment in Shropshire is four rather than three jobs. Third, in Shropshire, the top 5 per cent of businesses only contribute about one-quarter of jobs rather than one-third in the other two counties, suggesting that employment generation is more evenly distributed than elsewhere. Despite these three differences, more than four out of ten businesses in all three counties experienced no employment change, confirming our findings for Teesside in Chapter 8.

*Table 9.3*   Job generation capabilities by region

|  | Teesside | Buckinghamshire | Shropshire |
|---|---|---|---|
| Total jobs | 1,989 | 833 | 951 |
| Mean | 6.21 | 5.31 | 6.48 |
| Std. Dev. | 10.68 | 10.29 | 7.86 |
| Median | 3 | 3 | 4 |
| No employment change | 42.4% | 43.9% | 45.4% |
| Jobs of top 10% of businesses | 47.2% | 43.0% | 39.3% |
| Jobs of top 5% of businesses | 35.3% | 33.7% | 26.9% |

These figures could, of course, mask very real differences in the employment trajectory of new businesses in the three counties. Again the expectation is that Buckinghamshire would outperform the two other counties. To trace this, Figure 9.1 shows the mean employment sizes of new businesses up to five years prior (t–5) to the initial study (2001) (t0) and for three years afterwards (t+3). Over this period, the new Buckinghamshire enterprises began smaller (mean of 2.7 jobs) than either Teesside (3.76 jobs) or Shropshire businesses (3.95 jobs). By the end of the period, Figure 9.1 suggests that Buckinghamshire businesses had largely caught up, in terms of employment, with the other two counties. By 2001, Buckinghamshire new businesses have an average of 5.3 employees, whilst Shropshire and Teesside businesses have 6.48 and 6.2, respectively. By 2004, Buckinghamshire businesses average 7.22, compared to 7.54 for Teesside and 7.9 for Shropshire.

However, these size differences between the three counties are not significant at any of the three points (t–5 F. Stat 2.886, p. value 0.057; t0 F. Stat 0.518, p. value 0.596; t+3 F. Stat 0.039, p. value 0.96). Growth rates also do not vary significantly, even though from Figure 9.1 the Buckinghamshire businesses appear to catch up with those in the two other counties over the eight-year period. To explain this, Table 9.4 shows the differing mean growth patterns on an annualised and relative growth basis. In each period (t–5 to t+3, t–5 to t0, and t0 to t+3), employment growth in the Buckinghamshire businesses is higher using either

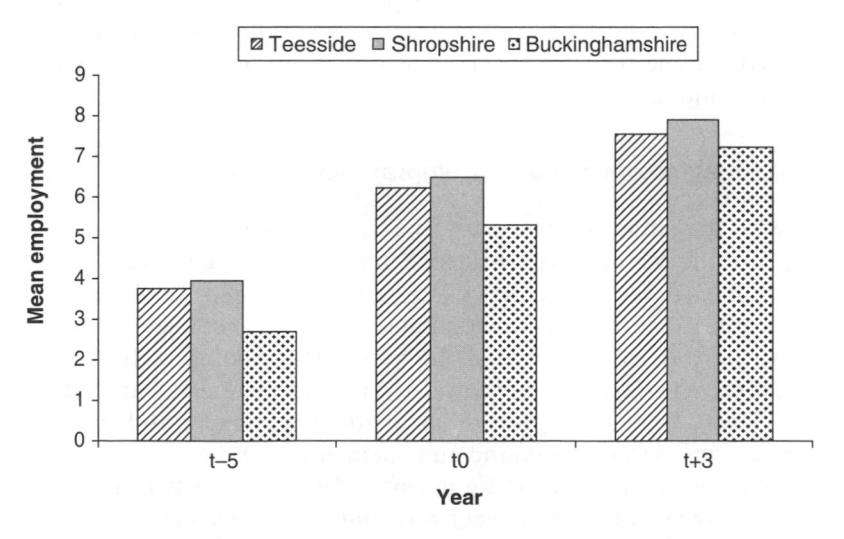

*Figure 9.1*   Employment growth in Teesside, Shropshire and Buckinghamshire

*Table 9.4*   Statistical tests of employment growth trajectories of the three counties

|  | t–5 to t+3 | t–5 to t0 | t0 to t+3 |
|---|---|---|---|
| Annualised |  |  |  |
| Teesside | 0.124 | 0.222 | 0.096 |
| Buckinghamshire | 0.224 | 0.430 | 0.188 |
| Shropshire | 0.127 | 0.277 | 0.172 |
| F. Stat | 1.939 | 2.616 | 1.946 |
| p. value | 0.145 | 0.074 | 0.144 |
| Relative |  |  |  |
| Teesside | 1.573 | 0.909 | 0.289 |
| Buckinghamshire | 2.473 | 1.625 | 0.565 |
| Shropshire | 1.499 | 0.874 | 0.516 |
| F. Stat | 0.575 | 1.681 | 1.946 |
| p. value | 0.563 | 0.187 | 0.144 |

measure, but these differences are not statistically significant at the 5 per cent level.

Similar results are also obtained when sales turnover – either relative or annualised – is considered with there being no significant differences either in terms of relative turnover growth (F. Stat 1.439, p. value 0.239) or in terms of annualised turnover growth (F. Stat 1.259, p. value 0.285). Equally, about 80 per cent of new businesses in each of the three counties report that they are profitable, implying the difference is not statistically significant (Chi 2: 2.879, p. value 0.237). Overall, therefore, there are few grounds from these simple profiles to suggest that new Teesside businesses perform any worse than businesses from the two other counties.

## Individual factors explaining employment growth

As with the earlier survival analysis, attention now turns to seeking to explain the factors that influence new business growth. As with Chapter 8, our favoured metrics of growth were employment and turnover, given that the data on profitability was less complete. Table 9.5 show the correlations between the four measures of growth. All four measures of performance are correlated with each other (all at the 1 per cent level). Our results are similar to the employment and turnover correlations found by Wiklund and Shepherd (2005).

Table 9.6 summarises the significant relationships between annualised employment and turnover growth and the explanatory variables. As with Table 9.2 earlier, we show only the statistically significant relationships at the 5 per cent level using F-tests and Pearson correlation tests.

*Table 9.5* Correlation matrix for employment and turnover

|  | Annualised employment | Relative employment | Annualised turnover |
| --- | --- | --- | --- |
| Annualised employment | 1 |  |  |
| Relative employment | 0.669* | 1 |  |
| Annualised turnover | 0.511* | 0.782* | 1 |
| Relative turnover | 0.485* | 0.744* | 0.922* |

Moreover, a further investigation was also undertaken of relative employment and turnover growth which showed little difference between the results of Table 9.6 except that there were some positive signs for relative employment growth (portfolio entrepreneur (All), having a degree (Shropshire), operating in Other sector (Shropshire)) and relative turnover growth (Shropshire and financial problems in the first year). These results, however, are not presented largely because annualised growth provides a smoother aspect to performance changes.

Table 9.6 suggests the influences on performance are different in the three counties. The factors common to all three counties are that prior managerial experience, size (VAT registration), being a limited company and being established for more years is associated with faster employment growth. Other important influences are some formalised managerial practices (e.g. computerised records), some move towards using email and the web, and the use of non-local suppliers and customers. What slows growth is a reliance on lower price strategies. It is interesting that this is significant for Teesside and Shropshire businesses. Indeed several factors that are significant in columns 1 and 5 also appear for Teesside and Shropshire businesses, but interestingly there is no factor that is 'common' to both Buckinghamshire and Teesside new businesses – perhaps implying the presence of very different factors at work.

Only three variables are significant for Buckinghamshire businesses in terms of employment growth. These are that businesses with a national customer grow faster, those that focus on lower prices grow more slowly and, most unexpectedly, those running the business on a part-time basis had faster growth.

In terms of sales turnover the picture is richer but, besides the importance of having a national customer, an important influence is the role of sectors. This is because the businesses reporting sales growth were likely to be in the Professional Services sector, where the owner has a professional qualification and a product or service that is innovative. These issues are closely linked to the other dimensions of professionalism (e.g. limited company, use of planning and controls).

Table 9.6 Summary of the statistically significant relationships between annualised employment and turnover growth

|  | Employment | | | | Turnover | | | |
|---|---|---|---|---|---|---|---|---|
|  | All | Tees | Bucks | Shrops | All | Tees | Bucks | Shrops |
| Manager | + | | | | | | | |
| Prior entrepreneurial Experience | | | | | | | | |
| Full time | | | − | | | | | |
| A level/HND qualification | | + | | + | + | | + | |
| Professional qualification | | | | | | | | |
| VAT registered | + | + | | | | | | |
| Limited company | | | | | | | | |
| Age of business | + | + | | | | | | |
| Problems in the 1st year with skilled labour | | | | + | + | | | + |
| Problems in the 1st year with labour turnover | | | | | + | | | + |
| Problems in the 1st year with wages | + | | | | | + | | |
| Problems in the 1st year with demand | − | | | | | | | |
| Innovatory product that was totally new | | | | | + | | + | + |
| Business records done by entrepreneur | | − | | | | | | |
| Business records done by employee of the business | | | | + | | | + | |

| | C1 | C2 | C3 | C4 | C5 | C6 | C7 | C8 |
|---|---|---|---|---|---|---|---|---|
| Business records kept in hand written form | – | – | | | | | | |
| Business records kept in computerized form | + | + | | | | | | |
| Made use of post start business plan | + | + | | + | | | | |
| Business uses e-mail | + | + | + | | + | | | |
| Business uses website | + | + | + | | + | + | | |
| Use made of -start-up savings | | | | | | | | |
| Use made of pre start-up finance company | + | + | | | | | | |
| Use made of post start-up finance company | + | + | | + | | | | |
| Use made of post start-up friends and family | | | | | + | | + | |
| % use of local supplier | | | | | | | | |
| % use of regional supplier | | + | | | | | + | |
| % use of inter/national supplier | + | – | | | | | + | |
| % use of local customer | | – | | | | – | | |
| % use of national customer | | + | | + | + | + | | |
| Competitive advantage based on lower prices | – | – | | – | | | | |
| Competitive advantage based on locational advantages | | | | | | | | |
| Construction | | | | | | | | + |
| Professional services | + | | | + | | + | | + |

## An unhinged relationship? The interplay of survival and growth

So far, it has largely been the conditions of entry (e.g. legal form) rather than the entrepreneurs' characteristics *per se* that are associated with the early growth and exit of new businesses. What also seems to matter is post-entry behaviour rather than pre-entry characteristics. However, such results may be conditional on the relationship between growth and survival.

To formally test the inter-relationship between exit and growth we use a Heckman two-stage sample selection procedure. The central problem with the approach is that it ideally requires a variable that influences one performance measure but is unrelated to the other. In practice it is difficult to identify such a variable.

Cowling (2004) however makes the interesting suggestion that geographic location could play this role since it '…. impacts on the firm's supply of factor inputs, but not necessarily demand' (p. 3). In support of this, our evidence so far has suggested that the impact of geography on growth or exit has been modest. A second approach, is to use the variable – 'born and bred' in the county, on the grounds that it may enhance survival – because the individual wishes to stay in the area – but not influence growth.

Three measurement issues require resolution. The first is what is measured (e.g. employment and turnover growth). The second is how it is measured (e.g. relative or annualised growth) and the third is over what time period is it appropriate to measure (e.g. all of the period, the last three years or amongst those who actually did not exit).

Given all the measurement options there are, therefore, a considerable number of Heckman specifications that can be offered to investigate these relationships. Table 9.7 presents 19 variations based upon the three metrics and around geographic location and being 'born and bred'. For ease of exposition, Table 9.7 does not detail the full results for all variables included in the analysis (i.e. human capital, business characteristics, strategy, strategic orientation, geographic reach, problems in the first year, use of finance, sector). Instead it presents the outcome statistics (Wald and Chi. Square statistic) and the selection outcomes. Of these two the most important is the selection result for the inverse Mills ratio. If this is significant (e.g. p. value of less than 0.1 or 0.5 per cent) (column 8: Sig.) then there are grounds for believing that exits are linked to growth.

Our results show none of the seven annualised employment growth models have a significant Mills Ratio. This includes whether the

Table 9.7 Heckman selection models

| | | Censor | Uncensor | Outcome statistics | | Selection Statistics | |
| | N. | Ed N. | Ed N. | Wald | Chi.² | Coef. | Sig. |
|---|---|---|---|---|---|---|---|
| **Annualised employment models** | | | | | | | |
| All years growth (born & bred and location as identifier) | 422 | 98 | 324 | 122.29 | 0.000 | -0.0318 | 0.281 |
| All years growth (location as identifier) | 422 | 98 | 324 | 661.98 | 0.000 | .02033 | 0.881 |
| All years growth (born & bred as identifier) | 422 | 98 | 324 | 168.06 | 0.004 | -0.0338 | 0.331 |
| All years growth without lag | 422 | 98 | 324 | 788.41 | 0.000 | -.00411 | 0.617 |
| 3 years growth | 422 | 98 | 324 | 169.53 | 0.001 | -0.027 | 0.452 |
| 3 years growth without lag | 422 | 98 | 324 | 121.51 | 0.495 | -.0265 | 0.324 |
| 3 year growth (born & bred as identifier) | 422 | 98 | 324 | 123.41 | 0.574 | -.0314 | 0.286 |
| Sub-sample of growing businesses | 207 | 32 | 175 | 145.3 | 0.074 | 0.029 | 0.264 |
| **Relative employment models** | | | | | | | |
| All years growth (born & bred and location as identifier) | 422 | 98 | 324 | 674.76 | 0.000 | 0.0236 | 0.851 |
| All years growth (location as identifier) | 422 | 98 | 324 | 642.53 | 0.000 | 0.0608 | 0.672 |
| All years growth (born & bred as identifier) | 422 | 98 | 324 | 668.71 | 0.000 | -.00156 | 0.992 |
| All years growth without lag | 422 | 98 | 324 | 189.01 | 0.000 | -.0756 | 0.676 |
| 3 years growth | 422 | 98 | 324 | 123.04 | 0.482 | -0.0743 | 0.305 |
| 3 years growth without lag | 422 | 98 | 324 | 122.14 | 0.479 | -0.0712 | 0.325 |
| 3 year growth (born & bred as identifier) | 422 | 98 | 324 | 124.69 | 0.541 | -0.0818 | 0.301 |
| Sub-sample of Growing businesses | 249 | 38 | 211 | 559.8 | 0.000 | 0.0229 | 0.825 |
| **Absolute employment growth** | | | | | | | |
| All years growth (born & bred and location as identifier) | 422 | 98 | 324 | 209.17 | 0.000 | 0.00212 | 0.984 |
| **Relative turnover model** | | | | | | | |
| All years growth (born & bred and location as identifier) | 309 | 98 | 211 | 146.1 | 0.053 | 0.18096 | 0.356 |
| **Annualised turnover model** | | | | | | | |
| All years growth (born & bred and location as identifier) | 309 | 98 | 211 | 156.7 | 0.014 | 0.06095 | 0.374 |

identifier is location on its own, born and bred on its own or location in combination with born and bred is used. Additionally, we also looked at three-year growth and restricting the sample to those businesses who actually experienced some growth. The seven relative growth models are also insignificant. Further models, this time of absolute growth, annualised and relative turnover growth, are also insignificant.

## Multivariate determinants of survival

Given the absence of any significant relationship between exit and growth, Table 9.8 considers three different probit models to explain exit (where 1= survivor and 0= non-survivor). The first model – General I – is insignificant (p. value 0.1459), indicating that it is no more likely than chance to explain why some businesses exit and some do not. Further tests of significance on individual and groups of determinants suggest that pre-entry factors such as use of finance (chi2: 2.43, p. 0.7863) and problems in the first year (chi2: 1.10, p. 0.9818) were also insignificant. This is reflected in the marginal effects in the second model. In moving from a general to a specific model, further early stage variables such as pre start support (chi2: 0.45, p. 0.5027) and pre start business planning (chi2: 0.14, p. 0.7097) were found to be insignificant. Much the same was also true of the available human capital factors (chi2: 9.02, p. 0. 5303) and geographic location (chi2: 0.78, p. 0. 6769).

The effects for the specific model show that exit behaviour is largely influenced by entry conditions. In keeping with earlier results, businesses that are older and are limited companies are more likely to persist. So, too, are businesses that have reinvested prior profits into the business. The factors reducing the likelihood of exit are where the owner has A Level/HND qualifications, relative to other forms of qualification and being VAT registered. Finally, new businesses with a strategy that emphasises low prices are more likely to exit.

Our findings therefore do broadly support the thrust of other empirical work. We, like some others, find older businesses and limited companies are less likely to exit. One interesting twist on this, though, is that reaching a certain sales turnover threshold (VAT registration) does not insulate a business from exiting. Equally, of practical significance is the finding that those following a low price strategy are more likely to exit. Nevertheless the overall impression, following on from the Heckman analyses, is that exit is not clearly and powerfully related to the factors we have examined. In essence, regardless of geographic location, having higher levels of human capital, better education, using

Table 9.8  Probit models for exit (marginal effects)

| | General I | | General II | | Specific I | |
|---|---|---|---|---|---|---|
| | dF/dx | P>\|z\| | dF/dx | P>\|z\| | dF/dx | P>\|z\| |
| Entrepreneur characteristics | | | | | | |
| Age | 0.00138 | 0.94 | 0.00437 | 0.805 | | |
| Age$^2$ | -2E-05 | 0.913 | -7E-05 | 0.741 | | |
| Male | -0.0269 | 0.623 | -0.0467 | 0.37 | | |
| Prior entrepreneur experience | -0.0196 | 0.684 | -0.0181 | 0.697 | | |
| Portfolio entrepreneur | 0.02754 | 0.626 | 0.01264 | 0.815 | | |
| Managerial experience | -0.0503 | 0.276 | -0.0434 | 0.336 | | |
| Sectoral experience | -0.0015 | 0.975 | 0.0097 | 0.838 | | |
| Previously unemployed | -0.0356 | 0.512 | -0.0474 | 0.362 | | |
| Full time in business | 0.17216 | 0.083 | 0.11666 | 0.202 | | |
| Indigenous | 0.06124 | 0.214 | 0.05437 | 0.255 | | |
| Education | | | | | | |
| Degree | 0.08577 | 0.209 | 0.06659 | 0.331 | | |
| A level/HND qualification | -0.0284 | 0.68 | -0.0626 | 0.356 | -0.0947 | 0.051 |
| Vocational qualification | 0.03986 | 0.513 | 0.03526 | 0.556 | | |
| Professional qualification | 0.06539 | 0.383 | 0.05355 | 0.474 | | |
| Business level characteristics | | | | | | |
| Age of business | 0.07943 | 0.403 | 0.09981 | 0.273 | 0.02514 | 0.015 |
| Age of business$^2$ | -0.0059 | 0.395 | -0.0064 | 0.34 | | |
| Limited company | 0.0657 | 0.213 | 0.0611 | 0.227 | 0.1032 | 0.013 |
| VAT registered | -0.1247 | 0.024 | -0.1161 | 0.03** | -0.0792 | 0.059 |
| Employment size in 2001 | 0.0013 | 0.665 | 0.00185 | 0.531 | | |
| Use of support | | | | | | |
| Pre start support | 0.04437 | 0.504 | 0.04809 | 0.456 | | |
| Post start support | 0.04191 | 0.4 | 0.02961 | 0.534 | | |

Continued

Table 9.8 (Continued)

| | General I | | General II | | Specific I | |
|---|---|---|---|---|---|---|
| | dF/dx | P>|z| | dF/dx | P>|z| | dF/dx | P>|z| |
| **Problems in the first year** | | | | | | |
| Supplies | 0.05686 | 0.485 | | | | |
| Skilled labour | 0.02199 | 0.681 | | | | |
| Labour turnover | −0.041 | 0.724 | | | | |
| Wages | −0.0126 | 0.848 | | | | |
| Demand | −0.0014 | 0.979 | | | | |
| Finance | −0.1016 | 0.624 | | | | |
| **Strategy** | | | | | | |
| Totally new product or service | −0.0213 | 0.794 | 0.01053 | 0.89 | | |
| Research and Development | −0.1047 | 0.037 | −0.089 | 0.066 | | |
| Self-records | −0.0923 | 0.097 | −0.0874 | 0.114 | | |
| Internal records | −0.0472 | 0.508 | −0.0365 | 0.592 | | |
| Computer | 0.05059 | 0.354 | 0.03717 | 0.474 | | |
| Used pre start business plan | −0.0186 | 0.713 | −0.0211 | 0.654 | | |
| Use post start business plan | 0.02489 | 0.636 | 0.04678 | 0.357 | | |
| Use email | 0.06852 | 0.288 | 0.07885 | 0.198 | | |
| Have a website | 0.08598 | 0.109 | 0.07852 | 0.123 | | |
| **Use of finance** | | | | | | |
| *Pre start-up* | | | | | | |
| Savings | 0.05449 | 0.382 | | | | |
| Mortgage | −0.093 | 0.562 | | | | |
| Bank | 0.05182 | 0.49 | | | | |
| Finance company | 0.08132 | 0.574 | | | | |
| Public authorities | −0.0704 | 0.541 | | | | |
| *Post start-up* | | | | | | |
| Savings | −0.0262 | 0.802 | −0.036 | 0.714 | | |

| | | | | | | |
|---|---|---|---|---|---|---|
| Profits | 0.04939 | 0.52 | 0.06161 | 0.362 | 0.10405 | 0.008 |
| Bank | -0.0324 | 0.72 | -0.0277 | 0.734 | | |
| Finance company | -0.2885 | 0.185 | -0.3358 | 0.119 | | |
| Public authorities | -0.1929 | 0.42 | -0.2411 | 0.311 | | |
| Source of competitive advantage | | | | | | |
| Understanding competition | 0.0327 | 0.317 | 0.0071 | 0.82 | | |
| Lower prices | -0.0756 | 0.001 | -0.0648 | 0.003* | -0.0487 | 0.007 |
| Novelty of product/service | 0.01453 | 0.545 | 0.02592 | 0.253 | | |
| Low cost base | 0.00741 | 0.739 | -0.0014 | 0.947 | | |
| Skills of our workforce | -0.0287 | 0.408 | -0.0295 | 0.369 | | |
| Owners managerial skills | 0.04206 | 0.155 | 0.04258 | 0.131 | | |
| Better administration | -0.0398 | 0.119 | -0.0307 | 0.207 | | |
| Geographic reach | | | | | | |
| Regional supplier | 0.00191 | 0.034 | 0.0016 | 0.062 | 0.00207 | 0.003 |
| Inter/national supplier | 0.00047 | 0.486 | 0.00032 | 0.62 | | |
| Regional customer | -0.0005 | 0.616 | -0.0005 | 0.601 | | |
| National customer | 0.00114 | 0.247 | 0.00089 | 0.33 | | |
| Sector | | | | | | |
| Motor Repairs and Beauty | 0.04008 | 0.588 | 0.06183 | 0.381 | | |
| Manufacturer | -0.0448 | 0.625 | -0.052 | 0.562 | | |
| Construction | 0.03055 | 0.675 | -0.0164 | 0.819 | | |
| Professional services | 0.10796 | 0.118 | 0.09587 | 0.173 | | |
| Other | 0.03647 | 0.622 | 0.05876 | 0.401 | | |
| County | | | | | | |
| Buckinghamshire | 0.05577 | 0.42 | 0.09665 | 0.121 | | |
| Shropshire | -0.0472 | 0.527 | -0.0276 | 0.69 | | |
| N. | 421 | | 448 | | 516 | |
| LR chi$^2$ | 75.94 | | 74.81 | | 36.73 | |
| Sig. | 0.1459 | | 0.0259 | | 0.000 | |
| Pseudo R$^2$ | 0.1662 | | 0.1526 | | 0.0643 | |
| Log likelihood | -190.47 | | -207.71 | | -267.32 | |

business planning, indulging in innovation or making use of public support explain very little of why some new businesses survive and others do not.

## Multivariate determinants of growth

We now present six models seeking to explain employment growth (Table 9.9) and four models of sales turnover growth (Table 9.10). For employment growth, annualised employment growth and a tobit model taking account of left censoring are presented. Identical employment models are also presented for relative and absolute employment growth. Table 9.10 shows annualised and relative growth and tobits for sales growth.

Table 9.9 shows the only significant human capital attribute in two of the tobit (annualised and relative) models is that businesses where the owner is full time in the business are more likely to grow. The education of the founder also has an influence on employment growth, so that businesses where the founder has a degree/A levels/HND are more likely to report absolute employment growth.

Early business conditions seem to have a patchy impact on performance. For instance, experiencing labour turnover and demand problems in the first year, and a reliance on some forms of pre start finance (particularly the bank), seem to have a positive impact on employment growth. More powerful influences are exerted by the now familiar framing conditions: such as prior growth patterns, legal form, professional services, regional suppliers and business age. The only unexpected result is that the annualised employment growth results suggest it is younger, rather than older businesses, that are more likely to experience employment growth. Although this is only a slight impact, it is more in line with prior theoretical and empirical work. However, using the measure of absolute growth, Table 9.9 confirms our earlier result that older businesses that are much more likely to have experienced employment growth, perhaps emphasising our central point that outcomes are extremely sensitive to the way in which growth is measured.

Equally, interesting is the seeming importance of post-entry factors in explaining employment growth. For example, using profits for reinvestment and using finance companies are characteristic of growing businesses. We also find factors reflecting research and development, the use of a website and the strategic advantage of having a novel product or service are associated with growth. Another important factor

Table 9.9 Annualised, relative and absolute employment growth: regression of all years and tobit of growers

| | Annualised | | | | Relative | | | | Absolute | | | |
| --- | --- | --- | --- | --- | --- | --- | --- | --- | --- | --- | --- | --- |
| | All years | | Growers | | All years | | Growers | | All Years | | Growers | |
| | Coef. | P>\|t\| | Coef. | P>\|t\| | Coef. | P>\|t\| | Coef. | P>\|t\| | Coef. | P>\|t\| | Coef. | P>\|t\| |
| **Entrepreneur characteristics** | | | | | | | | | | | | |
| Age | 0.000 | 0.274 | 0.000 | 0.973 | 0.003 | 0.262 | 0.000 | 0.998 | 0.001 | 0.431 | −0.006 | 0.463 |
| Age² | 0.000 | 0.444 | 0.000 | 0.972 | 0.000 | 0.258 | 0.000 | 0.959 | 0.000 | 0.298 | 0.000 | 0.502 |
| Male | 0.000 | 0.699 | −0.002 | 0.805 | −0.015 | 0.098 | −0.007 | 0.778 | 0.001 | 0.906 | 0.023 | 0.362 |
| Prior entrepreneurial experience | 0.000 | 0.114 | 0.004 | 0.633 | −0.004 | 0.572 | 0.010 | 0.653 | 0.006 | 0.135 | 0.025 | 0.248 |
| Portfolio entrepreneur | 0.000 | 0.759 | 0.006 | 0.491 | −0.010 | 0.255 | 0.016 | 0.527 | −0.006 | 0.222 | 0.013 | 0.617 |
| Manager | 0.000 | 0.147 | −0.011 | 0.138 | 0.005 | 0.513 | −0.030 | 0.145 | 0.000 | 0.998 | 0.005 | 0.816 |
| Sectoral experience | 0.000 | 0.431 | 0.013 | 0.093 | 0.010 | 0.209 | 0.037 | 0.093 | −0.002 | 0.714 | −0.007 | 0.733 |
| Previously unemployed | 0.000 | 0.154 | 0.011 | 0.203 | −0.011 | 0.186 | 0.032 | 0.19 | 0.003 | 0.531 | −0.010 | 0.683 |
| Full time | 0.000 | 0.906 | 0.035 | 0.043** | 0.019 | 0.184 | 0.093 | 0.044** | 0.001 | 0.888 | 0.073 | 0.082 |
| **Education** | | | | | | | | | | | | |
| Degree | 0.000 | 0.948 | 0.012 | 0.312 | 0.005 | 0.648 | 0.033 | 0.304 | 0.014 | 0.028** | 0.017 | 0.603 |
| A level/HND | 0.000 | 0.137 | 0.001 | 0.901 | 0.006 | 0.579 | 0.005 | 0.859 | 0.012 | 0.040** | 0.037 | 0.222 |
| Vocational qualification | 0.000 | 0.685 | −0.012 | 0.240 | −0.009 | 0.347 | −0.032 | 0.249 | 0.002 | 0.657 | −0.017 | 0.565 |
| Professional qualification | 0.000 | 0.329 | −0.012 | 0.392 | −0.019 | 0.130 | −0.030 | 0.41 | 0.009 | 0.183 | 0.021 | 0.554 |
| **Business level characteristics** | | | | | | | | | | | | |
| Business age | −0.001 | 0.000* | 0.025 | 0.137 | −0.029 | 0.062 | 0.064 | 0.156 | 0.010 | 0.249 | 0.102 | 0.028** |
| Business age² | 0.000 | 0.000* | −0.002 | 0.112 | 0.002 | 0.109 | −0.005 | 0.128 | −0.001 | 0.236 | −0.007 | 0.037** |
| Limited co. | 0.000 | 0.129 | 0.003 | 0.732 | 0.011 | 0.211 | 0.009 | 0.708 | 0.010 | 0.031** | 0.044 | 0.064 |
| VAT registered | 0.000 | 0.662 | 0.010 | 0.285 | 0.008 | 0.383 | 0.027 | 0.294 | 0.010 | 0.057 | 0.017 | 0.531 |
| Lagged growth | 0.588 | 0.000* | −0.008 | 0.878 | 0.936 | 0.000* | −0.012 | 0.824 | 0.231 | 0.000* | 0.522 | 0.000* |
| **Use of support** | | | | | | | | | | | | |
| Pre start support | 0.000 | 0.818 | 0.003 | 0.804 | −0.006 | 0.537 | 0.005 | 0.858 | 0.005 | 0.370 | 0.033 | 0.269 |

Continued

Table 9.9 (Continued)

| | Annualised | | | | Relative | | | | Absolute | | | |
| | All years | | Growers | | All years | | Growers | | All Years | | Growers | |
| | Coef. | P>\|t\| | Coef. | P>\|t\| | Coef. | P>\|t\| | Coef. | P>\|t\| | Coef. | P>\|t\| | Coef. | P>\|t\| |
|---|---|---|---|---|---|---|---|---|---|---|---|---|
| Post start support | 0.000 | 0.573 | 0.002 | 0.837 | 0.000 | 0.962 | 0.005 | 0.828 | -0.004 | 0.348 | 0.002 | 0.944 |
| Problems in the first year | | | | | | | | | | | | |
| Supplies | 0.000 | 0.649 | -0.002 | 0.856 | -0.002 | 0.879 | -0.005 | 0.888 | -0.010 | 0.158 | -0.046 | 0.206 |
| Skilled labour | 0.000 | 0.060 | 0.013 | 0.114 | -0.005 | 0.558 | 0.036 | 0.111 | -0.007 | 0.144 | -0.009 | 0.704 |
| Labour turnover | 0.000 | 0.710 | 0.014 | 0.370 | 0.036 | 0.023** | 0.042 | 0.33 | 0.028 | 0.002* | 0.059 | 0.188 |
| Wages | 0.000 | 0.882 | -0.015 | 0.175 | -0.016 | 0.108 | -0.042 | 0.167 | -0.006 | 0.264 | 0.006 | 0.831 |
| Demand | 0.000 | 0.781 | -0.005 | 0.558 | 0.012 | 0.155 | -0.013 | 0.582 | -0.002 | 0.668 | -0.049 | 0.043** |
| Finance | 0.000 | 0.623 | -0.058 | 0.085 | 0.023 | 0.444 | -0.155 | 0.089 | -0.001 | 0.947 | -0.107 | 0.228 |
| Strategy | | | | | | | | | | | | |
| Totally new product or service | 0.000 | 0.386 | -0.005 | 0.651 | 0.000 | 0.970 | -0.014 | 0.675 | -0.007 | 0.292 | 0.016 | 0.631 |
| R&D | 0.000 | 0.617 | 0.009 | 0.272 | 0.017 | 0.025** | 0.025 | 0.229 | 0.003 | 0.495 | -0.003 | 0.878 |
| Self-records | 0.000 | 0.976 | 0.015 | 0.096 | 0.017 | 0.052 | 0.041 | 0.101 | 0.006 | 0.205 | 0.032 | 0.202 |
| Internal records | 0.000 | 0.359 | 0.009 | 0.410 | 0.007 | 0.460 | 0.022 | 0.454 | 0.011 | 0.043 | 0.010 | 0.721 |
| Computer | 0.000 | 0.956 | 0.003 | 0.707 | 0.000 | 0.980 | 0.011 | 0.649 | 0.002 | 0.736 | 0.040 | 0.100 |
| Used pre start business plan | 0.000 | 0.731 | 0.002 | 0.781 | -0.008 | 0.336 | 0.005 | 0.826 | -0.009 | 0.047 | -0.021 | 0.347 |
| Use post start business plan | 0.000 | 0.669 | 0.010 | 0.244 | 0.008 | 0.366 | 0.027 | 0.237 | 0.011 | 0.018** | 0.069 | 0.004** |
| Use email | 0.000 | 0.697 | 0.004 | 0.659 | 0.006 | 0.559 | 0.012 | 0.654 | -0.006 | 0.280 | -0.045 | 0.098 |
| Have a website | 0.000 | 0.597 | 0.018 | 0.038** | 0.011 | 0.205 | 0.050 | 0.034** | 0.015 | 0.001* | 0.120 | 0.000* |
| Use of finance | | | | | | | | | | | | |
| Pre start-up | | | | | | | | | | | | |
| Savings | 0.000 | 0.090 | 0.000 | 0.967 | 0.010 | 0.295 | 0.001 | 0.972 | 0.005 | 0.328 | -0.005 | 0.863 |
| Mortgage | 0.000 | 0.366 | 0.000 | 0.999 | 0.025 | 0.277 | 0.003 | 0.961 | 0.005 | 0.687 | -0.037 | 0.552 |

|  |  |  |  |  |  |  |  |  |  |  |  |  |
|---|---|---|---|---|---|---|---|---|---|---|---|---|
| Bank | 0.000 | 0.146 | 0.005 | 0.668 |  |  | 0.016 | 0.632 | 0.019 | 0.006* | 0.008 | 0.806 |
| Finance company | 0.000 | 0.596 | 0.024 | 0.411 |  |  | 0.071 | 0.38 | -0.001 | 0.974 | 0.246 | 0.001* |
| Public authorities | 0.000 | 0.166 | -0.010 | 0.597 |  |  | -0.026 | 0.621 | -0.001 | 0.956 | -0.092 | 0.110 |
| **Post start-up** |  |  |  |  |  |  |  |  |  |  |  |  |
| Savings | 0.000 | 0.503 | 0.014 | 0.440 | 0.011 | 0.475 | 0.038 | 0.439 | -0.006 | 0.533 | 0.001 | 0.980 |
| Profits | 0.000 | 0.391 | 0.023 | 0.091 | 0.031 | 0.009* | 0.063 | 0.086 | 0.013 | 0.056 | 0.061 | 0.100 |
| Bank | 0.000 | 0.430 | 0.010 | 0.508 | 0.010 | 0.453 | 0.028 | 0.498 | 0.002 | 0.756 | 0.039 | 0.341 |
| Finance company | 0.000 | 0.744 | 0.028 | 0.436 | 0.013 | 0.662 |  |  | 0.005 | 0.779 | 0.250 | 0.002* |
| Public authorities | 0.000 | 0.801 |  |  | 0.039 | 0.250 | 0.073 | 0.448 | 0.006 | 0.768 | 0.030 | 0.772 |
| **Source of competitive advantage** |  |  |  |  |  |  |  |  |  |  |  |  |
| Understanding competition | 0.000 | 0.621 | 0.006 | 0.305 | 0.003 | 0.605 | 0.015 | 0.336 | 0.002 | 0.427 | 0.033 | 0.037** |
| Lower prices | 0.000 | 0.838 | 0.004 | 0.299 | -0.001 | 0.873 | 0.009 | 0.35 | -0.001 | 0.509 | -0.021 | 0.037** |
| Novelty of product/service | 0.000 | 0.004* | -0.002 | 0.563 | -0.008 | 0.029** | -0.006 | 0.532 | 0.000 | 0.944 | -0.011 | 0.295 |
| Low cost base | 0.000 | 0.114 | 0.001 | 0.591 | 0.004 | 0.230 | -0.005 | 0.65 | -0.001 | 0.629 | -0.007 | 0.510 |
| Skills of our workforce | 0.000 | 0.292 | 0.001 | 0.815 | 0.000 | 0.961 | 0.004 | 0.792 | -0.004 | 0.202 | 0.002 | 0.910 |
| Owners managerial skills | 0.000 | 0.113 | -0.006 | 0.206 | 0.007 | 0.148 | -0.016 | 0.205 | 0.002 | 0.386 | -0.017 | 0.204 |
| Better administration | 0.000 | 0.025** | -0.001 | 0.788 | -0.002 | 0.577 | -0.003 | 0.787 | -0.002 | 0.370 | 0.010 | 0.392 |
| **Geographic reach** |  |  |  |  |  |  |  |  |  |  |  |  |
| Regional supplier | 0.000 | 0.891 | 0.000 | 0.018** | 0.000 | 0.120 | 0.001 | 0.014** | 0.000 | 0.064 | 0.001 | 0.028** |
| International supplier | 0.000 | 0.145 | 0.000 | 0.298 | 0.000 | 0.433 | 0.000 | 0.271 | 0.000 | 0.330 | 0.000 | 0.829 |
| Regional customer | 0.000 | 0.982 | 0.000 | 0.292 | 0.000 | 0.627 | 0.000 | 0.269 | 0.000 | 0.274 | -0.001 | 0.044** |
| National customer | 0.000 | 0.309 | 0.000 | 0.801 | 0.000 | 0.754 | 0.000 | 0.852 | 0.000 | 0.063 | 0.000 | 0.372 |
| **Sector** |  |  |  |  |  |  |  |  |  |  |  |  |
| Motor Repairs and Beauty | 0.000 | 0.280 | -0.005 | 0.716 | 0.002 | 0.890 | -0.012 | 0.723 | -0.010 | 0.154 | -0.012 | 0.729 |
| Manufacturer | 0.000 | 0.678 | 0.015 | 0.308 | 0.014 | 0.339 | 0.042 | 0.295 | 0.005 | 0.502 | 0.086 | 0.036** |
| Construction | 0.000 | 0.639 | 0.008 | 0.508 | 0.006 | 0.624 | 0.021 | 0.508 | -0.009 | 0.171 | 0.028 | 0.383 |
| Professional services | 0.000 | 0.753 | 0.035 | 0.008* | 0.006 | 0.653 | 0.094 | 0.009* | 0.005 | 0.458 | 0.080 | 0.030** |
| Other | 0.000 | 0.989 | -0.003 | 0.846 | -0.004 | 0.750 | -0.008 | 0.823 | -0.012 | 0.075 | 0.023 | 0.505 |
| **County** |  |  |  |  |  |  |  |  |  |  |  |  |
| Buckinghamshire | 0.000 | 0.538 | 0.007 | 0.521 | 0.000 | 0.989 | 0.017 | 0.57 | 0.003 | 0.577 | 0.002 | 0.948 |
| Shropshire | 0.000 | 0.907 | -0.008 | 0.482 | -0.015 | 0.190 | -0.026 | 0.412 | -0.009 | 0.133 | 0.002 | 0.947 |

Continued

Table 9.9 (Continued)

| | Annualised | | | | Relative | | | | Absolute | | | |
| | All years | | Growers | | All years | | Growers | | All Years | | Growers | |
| | Coef. | P>|t| | Coef. | P>|t| | Coef. | P>|t| | Coef. | P>|t| | Coef. | P>|t| | Coef. | P>|t| |
|---|---|---|---|---|---|---|---|---|---|---|---|---|
| Constant | 0.950 | 0.000* | 2.102 | 0.000* | 0.107 | 0.245 | 1.753 | 0.000* | 4.101 | 0.000* | 3.632 | 0.000* |
| N. | 421 | | 421 | | 421 | | 421 | | 421 | | 421 | |
| F. Stat | 132.93 | | | | 10.33 | | | | 1.99 | | | |
| Sig. | 0.000 | | 0.097 | | 0.000 | | 0.0895 | | 0.000 | | 0.000 | |
| R-squared | 0.960 | | | | 0.650 | | | | 0.260 | | | |
| Adj R-squared | 0.953 | | | | 0.587 | | | | 0.130 | | | |
| Root MSE | 0.010 | | | | 0.158 | | | | 0.138 | | | |
| LR Chi | | | 78.39 | | | | 79.67 | | | | 147.78 | |
| Censored N. | | | 261 | | | | 261 | | | | 173 | |
| Uncensored N. | | | 160 | | | | 160 | | | | 248 | |

*Table 9.10* Annualised and relative turnover growth: regression of all years and tobit of growers

| | Annualised | | | | Relative | | | |
| --- | --- | --- | --- | --- | --- | --- | --- | --- |
| | All years | | Growers | | All years | | Growers | |
| | Coef. | P>\|t\| | Coef. | P>\|t\| | Coef. | P>\|t\| | Coef. | P>\|t\| |
| Entrepreneur characteristics | | | | | | | | |
| Age | 0.016 | 0.158 | 0.020 | 0.123 | 0.006 | 0.303 | 0.027 | 0.147 |
| Age² | 0.000 | 0.141 | 0.000 | 0.103 | 0.000 | 0.249 | 0.000 | 0.118 |
| Male | 0.014 | 0.698 | 0.031 | 0.466 | -0.028 | 0.140 | 0.030 | 0.616 |
| Prior entrepreneurial experience | 0.037 | 0.193 | 0.045 | 0.170 | 0.016 | 0.282 | 0.058 | 0.203 |
| Portfolio entrepreneur | -0.040 | 0.262 | -0.053 | 0.202 | -0.033 | 0.077 | -0.066 | 0.261 |
| Manager | -0.064 | 0.029 | -0.088 | 0.011** | 0.006 | 0.692 | -0.102 | 0.033** |
| Sectoral experience | -0.038 | 0.232 | -0.068 | 0.065 | -0.006 | 0.715 | -0.086 | 0.094 |
| Previously unemployed | 0.078 | 0.024 | 0.081 | 0.047 | 0.018 | 0.331 | 0.106 | 0.063 |
| Full time | -0.001 | 0.988 | -0.011 | 0.878 | -0.015 | 0.648 | -0.026 | 0.797 |
| Education | | | | | | | | |
| Degree | 0.027 | 0.564 | 0.043 | 0.443 | 0.007 | 0.784 | 0.048 | 0.540 |
| A level/HND | 0.051 | 0.229 | 0.102 | 0.042** | 0.029 | 0.195 | 0.133 | 0.058 |
| Vocational qualification | 0.018 | 0.668 | 0.059 | 0.228 | 0.002 | 0.941 | 0.084 | 0.218 |
| Professional qualification | 0.025 | 0.607 | 0.066 | 0.247 | 0.045 | 0.080 | 0.102 | 0.204 |
| Business level characteristics | | | | | | | | |
| Business age | 0.036 | 0.623 | 0.059 | 0.481 | 0.089 | 0.022** | 0.109 | 0.348 |
| Business age² | -0.004 | 0.489 | -0.006 | 0.309 | -0.007 | 0.012** | -0.010 | 0.258 |
| Limited co. | 0.010 | 0.760 | 0.031 | 0.429 | 0.029 | 0.090 | 0.049 | 0.359 |
| VAT registered | 0.012 | 0.740 | 0.005 | 0.902 | 0.004 | 0.836 | 0.007 | 0.910 |
| Use of support | | | | | | | | |
| Pre start support | 0.068 | 0.104 | 0.099 | 0.045** | 0.035 | 0.111 | 0.141 | 0.041** |
| Post start support | -0.005 | 0.872 | -0.032 | 0.373 | -0.040 | 0.015** | -0.045 | 0.363 |

Continued

Table 9.10 (Continued)

| | Annualised | | | | Relative | | | |
| | All Years | | Growers | | All Years | | Growers | |
| | Coef. | P>\|t\| | Coef. | P>\|t\| | Coef. | P>\|t\| | Coef. | P>\|t\| |
|---|---|---|---|---|---|---|---|---|
| **Problems in the first year** | | | | | | | | |
| Supplies | 0.028 | 0.558 | 0.050 | 0.359 | 0.011 | 0.662 | 0.071 | 0.354 |
| Skilled labour | 0.004 | 0.902 | 0.000 | 0.998 | -0.020 | 0.246 | -0.002 | 0.977 |
| Labour turnover | -0.056 | 0.341 | -0.048 | 0.481 | 0.060 | 0.053 | -0.057 | 0.549 |
| Wages | 0.076 | 0.062 | 0.071 | 0.130 | 0.073 | 0.122 | 0.073 | 0.262 |
| Demand | -0.062 | 0.065 | -0.087 | 0.027** | -0.033 | 0.563 | -0.129 | 0.018** |
| Finance | 0.004 | 0.975 | -0.039 | 0.796 | 0.078 | 0.202 | -0.030 | 0.885 |
| **Strategy** | | | | | | | | |
| Totally new product or service | 0.082 | 0.070 | 0.127 | 0.015** | 0.054 | 0.026** | 0.199 | 0.006** |
| R&D | 0.023 | 0.465 | 0.006 | 0.876 | -0.011 | 0.501 | 0.002 | 0.972 |
| Self-records | 0.032 | 0.398 | 0.025 | 0.555 | -0.006 | 0.779 | 0.034 | 0.568 |
| Internal records | -0.004 | 0.931 | 0.010 | 0.837 | -0.012 | 0.588 | 0.005 | 0.946 |
| Computer | 0.041 | 0.243 | 0.064 | 0.121 | -0.005 | 0.791 | 0.092 | 0.114 |
| Pre start business plan | -0.024 | 0.473 | -0.052 | 0.183 | -0.021 | 0.232 | -0.067 | 0.224 |
| Post start business plan | 0.037 | 0.261 | 0.079 | 0.039 | 0.025 | 0.144 | 0.122 | 0.023 |
| Use email | 0.032 | 0.405 | 0.037 | 0.403 | 0.008 | 0.703 | 0.028 | 0.658 |
| Have a website | -0.003 | 0.917 | 0.021 | 0.580 | 0.030 | 0.085 | 0.047 | 0.378 |
| **Use of finance** | | | | | | | | |
| *Pre start-up* | | | | | | | | |
| Savings | 0.057 | 0.149 | 0.075 | 0.113 | 0.034 | 0.096 | 0.094 | 0.151 |
| Mortgage | -0.050 | 0.563 | -0.082 | 0.409 | 0.019 | 0.669 | -0.108 | 0.435 |
| Bank | -0.006 | 0.907 | 0.008 | 0.889 | 0.050 | 0.067 | -0.003 | 0.967 |
| Finance company | 0.069 | 0.618 | 0.058 | 0.743 | 0.135 | 0.066 | 0.101 | 0.679 |
| Public authorities | 0.014 | 0.851 | 0.064 | 0.439 | 0.070 | 0.066 | 0.078 | 0.499 |

| Post Start-up | | | | | | | | |
|---|---|---|---|---|---|---|---|---|
| Savings | -0.052 | 0.450 | -0.054 | 0.509 | 0.005 | 0.896 | -0.081 | 0.479 |
| Profits | -0.047 | 0.350 | 0.006 | 0.925 | 0.022 | 0.411 | 0.018 | 0.827 |
| Bank | -0.082 | 0.161 | -0.051 | 0.449 | 0.013 | 0.683 | -0.057 | 0.545 |
| Finance company | -0.065 | 0.565 | -0.045 | 0.734 | 0.076 | 0.207 | -0.031 | 0.865 |
| Public authorities | -0.123 | 0.589 | 0.042 | 0.864 | 0.126 | 0.293 | 0.091 | 0.794 |
| **Source of competitive Advantage** | | | | | | | | |
| Understanding competition | 0.032 | 0.161 | 0.030 | 0.247 | -0.011 | 0.354 | 0.039 | 0.283 |
| Lower prices | 0.006 | 0.643 | -0.001 | 0.949 | -0.009 | 0.209 | -0.004 | 0.839 |
| Novelty of product/service | 0.019 | 0.212 | 0.024 | 0.159 | -0.002 | 0.816 | 0.028 | 0.241 |
| Low cost base | -0.015 | 0.315 | -0.011 | 0.516 | 0.004 | 0.632 | -0.014 | 0.560 |
| Skills of our workforce | -0.018 | 0.369 | -0.015 | 0.527 | -0.008 | 0.451 | -0.020 | 0.540 |
| Owners managerial skills | 0.006 | 0.752 | 0.018 | 0.376 | 0.021 | 0.025** | 0.025 | 0.383 |
| Better administration | -0.027 | 0.081 | -0.042 | 0.018** | -0.003 | 0.696 | -0.058 | 0.021** |
| **Geographic reach** | | | | | | | | |
| Regional supplier | 0.000 | 0.634 | 0.000 | 0.806 | 0.000 | 0.491 | 0.000 | 0.650 |
| International supplier | -0.001 | 0.171 | -0.001 | 0.079 | 0.000 | 0.312 | -0.001 | 0.129 |
| Regional customer | -0.001 | 0.258 | 0.000 | 0.532 | 0.000 | 0.616 | 0.000 | 0.705 |
| National customer | 0.000 | 0.636 | 0.000 | 0.635 | 0.000 | 0.923 | 0.000 | 0.797 |
| **Sector** | | | | | | | | |
| Motor Repairs and Beauty | 0.044 | 0.359 | 0.059 | 0.290 | -0.006 | 0.810 | 0.068 | 0.384 |
| Manufacturer | 0.103 | 0.069 | 0.146 | 0.022** | 0.015 | 0.618 | 0.213 | 0.017** |
| Construction | 0.057 | 0.190 | 0.046 | 0.370 | -0.004 | 0.855 | 0.071 | 0.318 |
| Professional services | 0.060 | 0.254 | 0.118 | 0.048** | 0.041 | 0.134 | 0.159 | 0.057 |
| Other | 0.002 | 0.969 | -0.013 | 0.810 | -0.007 | 0.779 | -0.016 | 0.836 |
| **County** | | | | | | | | |
| Buckinghamshire | -0.012 | 0.779 | -0.011 | 0.826 | -0.004 | 0.862 | -0.016 | 0.819 |
| Shropshire | 0.115 | 0.013 | 0.127 | 0.018** | -0.020 | 0.411 | 0.159 | 0.034** |
| Constant | 0.583 | 0.110 | 0.345 | 0.409 | 1.990 | 0.000* | 1.216 | 0.039** |

Continued

Table 9.10 (Continued)

| | Annualised | | | | Relative | | | |
| | All Years | | Growers | | All Years | | Growers | |
| | Coef. | P>\|t\| | Coef. | P>\|t\| | Coef. | P>\|t\| | Coef. | P>\|t\| |
|---|---|---|---|---|---|---|---|---|
| N. | 225 | | 255 | | 255 | | 255 | |
| F.Stat | 1.46 | | | | 1.26 | | | |
| Sig. | 0.0261 | | 0.0179 | | 0.119 | | 0.0491 | |
| R-squared | 0.3256 | | | | 0.294 | | | |
| Adj R-squared | 0.1032 | | | | 0.061 | | | |
| Root MSE | 0.0930 | | | | 0.271 | | | |
| LR Chi | | | 88.78 | | | | 82.65 | |
| Censored N. | | | 80 | | | | 80 | |
| Uncensored N. | | | 175 | | | | 175 | |

is, as with the exit results, avoidance of a low price strategy as this, at least in comparison with understanding the competitor, appears to slow employment growth. Equally, there is also evidence, albeit only for absolute employment growth, of the positive impact of having a post start-up business plan.

A similar pattern emerges when turnover is considered in Table 9.10. In the tobit model for relative turnover growth, using pre start-up support and post start-up business planning have a positive impact on sales. So, too, does, innovation capacity although, unlike employment growth, this is apparent in terms of having totally new products/services rather than developing such products or services. Being better at administration, however, has a negative association with turnover growth as does, if only in terms of the two tobits, prior managerial experience. Having such a background seems to detract from growth.

For the turnover models – with the exception of annualised turnover growth for all businesses which has no factors significant at the 5 per cent level – the framing conditions seem less important with only older business being more likely to experience relative turnover growth. What seems more important is sector and location. Both manufacturing and professional services and Shropshire emerge as positive factors in explaining turnover growth.

## Summary

We began this chapter by expecting there would be clear performance differences between new businesses in the three counties because, if nothing else, they have very differing entrepreneurship profiles. Buckinghamshire was expected to produce the most dynamic and competitive new businesses, one consequence of which might be heightened levels of exit. Shropshire, meanwhile, might be expected to amble along, allowing businesses to persist but providing unspectacular growth. Teesside was expected to bring up the rear, with a decidedly un-dynamic set of new businesses.

These stereotypes were not borne out by the results. Far from being the area with the highest level of exits, Buckinghamshire new businesses were no more likely to exit than those in the other two counties. This could be an outcome of our methodological approach. We went to extreme lengths to identify *de novo* businesses rather than the more all embracing definition of 'new' businesses in UK official statistics – defined as a business newly registered for Value Added Tax. However, whilst the results showed some evidence that being registered promoted growth, there was also evidence that it led to a business exiting.

A second explanation is that the low and middling enterprise areas have new businesses owned by individuals with lower human capital than new businesses started by those in Buckinghamshire. The simple interpretation of the Jovanovic (1982) theory of why businesses close is that their owners realise they have made a mistake. Prior to actually starting a business the individual did not know what was involved; they are unable to assess their suitability for running a business. Once in business they are able to better estimate their ability – because they have learnt how good or bad they are – and hence are able to make a better informed choice about whether to exit or whether to continue. Other choice-based factors such as a willingness to forgo financial for non-financial rewards or the lack of an alternative and viable employment option may also influence this decision. Finally, most business owners would recognise that, if their costs were greater than their revenues then – at some point – it is time to do something else. In essence, then exit rates also reflect the presence of poorer performing businesses. Our result that new business exit rates do not vary spatially across the three counties could imply that some explanations are more important in one county than elsewhere. The most plausible explanation is that Teesside new businesses may have lower human capital – implying higher exit rates – but their owners have fewer options than those in Buckinghamshire – implying they are more motivated to 'struggle on'.

However, we were also surprised by the small differences between the counties in terms of profitability or turnover differences. The employment growth patterns of new businesses in the three areas suggests that those in the low and middle enterprise areas start off larger, but over time, the businesses in high areas catch up. If perhaps we had been able to continue the tracking this might have found that the Buckinghamshire businesses did end up, on average, larger than the new businesses from the other counties.

This seems in line with Bartelsman et al. (2003). They found US new businesses start-up smaller than their European counterparts but over the course of time, catch up and eventually overtake the European businesses. As noted in the above paragraph, the overtaking is not observable from our data, but it is clearly a possibility for the future.

Nevertheless, Buckinghamshire remains something of a puzzle if the goal is to identify particular business features elucidating survival and growth. Of course, there are some factors that explain the performance of new businesses in this county – but the explanations are weak. In part, this may be because the data set is too modest or because it does not consider the appropriate measures. There is little we can do about the former critique but, in response to the latter, we emphasise that this chapter has considered around eighty determinants that have been shown by others to be associated with business performance. For Buckinghamshire's new businesses, apart from some evidence of professional qualifications or working in such sectors and innovation, links with survival or growth are hard to identify.

Equally, despite taking careful note of the various ways performance is open to measurement sensitivities, our findings are not strong. Table 9.11 summarises the significant factors from the survival and growth models, using the convention followed earlier of + being positive and – being negative. It also provides another two columns, derived from the results of the review in Chapter 8 (Table 8.2), of what prior research has found in terms of exit and growth. Table 9.11 then identifies any consistencies between our findings and that of other studies; a lack of consistency is denoted as a '?'.

For exiting, what matters is avoiding a lower price strategy. This is an important finding. Although this study does not focus principally on the practice of new business ownership it does suggest that a heavy price-based focus increases the likelihood of exit (see Saridakis et al., 2008 for a further exposition of this relationship). Instead, what seems to matter is the reinvestment of profits. Human capital turns on having some minimum of post-secondary schooling (A Level/HND) to reduce the likelihood of exit. The role of the age of the business and its choice of legal form of the businesses, found to be important in earlier work, are confirmed here.

Much the same can be said of growth performance. Table 9.11 summarises our findings using the annualised employment and sales turnover growth, both for all businesses and just for growers (tobit). We emphasise again that performance is sensitive to how it is measured and that there appear to be very different factors that explain survival and performance. Indeed, the only variable appearing in both equations is the value of regional suppliers. Elsewhere, other features seem apparent such as VAT registration or business age but these are not consistently signed between survival and growth.

From a statistical perspective the results are a disappointment. The explanatory power of the models is consistently low and different independent variables appear in the equations relating to survival and growth. Even more disconcerting is that, when different metrics of growth are examined the significant independent variables also change. Of course,

*Table 9.11*   Summary of review and results

| | Exit | | Growth | | | |
|---|---|---|---|---|---|---|
| | Review | Results | Review | All | Tobit | Tobit |
| Managerial experience | n.s | | n.s | | | − |
| Full time in business | ? | | | | + | |
| A level/HND qualification | + | − | + | | | + |
| Age of business | − | + | − | − | | |
| Business age$^2$ | + | | + | + | | |
| Limited company | + | + | + | | | |
| VAT registered | ? | − | ? | + | | |
| Used pre start support | + | | +/− | | | + |
| Problems in 1st year with demand | ? | | ? | | | − |
| Totally new product or service | + | | +/− | | | + |
| Use a website | n.s | | ? | | + | |
| Used post start-up profits | + | + | + | | | |
| Competitive advantage based on lower prices | ? | − | ? | | | |
| Competitive advantage based on better administration | ? | | ? | + | | − |
| % use of regional supplier | ? | + | ? | + | + | |
| Manufacturer | +/− | | + | | | + |
| Professional services | + | | +/− | | | + |
| Other sector | − | | ? | | | − |
| Shropshire | ? | | ? | | | + |

this may partly reflect the size of the sample, but since it has been collected with great care, it is expected to be considerably closer to being an accurate reflection of new businesses than many much larger samples.

We, therefore, feel forced to conclude that there is a strong chance element in business performance – indeed it is probably the most powerful influence. Of course, there are other factors at work – some under the control of the business owner and some not. In the latter category is to start in professional services, sell outside the local market, choose limited company legal status, and to reinvest the profits from the business as a key source of post start finance. What our research tells us, however, is that none of these individually or taken as a group is either an insurance against exit or an assurance of growth.

# 10
# An Audit of the Three Decades and Three Regions

## Introduction

This book has sought to observe new businesses primarily through the lens of public policy makers. Its prime concern has been to examine the characteristics of new businesses created in arguably the UK's least entrepreneurial area – Teesside – in the 1970s, the 1980s and the 1990s and, during the 1990s to compare them with other more entrepreneurial parts of the UK. Our central policy question has been: 'Given the objective of policy in the 1980s and 1990s was to make Teesside more entrepreneurial – did it work?' Our supplementary concern is – based on our and other evidence – to offer guidance of the direction of new policies.

We were also concerned to what extent new businesses to what extent new businesses in the low enterprise area (Teesside) differed from those in the medium and high enterprise areas of Shropshire and Buckinghamshire, respectively. Data on businesses in the three counties is available only for the 1990s, but this disadvantage is compensated to some extent by being able to track this cohort of new businesses for three years. Here our central policy question is 'What lessons can be learnt by Teesside policy makers by observing the factors influencing the performance of new businesses in Shropshire and Buckinghamshire?'

We began by pulling together a range of data to describe new business formation – or entrepreneurship – over a long period. The picture that emerged was one of striking stability, or less politely expressed, one of ossification. Identifying an English regional entrepreneurship index for the 1970s, 1980s and 1990s, we showed the Southern regions of England scored far higher than the Northern English regions during each decade. Perhaps even more strikingly is that the 'league' position

233

of almost every region is virtually identical in every decade. This is confirmed by official data on new VAT registrations which first became available in 1980. So, if there has been some form of enterprise/ entrepreneurship policy over these decades it has clearly not resulted in any shift whatever in the relative positions of the regions.

We then introduced our chosen three regions – or technically – counties. The first of these was Teesside in the North East of England and, on all criteria, it is clearly a low enterprise area. Here we showed in Chapter 1 (Figure 1.2) that it has about 20 new businesses per 10,000 population. In contrast, Buckinghamshire in the South East of England (a 'high' enterprise area) has almost 60 new VAT registrations per 10,000 population. The West Midlands county of Shropshire is a middling enterprise area with almost 40 new VAT registrations per 10,000 population.

Teesside, however, was not always an area of low promise. During the 1960s and early 1970s it was regarded as being the most economically vibrant area in Northern England, but the last 40 years have been one of decline.

In parallel with charting the decline of Teesside since the 1970s, this book also described the considerable policy shifts in enterprise policy that have taken place in Britain during the same period. The first, during the 1970s, we described as an era of 'policy off'. This was replaced in the 1980s with a focus on improving the 'quantity' of new businesses in the economy – maximising the number of new businesses. In the 1990s this changed again, with a greater emphasis being placed upon improving the 'quality' of existing businesses. The election of a Labour government in 1997 saw a further change towards more of a 'balanced portfolio' approach to small business support – with a much greater emphasis upon linking enterprise and disadvantage.

Having outlined the economic and policy background, the book then proceeded to empirically examine interviews with over 900 *de novo* entrepreneurs over these three decades and across the three regions. Here the focus was on understanding what characterised the entrepreneurs and their sectoral choices (Chapter 4), what typified how they did business (Chapter 5), what support they received (Chapter 6) and how they used and valued finance (Chapter 7). In subsequent chapters (8 and 9), the focus was on identifying the performance of these new business and their likely impact on the local economy.

The focus of this final chapter is on examining the lessons learnt. It is principally organised around two tables. The first synthesises the evidence from Chapters 8 and 9 to provide a clear focus on the factors that promote or restrict the performance of new businesses across the three decades and between the three regions.

The second table assumes our audience comprises four groups: new business owners, finance providers, researchers and students and finally public policy makers. It seeks to address each audience in turn by highlighting those of our findings which we believe are relevant for them.

## A synopsis of performance

In this section, the focus is on providing an overview of the main findings that may be drawn from Chapters 8 and 9, allowing us to trace the impact of factors that are spatially and temporally invariant. The overview then acts as an empirical introduction to the policy review.

Table 10.1 identifies four aspects of this study into *de novo* entrepreneurs. First, it examines the factors that were found to be significant in explaining performance in both the three decades and the three regions. For the three decades, it summarises the direction ('+' or '−') of the influence a particular factor exerts on new enterprise growth during these periods. This is complemented by a synopsis of the factors that were found to influence survival (column 3) and growth performance (column 6) in the review of 54 performance studies (Chapter 8, Table 8.2). Finally, columns 2 and 4 itemise the suggested direction for survival and growth, respectively.

There are obviously data limitations in seeking to compare and contrast performance between the three decades and the regions. First, there was a greater range of factors examined in the three region study than in the earlier decades. Second, the three decades results only apply to surviving businesses, whereas the regional study is able to control for the influence of survival on performance. Finally, in seeking to provide an aggregate synopsis of the results, we are conscious of the risk of oversimplification.

So, acknowledging these limitations, the following findings emerge from Table 10.1. The first of these is that the age of the business has a strong impact on its likelihood of survival and subsequent growth. In terms of survival, Table 10.1 follows the expected direction that older businesses are more likely to persist. Similarly, the balance of evidence suggests that younger businesses are more likely to grow faster, but that this effect does tail off. What is also evident is that being a limited company is associated with survival and growth. This, though, does not hold for the three-region growth results.

*Table 10.1*   Synopsis of performance factors

| | Exit | | Growth | | |
|---|---|---|---|---|---|
| | | | | Three | Three |
| | Review | Results | Review | decades | regions |
| Managerial Experience | n.s. | | n.s. | | − |
| Indigenous | | | +/n.s. | − | |
| Previously Unemployed | | | - | − | |
| Prior Entrepreneurial experience | | | n.s. | − | |
| Full time in business | ? | | | | + |
| Education | + | − | + | + | + |
| Age of Business | + | + | − | −/+ | − |
| Business age$^2$ | + | | + | + | + |
| Limited Company | + | + | + | + | |
| VAT registered | ? | − | ? | | + |
| Used pre start support | + | | +/− | + | + |
| Problems in 1st year with demand | ? | | ? | − | − |
| Totally new product or service | + | | +/− | | + |
| Use a website | ? | | ? | | + |
| Use of pre start mortgage | ? | | ? | +/− | |
| Use of pre start bank | ? | | ? | + | |
| Use of pre start finance company | ? | | ? | + | |
| Use of post start savings | ? | | ? | − | |
| Use of post start profits | ? | + | ? | + | |
| Competitive advantage based on lower prices | ? | − | ? | | |
| Competitive advantage based on better administration | ? | | ? | | +/− |
| % use of regional supplier | ? | + | ? | | + |
| Manufacturer | +/− | | + | | + |
| Professional services | + | | +/− | | + |
| Other sector | − | | ? | | − |
| Shropshire | ? | | ? | | + |
| 1980s | ? | | ? | + | |
| 1970s | ? | | ? | + | |

The third finding relates to the educational qualifications of the entrepreneur. Although there is no evidence of a positive impact of qualifications on business survival, the weight of the historical and spatial evidence suggests that formal qualifications, particularly those around post-compulsory education (A Level/HND), promotes business growth.

A fourth area is that of the prior business ownership experience of the entrepreneur. Here we find that prior business ownership experience lowers performance. To some this may be a surprising result since policy makers in the UK and elsewhere have sought to make it easier for individuals whose businesses have failed to restart. This policy change has been on two grounds. The first is that failure will have taught that individual valuable lessons, and the second is that, by excluding these individuals from implementing the lessons that they have learnt by starting a new business, the economy is incurring a possibly high opportunity cost. However, we feel reassured by our results since they fit closely with Metzger (2006). He found, using a large German data set, that whilst prior business experience of the entrepreneur improved the likelihood of new businesses showing employment growth, if the entrepreneur had failed in business this lowered the likelihood of employment growth. We are unable to distinguish in our data between businesses founded by individuals that have failed and those that made a voluntary choice to close their business. Nonetheless, the negative finding by Metzger is in line with our results, and does again lead to a serious questioning of the concept of entrepreneurial learning. We return to this issue later.

Another interesting finding from both the three decades and three regions study is the impact that a lack of demand during the first year of operations has on business performance. It would appear that suffering from this problem effectively retards growth, although curiously it does not appear to have any impact on survival.

These results and the other findings from Table 10.1 are discussed more fully in the following section.

## Auditing the new business

We now turn to examine the findings from Table 10.1 from the perspective of our four groups: entrepreneurs, finance providers, researchers and students and, finally, public policy makers (see Table 10.2).

### Entrepreneurs

Although the principal focus of this book has not been on how to improve the practice of individuals setting up their own business, there are nevertheless some practical issues that emerge from this study. Before considering these issues, it is important to remember that our overall finding is that performance is idiosyncratic. In highlighting this point we emphasise that there are no simple rules that may be

*Table 10.2*   An audit of the three decades and three regions

| Areas of interest | Positives | Negatives |
|---|---|---|
| Entrepreneurs | • Limited companies<br>• Importance of sectoral choice (innovation, professional services, website)<br>• Value of finance | • Low cost pricing strategy<br>• 'Me too' businesses (sectoral choices, lack of demand) |
| Finance Providers | • Lack of evidence of any access to finance problems | • Potential 'over' supply of finance: weight of public sector support |
| Researchers and students | • Entrepreneurial learning<br>• Public policy<br>• New businesses | • The importance of chance |
| Public policy makers | • Many policy initiatives<br>• Value of public support<br>• Improvement of the UK in Enterprise "league tables" | • Cost-effectiveness open to question<br>• Not improved the Teesside problem |

applied by entrepreneurs that will, in all circumstances, ensure the success of their business. If anything our message is the reverse. It is that business ownership is risky and so, whilst 'doing the right things' is helpful, it provides only a very modest level of protection against the chance events that can easily overwhelm a new business.

It might, for example, have been thought that entrepreneurial experience either gained from previously owning a business (serial entrepreneurship) or owning concurrent businesses (portfolio entrepreneurship) would enhance the performance of a new venture. After all, one of the main theories of entrepreneurship (Jovanovic, 1982) argues that individuals can only assess their entrepreneurial ability accurately once they have started running their own business. Our evidence, however, is that portfolio entrepreneurs performed no better than others who did not own another business. Moreover, the performance of serial entrepreneurs was even worse.

The evidence that entrepreneurs learn is being increasingly questioned (Parker, 2006; Metzger, 2006), leading to a greater emphasis being placed on the role of chance. Indeed, our finding that portfolio entrepreneurs performed no better is compatible with the view that entrepreneurs recognise the nature of the uncertainty they face and, therefore, seek to limit their exposure to this by diversifying their risks.

A second finding is that new business founders with some formal education, particularly post-compulsory education, perform better than those without such educational qualifications. This remains a puzzle rather than a prescription for entrepreneurial success, on the grounds that many successful entrepreneurs delight in trumpeting their success in business by emphasising that this has been achieved in spite of, for example, either never going to college or dropping out. The clear implication of such assertions is that education cannot 'claim' the credit for the success of the business – and by implication the success is clearly attributable to the entrepreneur, and the entrepreneur alone. Our results, and that of much other research, instead points to the presence of thresholds. Our view is that entrepreneurs may also not need high educational qualifications to possess the necessary minimum skills to own and manage a new business: much of this is because what is required is humdrum, either because it focuses on personal sectors (e.g. clothes, food, entertainment) or living needs (e.g. house repair).

The challenge, then, is whether the entrepreneur is suited to their chosen environment and how lucky they are in this environment. An alternative explanation for the importance of a modicum of education may be that entrepreneurship requires people who are 'jack of all trades but masters of none' (Lazear, 2005). This may help explain the importance of post-compulsory education and, potentially why it is that so many of the other human capital attributes investigated in this study were not shown to be significant.

That said, there was little from the review of other studies (Chapter 8) that gave practical pointers towards the successful entrepreneur. One partial exception was the need to concentrate on the entry conditions. Whilst starting a business is often difficult, a positive practical choice would be to become a limited company. There is also evidence to suggest that the more dynamic or just plain different business (e.g. involved in innovation, having a website and being in the professional services sector) did relatively better. Similarly, Table 10.1 indicated that there were some grounds for assuming that businesses with diverse sources of finance performed better.

Entrepreneurs can also make choices that lower the likelihood of performing well. One is to focus on low price strategies as the basis of a perceived competitive advantage. A second is to start a business in a sector that is already crowded with businesses and where growth prospects are modest. In the low enterprise county of Teesside it was found that around one-fifth of all new businesses operated in either Motor repairs or in some form of beauty treatment (e.g. hairdressing). Whilst it is recognised that such businesses do provide essential services, their growth opportunities are likely to be modest. Unsurprisingly, Table 10.1 suggested that a lack of demand in the first year of operations was a central problem in dampening the performance of new businesses. This fits in with the idea of businesses that enter in the hope that they will prosper, but soon find that there is just too little demand for their goods and services and/or that the competition is more challenging than was expected.

Overall, we emphasise again that there is no silver bullet that leads inevitably and invariably to entrepreneurial success. Mostly, it is a matter of luck. What does appear to help is to offer something a little different and what the market actually wants rather than a 'me too' prescription. This may seem blindingly obvious, but the frequency with which it is contravened in practice suggests it does merit continual emphasis.

## Finance providers

This study found that, by most measures, the provision of finance for new businesses, at least in Teesside, has improved over the three decades. New entrepreneurs appeared to adhere to a finance formula which saw them access their own funding first and then proceed to make use of outside funding. As is evident from Table 10.1, some forms of external finance did enhance the performance of the business. So, whilst individual businesses did experience financing problems, there was little to suggest that lack of access to external finance providers was generally a barrier to the start-up and growth of new businesses. It also appeared, in line with other research, that in comparison with other issues, access to finance is now less of a problem for new businesses than was the case one, two and three decades ago. Indeed Chapter 7 suggested that, if anything, there was too much finance on offer to new businesses.

De Meza's (2002) suggests that this is a problem because it encourages ill-suited individuals into entrepreneurship which has unfortunate consequences for those individuals and those that financially support them. Each new business represents the expenditure of some sunk costs, whether this is in terms of the efforts of the entrepreneur (sweat equity) or in terms of equipment, overheads or day to day costs. It is likely that some, much, or even all of this may be unrecoverable if the business fails. Banks in a modern economy, with their ability to process vast quantities of information on customers, have a considerably better overview than the individual entrepreneur of the likely risks faced by a particular business. On those grounds they are unlikely to lend consistently to the 'wrong' sorts of people. However, banks are both political as well as commercial organisations, and they are managed by individuals rather than computers. So, there is a strong chance that banks may be prepared, in the face of political pressure, to over-lend to those that they know are unsuited to entrepreneurship in order to avoid conflict with governments. There is also a risk that, whilst credit-scoring models may be valid in buoyant macro-economic conditions, drawing inferences from such models would be unwise if macro-economic conditions were to deteriorate sharply. In short, there are situations in which de Meza's (2002) position that giving money to the 'wrong' sorts of people has welfare costs for the rest of society becomes a valid risk.

One clear example of this is the provision of public finance in an area like Teesside. It seems to us that there is little evidence of a market failure in the provision of finance to new businesses, and yet over a quarter of new businesses in this area received public financial assistance at start-up. This is higher than the proportion of new businesses using bank finance in either Shropshire or Buckinghamshire. Of course, the argument here is that such public provision is necessary because of the access to finance difficulties faced by new entrepreneurs either in terms of their limited pool of capital or their difficulty in leveraging bank finance. Our view on this aligns with that of Parker (2004) who suggests it is possible to go on a theoretical merry-go-round pointing to various potential access to finance issues. The central question remains: is such public finance propitious or does it just signal the existence of an economy that has grown too used to public financial assistance?

To answer this question, Chapter 7 showed that Teesside businesses were less likely to have experienced financial problems in their first year compared with new businesses in the other two regions. This may be seen as a positive outcome, although there is another school of thought suggesting that the most productive businesses are those that have to struggle to become the fittest (Disney et al., 2003). Nonetheless, businesses that made use of public finance did survive just as well – but not better – than those who did not receive such support. However, there was no evidence that supported businesses had more positive growth outcomes. The simple statistics in Chapter 7 showed that new businesses in receipt of public financial support performed worse than other businesses but, when a range of other factors was included in the multivariate analysis, no impact either way was identifiable.

Our overall view is that there are no clear inefficiencies in the finance market for the vast majority of new enterprises. This does not imply that all individuals seeking external funding obtain that funding in the quantities and at the price they would choose. What it does suggest is that access to funding broadly reflects the risk and expected returns from the project. If anything, the risk is greater that high risk/low return projects are funded than that low risk/high return projects are rejected. We are, therefore, unpersuaded that taxpayers' money should be used on the scale that it has in the past to provide financial support for new businesses, even in a low enterprise area such as Teesside.

The above focus has been on short term funding – most notably from banks and finance houses. There has been no discussion of external equity because this is virtually irrelevant for new businesses. For example, Bygrave and Hunt (2007) suggested that only 799 businesses in the US were supported by venture capital in the year 2004. Despite this only representing 0.26 per cent of new businesses and financial support of just 1.63 per cent of available finance, the topic of venture capital continues to excite attention. To give some sense of this, a simple search was conducted on a bibliographic website (Web of Science) to see how many peer review articles were captured by the search term 'venture capital' over the period 1992–2007. The answer was 685 articles. This is nearly one for each of the 799 venture capital businesses supported in 2004.

This, of course, is not to say that venture capital supported businesses are not important to the development of new businesses and economies. They are. What is really the issue is having some sense of proportion: whilst venture capital may have been central to the subsequent fortunes of internet monoliths like Google, it is wise to remember that such businesses began by also making use of the same sorts of finance used by virtually every other new business in this survey.

## Researchers and students

This section reviews three areas of interest to the research community. We begin by re-emphasising our dissatisfaction with the rarely acknowledged role, at least within the management literature, of chance. Our review both of our own results, and those of other scholars has emphasised that chance plays *a*, if not *the*, key role in the survival and growth of new businesses. Researchers, in our view, have to highlight this, rather than brush it under the carpet by placing their emphasis upon the factors that do only modestly influence performance. This requires some humility on the part of researchers.

A second issue that has emerged in recent empirical work, and appears to be supported from our findings is scepticism about the topic of entrepreneurial learning. Without repeating our earlier discussion, it is appropriate to emphasise that our results are compatible with the absence of entrepreneurial learning from those with prior business experience. Those researchers that have championed this approach should, in our view, look for more persuasive evidence if they wish to be convincing.

A third issue of interest to researchers is the effectiveness of public policy seeking to enhance rates of new business formation in the expectation that this will lead to greater economic welfare. The research reported here and elsewhere that we have undertaken questions these links at all stages in the causal chain. It questions whether, in low enterprise areas it is possible to raise new business formation rates – other than perhaps by inducing a recession or by offering incentives for existing informal businesses to 'convert' to the formal sector by potentially reducing registration costs and times for new businesses (Djankov et al., 2002). The second step in the chain is that the businesses created (always) enhance welfare. Certainly, the results from van Stel and Storey (2004) and from Mueller et al. (2008) suggest there are circumstances in which new businesses do lead to increased employment, but that there are also circumstances when they do not. These circumstances are those most likely to occur in areas such as Teesside where existing rates of new business formation are already low. So, even if it is possible to raise new business formation, 'more of the same' is not necessarily the solution.

## Public policy makers

Table 10.2 summarises both the positive and negative issues relevant to public policy makers that have emerged in this book.

On the positive side, the UK has been almost an enterprise laboratory over a 30-year period. It has seen the introduction of a huge diversity of policy initiatives to assist and promote new and small businesses. The efforts of the policy makers cannot, therefore, be questioned and, in return, there is much to show. Compared with 30 years ago there is a greater awareness of the entrepreneurial option and there is greater credibility in being an entrepreneur. The extent to which these changes have been caused by government policies to promote enterprise, and the extent to which they would have happened given the technical changes that have occurred throughout the world is a valid subject for debate. What is not up for debate is the scale of the change. Van Stel (2005) using the COMPENDIA data base shows that business ownership rates in the UK in 1976 were 7.4 per thousand in the labour force. This placed it in seventeenth equal position out of 23 OECD countries. 20 years later its rate had risen to 10.9, placing it in tenth place.

Table 10.2 shows, however, two important negatives. The first is a major reservation about whether the spending on enterprise policy has been cost-effective, and the second is the inability to make much observable progress on solving what we refer to as 'the Teesside problem'. We now deal with each of these issues in turn.

We have two central concerns on cost-effectiveness. The first is what is referred to as the 'flip-flop' policies. We observed that enterprise policies in the 1980s moved from being virtually non-existent to having an almost desperate focus upon seeking to persuade/bribe unemployed individuals to become self-employed. The folly of such measures was recognised in the 1990s when policy focussed more heavily upon businesses with the potential to grow, rather than upon maximising the number of start-up businesses. This policy was also later incorporated into a broader approach to enterprise that included not only new and growing businesses, but also emphasised the role of minority and other groups. This continual switching of policy focus, together with an even faster shuffling of policy instruments and methods of delivering policy, implies that governments themselves were unconvinced they had ever found the right recipe.

What has become clear, though, are the amounts spent on behalf of the taxpayer to support small businesses. Figures vary with the DTI/Treasury (2002) review identifying £7.98 billion or 0.8 per cent of UK GDP. This compares with the NAO (2006) report which added up small business expenditure differently by including an 'extra' £1.7 billion spent by the Learning and Skills Council but omitting the £2.6 billion on small business tax relief to arrive at a figure of £4.3 billion spent on small business support. Our view is that somewhere in the region of £7 billion of taxpayers' funds are used for the support of small businesses. What this means is that taxpayers spend approximately the same amount on supporting small businesses as they do on the police service or universities.

The central difference is that whilst the police or universities are primarily the responsibility of a single department of government, small businesses are not. The expenditure of the Small Business Service – was less than the small business budgets of the Department of Culture Media and Sport.

The clear picture that emerges is that public expenditure and tax relief devoted to supporting small businesses are huge, in part because so many agencies and departments of government have substantial budgets. In this situation where no single agency or department within central government exercises an overall function the inevitable outcome is the strong suspicion that policy is not cost effectively delivered. Our view is that whilst policy has lead to improvements in the last 20 or more years, it has been unduly expensive for the taxpayer and will continue to be expensive until an overarching policy role is exercised. The only organisation capable of exercising such a role is HM Treasury.

We now turn to our central concern in Table 10.2. It is the inability over 30 years to solve 'the Teesside problem'.

Fair minded observers might emphasise that Teesside has seen important improvements in the entrepreneurial environment. For example there has been a huge increase in the take-up and appreciation of publicly funded advisory services. In the 1970s, 36 per cent of businesses took business advice from the public sector before they began to trade. By the 1980s, this had risen to 44 per cent and on to 46 per cent in the 1990s. Second, there was also a sharp rise in the proportion of new businesses reporting this advice to be helpful. In the 1970s it was 17 per cent, rising to 33 per cent in the 1980s and 37% in the 1990s. Given that this has been a major plank of policy, our results point to a clear success.

Tempering the value of these positives there are powerful negatives. First, the evidence that the provision of public support led to superior performance outcomes is weak at best. Second, although rates of new business formation did rise in the 1980s, the new businesses made only a modest contribution to employment. Indeed, Teesside would have to raise its start-up rate to more than 30 times over just to replace the jobs lost to the local economy. Third, despite some increases in rates of new business formation, Teesside, along with almost every UK county and region remains in the same relative position as it did 10, 20 and probably 30 years ago. Climbing out from the lower reaches of the enterprise league table appears to be impossible. Fourth, when comparisons are made, particularly with Buckinghamshire new businesses, the sectoral composition of Teesside's new businesses is striking. In the 1990s, perhaps one in four of Teesside's new businesses were in the motor repairs and beauty sectors. There is a tangible absence of new businesses in professional and business services. The sectoral contrast with Buckinghamshire's new businesses, where there is a strong IT and professional services presence, could hardly be more stark. Policy has clearly failed to change that sectoral mix on Teesside over decades.

We do not regard it as our task to offer a blueprint for accelerating enterprise and entrepreneurship on Teesside. Even so, having examined these matters at such length we feel that some strategic pointers are expected from us.

What is clear is that more of the same is unlikely to enhance economic welfare of the residents of Teesside. By this we mean that efforts to raise new business formation will, if they have any effect at all, merely lead to more businesses established by individuals with low human capital, who are starting businesses in easy-to-enter industries because of a lack of alternative employment opportunities in the locality.

We are also unpersuaded that the provision of public funds either to provide advisory services to such businesses, or to provide them with grants of one form or another, is likely to enhance their economic performance. The businesses themselves clearly appreciate the support, and an 'enterprise industry' has emerged to provide this support, but our evidence is that its impact is small. Whilst there have been no recent other studies of new entrepreneurs on Teesside, our view is that it is of questionable benefit for individuals to be enticed into enterprise without being made aware of the potentially considerable expected downside losses.

A familiar response to this issue is to issue a clarion-call that what is needed is to change attitudes. For example, this may involve teaching enterprise to school children or to University students. It may also involve ensuring that entrepreneurs are presented as attractive role models in the media. Arguably, the attempts to create an "enterprise culture" in the 1980s illustrate such a policy response, and such initiatives continue today with TV programmes seeking to portray business and enterprise in a positive light. However, the reality is that attributing any attitudinal changes to enterprise in Britain (Fraser and Greene, 2006) to policy initiatives is extraordinarily difficult, in part because of the perhaps 30-year time-lag between an individual receiving enterprise education and starting a business. Linking one to the other, given all the other events in that individual's life, is difficult.

Our view corresponds more closely to that of Baumol (1990). He argued that there was not, and never has been, a shortage of entrepreneurs. Memorably he said 'the entrepreneur is always with us'. In economic-speak, he said that for most purposes there is a fairly fixed supply of entrepreneurs.

At first reading this seems totally at odds with the situation we have described on Teesside, until the second element of Baumol's thesis is presented. Baumol argues that these entrepreneurs are in one of three groups: productive, unproductive and destructive and that this allocation depends on 'the rules of the game'. By this Baumol meant that, for those with entrepreneurial talent, they made a choice between entrepreneurship that benefits themselves but also benefits others – productive entrepreneurship – and entrepreneurship that is unproductive or destructive (benefits them but not others e.g. 'ambulance chasing' lawyers, organised criminals).

The task of policy makers is to set 'the rules of the game' so that productive entrepreneurship is the rational and informed choice for individuals with entrepreneurial talent. It has to be favoured by them over either unproductive or destructive entrepreneurship. What Baumol was clear about was that society should not devote its resources to the fruitless task of seeking to increase the supply of entrepreneurs – by seeking to change attitudes.

So what does this mean for Teesside? The first is that it is compatible with our reservations about the impact of seeking to convert individuals to become enterprising. The second, and positive, implication is that it forces policy makers to consider the key phrases used by Baumol, of 'choice' and 'rules of the game'.

So, how might the rules be changed? Before answering that question we draw the reader's attention to some key research findings. The first, confirmed from our own data for Teesside, is that businesses established by individuals classifying themselves as born and bred on Teesside are, all else equal, likely to have slower growing new businesses than business founded by those coming from outside. It, therefore, implies that, if Teesside is to have businesses that are more likely to create jobs then they may have to look to outsiders to provide this function. This is also compatible with the findings for California that point to the scale and economic significance of businesses established by in-migrants – particularly educated in-migrants – in areas such as Silicon Valley. Saxenian (1999) for example found that companies in Silicon Valley established by Asians coming to the US to study had created close to 60,000 jobs. This also emphasises the economic significance of technology-based entrepreneurship to job creation as documented by Acs and Armington (2006).

Again the question arises as to how this fits with a Teesside agenda. The answer is that the UK is an extremely attractive location for overseas students and that the University of Teesside could, given its skill base, provide education to such individuals. Having studied in Britain the evidence provided by Saxenian suggests that many individuals might choose to stay in the UK, as enterprise creation is a favoured way to provide an income source in much the same way the Jews did in the 1930s (see Chapter 3). The disadvantage noted by Greene and Saridakis (2007) is that graduates are highly mobile, and likely to be attracted to the currently prosperous areas of London and South East England. Nevertheless many may also recognise the better quality of life and lower cost base of Northern England. Central government may be able to commit resources to help Universities in the area both to become attractive to overseas students and provide them with infrastructure for business support, such as premises.

The essence of the current proposal is therefore that new policies are required to promote enterprise on Teesside. More of the same is not good enough, and the role of in-migrants has to be considered. Since migration of UK citizens is away from, rather than towards, Teesside, those for whom Teesside constitutes an improvement have to be attracted, particularly if they bring with them technical and educational skills which enhance the locality.

We do not, of course, imply that this is the only route open to enhance enterprise creation and new business performance in Teesside. Our challenge is to others to identify novel ways of changing the rules of the game to enhance productive entrepreneurship in arguably England's least enterprising area.

# References

Acs, Z. J. and Armington, C. (2006) *Entrepreneurship, Geography, and American Economic Growth*, Cambridge University Press, New York.

Acs, Z. J. and Audretsch, D. B. (1990) *Innovation and Small Firms*, Cambridge, Mass.: MIT Press.

Acs, Z. J., Audretsch, D. B. and Carlsson, B. (1991) 'Flexible Technology and Firm Size', *Small Business Economics*, 3: 307–319.

Aghion, P. and Howitt, P. (1998) *Endogenous Growth Theory*, London: MIT Press.

Ajzen, I. (1991) 'The theory of planned behavior' *Organizational Behavior and Human Decision Processes*, 50: 179–211.

Almus, M. and Nerlinger, E. A. (1999) 'Growth of new technology-based firms: Which factors matter?' *Small Business Economics*, 13 (2): 141–154.

Appleyard, B. (1978) 'Bringing small business to the Boil', *The Times*, Monday, 2nd October, p. 16.

Arabsheibani, G., de Meza, D., Maloney, J. and Pearson, B. (2000) 'And a vision appeared unto them of great profit: evidence of self-deception among the self-employed', *Economics Letters*, 67: 35–41.

Archer, M. S. (2003) *Structure, Agency and the Internal Conversation*, Cambridge: Cambridge University Press.

Armington, C. and Acs, Z. J. (2002) 'The determinants of regional variation in new firm formation'. *Regional Studies*, 36 (1): 33–45.

Armington, C. and Odle, M. (1982) 'Small business – how many jobs?', *The Brookings Review*, Winter, 14–17.

Ashworth, J., Johnson, P. and Conway, C. (1998) 'How good are small firms at predicting employment?', *Small Business Economics*, 10 (4): 379–387.

Audretsch, D. B. (1995) 'Innovation, growth and survival', *International Journal of Industrial Organization*, 13 (4): 441–457.

Audretsch, D. B., and Fritsch, M. (1994) 'The Geography of Firm Birth in Germany', *Regional Studies*, 28: 359–365.

Audretsch, D. B., Houweling, P. and Thurik, A. R. (2000) 'Firm survival in the Netherlands', *Review of Industrial Organization*, 16 (1): 1–11.

Bank of England (1994) *Finance for Small Firms – A First Report*, Bank of England: London.

Bank of England (2004) *Finance for Small Firms – An Eleventh Report*, Bank of England: London.

Bannock, G. (1981) *The Economics of Small Firms*, Oxford: Blackwell.

Bannock, G. and Peacock, A. (1989) *Governments and Small Business*, London: PCP.

Barkham, R., Gudgin, G., Hart, M. and Hanvey, E. (1996) *The Determinants of Small Firm Growth*, Gateshead: Athenaeum.

Barnett, C. (1996) *The Lost victory: British dreams, British realities, 1945–1950*, London: Pan.

Barney, J. B. (1991) 'Business resources and sustained competitive advantage', *Journal of Management*, 17 (1): 99–120.

Barney, J. B. (1997) *Gaining and Sustaining Competitive Advantage*, Reading, MA: Addison-Wesley.

Barringer, B. R., Jones, F. F. and Neubaum, D. O. (2005) 'A quantitative content analysis of the characteristics of rapid-growth firms and their founders', *Journal of Business Venturing*, 20: 663–687.

Bartelsman, E., Scarpetta, S. and Schivardi, F. (2003) 'Comparative analysis of firm demographics and survival: Micro level evidence for the OECD countries', *OECD Economic Deparment Working Paper No. 348*, Paris: OECD.

Basu, A. and Goswami, A. (1999) 'Determinants of South Asian entrepreneurial growth in Britain: a multivariate analysis', *Small Business Economics*, 13 (1): 57–70.

Basu, A. and Parker, S. C. (2001) 'Family finance and new business start-ups', *Oxford Bulletin of Economics and Statistics*, 63 (3): 333–358.

Bates, T. (1995) 'Analysis of survival rates among franchise and independent small business startups', *Journal of Small Business Management*, 33 (2): 26–36.

Bates, T. (2005). 'Analysis of young, small firms that have closed: delineating successful from unsuccessful closures', *Journal of Business Venturing*, 20 (3): 343–358.

Baumol, W. J. (1990). 'Entrepreneurship: productive, unproductive, and destructive', *Journal of Political Economy*, 98: 893–921.

Becchetti, L. and Trovato, G. (2002) 'The determinants of growth for small and medium sized firms. The role of the availability of external finance', *Small Business Economics*, 19 (4): 291–306.

Becker, G. S. (1994) *Human Capital: A Theoretical and Empirical Analysis, with Special Reference to Education*, University Of Chicago Press: Chicago.

Beck, T. and Demirguc-Kunt, A. (2006) 'Small and medium-size enterprises: access to finance as a growth constraint', *Journal of Banking & Finance*, 30 (11): 2931–2943.

Beesley, M. E. and Wilson, P. E. B. (1984) 'Public policy and small firms in Britain', in *Small Business: Theory and Policy*, Levicki, C. (ed.), London: Croom Helm, 111–126.

Bennett, R. J. (1995) 'The Re-focusing of small business services in enterprise agencies: the influence of TECs and LECs', *International Small Business Journal*, 13 (4): 35–55.

Bennett, R. J. (1996) 'Memorandum submitted by Robert Bennett' in *Business Links*, Trade and Industry Committee, Fifth Report HC302-II, London: HMSO.

Bennett, R. J. and Robson, P. J. A. (2003) Changing use of external advice and government suports by SMEs in the 1990s, *Regional Studies*, 37: 795–811.

Bennett, R.J. and Robson, P.J.A. (2004) 'The role of trust and contract in the supply of business advice', *Cambridge Journal of Economics*, 28:4, 471-488.

Bennett, R. J. (2006) 'Government and Small Business', in *Enterprise and Small Business: Principles, Practice and Policy 2nd ed.* Carter, S. and Jones-Evans, D. (eds) FT Prentice Hall: London, 49–75.

Berger, A. N. and Udell, G. F. (1990) 'Collateral, loan quality and risk', *Journal of Monetary Economics*, 25: 21–42.

Berger, A. N. and Udell, G. F. (1998) 'The economics of small business finance: the roles of private equity and debt markets in the financial growth cycle', *Journal of Banking & Finance*, 22 (6–8): 613–673.

Berger, A. N. and Udell, G. F. (2002) 'Small business credit availability and relationship lending: the importance of bank organisational structure', *Economic Journal*, 112: F32–F53.

Bernhardt, I. (1994) 'Comparative advantage in self-employment and paid work', *Canadian Journal of Economics*, May, 273–289.

Beynon, H., Hudson, R. and Sadler, D. (1994) *A Place Called Teesside: A Locality in a Global Economy*, Edinburgh: Edinburgh University Press.

Bhide, A. V. (2000). *The Origin and Evolution of New Businesses*. Oxford University Press: New York.

Birch, D. (1979) *The Job Generation Process*, Cambridge, Mass.: MIT Program on Neighborhood and Regional Change.

Birch, D., Haggerty, A. and Parsons, W. (1997) *Who's Creating Jobs*, Cambridge, Mass.: Cognetics, Inc.

Birley, S., Muzyka, D., Dove, C. and Russel, G. (1995) 'Finding the high-flying entrepreneurs: a cautionary tale', *Entrepreneurship Theory and Practice*, 19 (4) 105–112.

Black, J., De Meza, D. and D. Jeffreys (1996) 'House prices, the supply of collateral, and the enterprise economy', *Economic Journal*, 106, January, 60–75.

Blackaby, F. eds. (1979) *De-industrialisation*, Oxford: Blackwell.

Blanchflower, D. G. (2000) 'Self-employment in OECD countries'. *Labour Economics*, 7 (5): 471–505.

Blanchflower, D. G. and Meyer, B. (1994) 'A longitudinal analysis of the young self-employment in Australia and the United States' *Small Business Economics*, 6: 1–20.

Blanchflower, D. G. and Oswald, A. J. (1998) 'What makes an entrepreneur?' *Journal of Labor Economics*, 16 (1): 26–60.

Bogenhold, D. and Staber, U. (1991) 'The Decline and Rise of Self-Employment', *Work Employment and Society*, 5(2): 223–39.

Bolton, J. (1971) *Report of the Committee of Inquiry on Small Firms*, Cmnd. 4811. London: HMSO.

Borjas, G. J. (1992) 'Ethnic Capital and Intergenerational Mobility', *Quarterly Journal of Economics*, 107(1): 123–50.

Borjas, G. J. and Bronars, S. G. (1989) 'Consumer discrimination and self-employment', *Journal of Political Economy*, 97, 581–605.

Bosma, N., van Praag M., Thurik, R. and de Wit, G. (2004). 'The value of human and social capital investments for the business performance of startups', *Small Business Economics*, 23 (3): 227–236.

Boswell, J. (1973) *The Rise and Decline of Small Firms*, London: George Allen and Urwin.

Box, T. M., Watts, L. R. and Hisrich, R. D. (1994). 'Manufacturing entrepreneurs – an empirical-study of the correlates of employment growth in the Tulsa Msa and rural East Texas', *Journal of Business Venturing*, 9 (3): 261–270.

Briggs, A. (1963) *Victorian Cities*, London: Odhams.

Brixy, U. and Kohaut, S. (1999). 'Employment growth determinants in new firms in eastern Germany', *Small Business Economics*, 13 (2): 155–170.

Broadberry, S. and O'Mahony, M. (2005) 'Britain's twentieth century productivity performance in international perspective', Working Paper Coventry: University of Warwick.

Broersma, L. and Gautier, P. (1997) 'Job creation and job destruction by small firms: an empirical investigation for the dutch manufacturing sector', *Small Business Economics*, 9 (3): 211–224.

Bruderl, J. and Preisendorfer, P. (1998) 'Network support and the success of newly founded businesses', *Small Business Economics*, 10 (3): 213–225.

Brush, C. G. and Chaganti, R. (1998), 'Business without glamour? an analysis of resources on performance by size and age in small service and retail firms', *Journal of Business Venturing*, 14, 233–257.

Bruton, G. D. and Rubanik, Y. (2002). 'Resources of the firm, Russian high-technology startups, and firm growth', *Journal of Business Venturing*, 17 (6): 553–576.

Bryson, J. R., Keeble, D. and Wood, P. (1997) 'The creation and growth of small business service firms in post-industrial Britain', *Small Business Economics*, 9: 345–360.

Burke, A. E., Fitzroy, F. R. and Nolan, M. A. (2000) 'When less is more: distinguishing between entrepreneurial choice and performance', *Oxford Bulletin of Economics and Statistics*, 62 (5): 565–587.

Burke, A. E., Fitzroy, F. R. and Nolan, M. A. (2002) 'Self-employment wealth and job creation: the roles of gender, non-pecuniary motivation and entrepreneurial ability', *Small Business Economics*, 19: 255–270.

Business Link Teesside (1996) *Business Link Teesside: Directory of Business Services*.

Bygrave, W. D. and Hunt, S. A. (2007) 'More for love than money?: financial returns on informal investments' *4th AGSE International Entrepreneurship Research Conference*, Brisbane, February.

Cairncross, A. and Cairncross, F. (1992) *The Legacy of the Golden Age: The 1960s and their Economic Consequences*, London: Routledge.

Capon, N., Farley, J. U. and Hoenig, S. (1990) 'Determinants of financial performance: a meta-analysis', *Management Science*, 36 (10): 1143–1159.

Carland, J. W., Hoy, F., Boulton, W. R. and Carland, J. C. (1984) 'Differentiating entrepreneurs from small business owners: a conceptualization', *Academy of Management Review*, 9 (3): 354–359.

Carlsson, B. (1989) 'Flexibility and the Theory of the Firm', *International Journal of Industrial Organisation*, 7, 179–203.

Carr, P. (2000) *The Age of Enterprise*, Dublin: Blackhall.

Carrasco, R. (1999) 'Transitions to and from self-employment in Spain: an empirical analysis', *Oxford Bulletin of Economics and Statistics*, 61 (3): 315.

Carree, M., van Stel, A., Thurik, R. and Wennekers, S. (2002) 'Economic development and business ownership: An analysis using data of 23 OECD countries in the period 1976–1996', *Small Business Economics*, 19 (3): 271–290.

Carroll, G. R. and Hannan, M. T. (2000) *The Demography of Corporations and Industries*, Princeton University Press: Princeton, New Jersey.

Carter, N. M., Williams, M. and Reynolds, P. D. (1997) 'Discontinuance among new firms in retail: The influence of initial resources, strategy, and gender', *Journal of Business Venturing*, 12 (2): 125–145.

Carter, R. B. and Van Auken, H. E. (1990) 'Personal equity investment and small business financial difficulties', *Entrepreneurship, Theory and Practice*, 15 (2): 51–60.

Cassar, G. (2004) 'The financing of business start-ups', *Journal of Business Venturing*, 19 (2): 261–283.

CCVS (1988) *Community Enterprise Directory*, Middlesbrough: CCVS.

Chandler, A. D. (1992) 'The emergence of managerial capitalism', in *The Sociology of Economic Life*, Granovetter, M. and Swedberg, R. (eds), Boulder: Westview Press.

Child J. (1972) 'Organization structures, environment, and performance: the role of strategic choice', *Sociology*, 6, 1–22.

Chrisman, J.J., and McMullan, W.E. (2000) 'A preliminary assessment of outsider assistance as a knowledge resource: The longer term impact of new venture counseling', *Entrepreneurship Theory and Practice*, 24(3), 37–53.

Chrisman, J. J. and McMullan, W. E. (2004) 'Outsider assistance as a knowledge resource for new venture survival', *Journal of Small Business Management* 42(3): 229–44.

Clark, K. and Drinkwater, S. (2000). 'Pushed out or pulled in? self-employment among ethnic minorities in England and Wales', *Labour Economics*, 7 (5): 603–628.

Cleveland County Council (1985) *The Economic Fortunes of Cleveland*, Middlesbrough: Cleveland County Council.

Cleveland County Council (1989) *Financial Incentives for Industry*, Middlesbrough: Cleveland County Council.

Cockett, R. (1994) *Thinking the Unthinkable*, London: HarperCollins.

Cognetics (2000) *Business Almanac*, Cambridge, MA: Cognetics.

Coles, B. (1995) *Youth and Social Policy: Youth Citizenship and Young Careers*, London: UCL Press.

Confederation of British Industry (CBI) (1980) *The Future Role of Government Organisations Which Assist Smaller Firms*, London: CBI (unpublished).

Cooke, P. and Morgan, K. (1998) *The Associational Economy: Firms, Regions, and Innovation*, Oxford: OUP.

Cooper, A. C. (1993) 'Challenges in predicting new firm performance', *Journal of Business Venturing*, 8: 241–253.

Cooper, A. C., Gimeno-Gascon, F. J. and Woo, C. Y. (1994) 'Initial human and financial capital as predictors of new venture performance'. *Journal of Business Venturing*, 9 (5): 371–395.

Cope, J. (2005) 'Toward a dynamic learning perspective of entrepreneurship', *Entrepreneurship Theory & Practice,* July, 373–397.

Cosh, A. and Hughes, A. (2003) *Enterprise Challenged: Policy and Performance in the British SME Sector 1999–2002*, ESRC Centre for Business Research: Cambridge.

Cowling, M. and Mitchell, P. (1997) 'The evolution of UK self-employment: a study of government policy and the role of the macroeconomy', *Manchester School of Economic and Social Studies*, September, 65 (4): 427–442.

Cowling, M. (2004) 'The growth – profit nexus', *Small Business Economics*, 22 (1): 1–9.

Cowling, M. and Hayward, R. (2000) *Out of Unemployment*, Birmingham: Research Centre for Industrial Strategy.

Cowling, M. and Taylor, M. (2001) 'Entrepreneurial women and men: Two different species?' *Small Business Economics*, 16 (3): 167–175.

Cressy, R. (1993) *The Startup Tracking Exercise: Third Year Report*, London: Natwest.

Cressy, R. (1995) 'Business borrowing and control – a theory of entrepreneurial types', *Small Business Economics*, 7 (4): 291–300.

Cressy, R. (1996) 'Pre-entrepreneurial income, cash-flow growth and survival of startup businesses: model and tests on UK data', *Small Business Economics*, 8 (1): 49–58.

Cressy, R. (2006) 'Why do most firms die young?' *Small Business Economics*, 26 (2): 103–116.

Cromie, S. and Birley, S. (1992) 'Networking by Female Business Owners in Northern Ireland', *Journal of Business Venturing*, 7: 237–251.

Curran, J. and Blackburn, R. (eds.) (1991) *Paths of Enterprise: The Future of the Small Business*, London: Routledge.

Curran, J. and Blackburn, R.A. (2000) 'Panacea or White Elephant? A Critical Examination of the Proposed New Small Business Service and Response to the DTI Consultancy Paper', *Regional Studies*, 34:2, 181–189.

Dale, I. and Kerr, J. (1995) 'Small and medium-sized enterprises: their numbers and importance to employment', *Labour Market Trends*, June, 461–466.

Davidsson, P. and Henrekson, M. (2002) 'Determinants of the prevalence of start-ups and high-growth firms' *Small Business Economics*, 19 (2): 81–104.

Davidsson, P. and Honig, B. (2003) 'The role of social and human capital among nascent entrepreneurs' *Journal of Business Venturing*, 18 (3): 301–331.

Davidsson, P., Achtenhagen, L. and Naldi, L. (2004) 'Research on small firm growth: a review', in *Proceedings European Institute of Small Business*.

Davidsson, P., Kirchhoff, B., Hatemi-J, A. and Gustavsson, H. (2002) 'Empirical analysis of business growth factors using Swedish data', *Journal of Small Business Management*, 40 (4): 332–349.

Davidsson, P., Lindmark, L. and Olofsson, C. (1998) 'The extent of over-estimation of small firm job creation – an empirical examination of the regression bias', *Small Business Economics*, 11 (1): 87–100.

Davis, J.J., Hatiwanger, J., and Schuh, S. (1996) 'Small Business and Job Creation: Dissecting the Myth and Reassessing the Facts', *Small Business Economics*, 8:4, 297–315.

Deakin, N. and Edwards, J. (1993) *The Enterprise Culture and the Inner City*, London: Routledge.

Deakins, D. and Freel, M. (2003) *Entrepreneurship and Small Firms*, 4th ed., London: McGraw-Hill.

de Meza, D. (2002) 'Overlending', *Economic Journal*, February, 112 (477): F17–F31.

de Meza, D. and Southey, C. (1996) 'The borrowers curse: optimism, finance and entrepreneurship', *Economic Journal*, 109: 153–163.

de Wit, G. (1993) 'Models of self-employment in a competitive market', *Journal of Economic Surveys*, 7 (4): 367–97.

de Wit, G. and Van Winden, F. A. A. M. (1990) 'An empirical analysis of self-employment in the Netherlands', *Economics Letters*, 32 (1): 97–100.

Delmar, F. (1997) 'Measuring growth: methodological considerations and empirical results', in *Entrepreneurship and SME Research: On its Way to the Next Millennium*, Donckels, R. and Miettinen, A. (eds) Ashgate: Aldershot, 199–216.

Delmar F. (2000) The psychology of the entrepreneur, in *Enterprise and Small Business*, Carter, S. and Jones-Evans, D. (eds) Harlow: Pearson Education.

Delmar, F. and Shane, S. (2003) 'Does business planning facilitate the development of new ventures?' *Strategic Management Journal*, 24 (12): 1165–1185.

Delmar, F. and Shane, S. (2004) 'Legitimating first: organizing activities and the survival of new ventures', *Journal of Business Venturing*, 19 (3): 385–410.

Delmar, F., Davidsson, P. and Gartner, W. B. (2003) 'Arriving at the high-growth firm', *Journal of Business Venturing*, 18 (2): 189–216.

Department of Trade and Industry (1980) *Aid for Enterprise*, London: HMSO.

Department of Trade and Industry (1982) *Source of Assistance to Small Firms in the North East*, London: HMSO.

Department of Trade and Industry (1988a) *DTI – the Department for Enterprise*, Cm. 278, London: HMSO.

Department of Trade and Industry (1988b) *Releasing Enterprise*, Cm. 512, London: HMSO.

Department of Trade and Industry (1988c) *Source of Assistance to Small Firms in the North East*, London: HMSO.

Department of Trade and Industry (1990) *A Directory of Small Business Management Training Experience in the UK*, HMSO: London.

Department of Trade and Industry (1995a) *A Guide to Help for Small Firms*, London: HMSO.

Department of Trade and Industry (1995b) *Competitiveness: Forging Ahead*, Cmnd 2867, HMSO: London.

Department of Trade and Industry (1996) *Competitiveness: Creating the Enterprise Centre of Europe*, London: HMSO.

Department of Trade and Industry (1998) *Our Competitive Future: Building and the Knowledge Driven Economy*, Cmnd 4176, DTI: London.

Department of Trade and Industry (2001a) *Industrial Development Act 1982: Annual Report*, London: The Stationery Office.

Department of Trade and Industry (2001b) *Business Clusters in the UK – A First Assessment*, HMSO: London.

Department of Trade and Industry (2005) *A Practical Guide to Cluster Development* HMSO: London.

Department of Trade and Industry/HM Treasury (2002) *Cross Cutting Review of Government Services for Small Business*, http://www.sbs.gov.uk/SBS_Gov_files/corporateinfo/ccr_finalreport.pdf

Dess, G. and Robinson, R. B. (1984) 'Measuring organizational performance in the absence of objective measures: The case of the privately held firm and conglomerate business unit', *Strategic Management Journal*, 5 (3): 265–273.

Disney, R., Haskel, J. and Heden, Y. (2003) 'Restructuring and productivity growth in UK manufacturing', *Economic Journal*, 113: 666–694.

Djankov, S., La Porta, R., Lopez-de-Silanes, F. and Schleifer, A. (2002) 'The regulation of entry', *Quarterly Journal of Economics*, February, CXVII (1): 1–37.

Dolton, P. J. and Makepeace, G. H. (1990) 'Self-employment among graduates', *Bulletin of Economic Research*, 42 (1): 35–53.

Doms, M., Dunne, T. and Roberts, M. J. (1995) 'The role of technology use in the survival and growth of manufacturing plants', *International Journal of Industrial Organization*, 13(4): 523–542.

Dorling, D. and Thomas, B. (2004) *People and Places: A 2001 Census Atlas of the UK*, Bristol: Policy Press.

Dunne, T., Klimek, S. D. and Roberts, M. J. (2005) 'Exit from regional manufacturing markets: The role of entrant experience', *International Journal of Industrial Organization*, 23(5–6): 399–421.

Dunning, J., Bannerman, E. and Lundan, S. M. (1998) *Competitiveness and Industrial Policy in Northern Ireland*, Monograph 5, March, Northern Ireland Research Council.

Edgerton, D. (1996) 'The white heat revisited: the british government and technology in the 1960s', *Twentieth Century British History*, 7 (1): 53–82.

European Commission (2000) *The Urban Audit – Volume I Overview and comparative section*, Brussels: European Commission.

European Commission (2003) *Green Paper: Entrepreneurship in Europe*, Brussels: European Commission.

EU (2005) *Eurostat News Release: STAT/05/13*, Brussels: EU, 25 January 2005.

Evans, D. and Jovanovic, B. (1989) 'An estimated model of entrepreneurial choice under liquidity constraints', *Journal of Political Economy*, 97: 808–827.

Evans, D. and Leighton, L. (1990) 'Small business formation by unemployed and employed workers', *Small Business Economics*, 2: 319–330.

Fairlie, R. W. (2002) 'Drug dealing and legitimate self-employment', *Journal of Labor Economics*, 20 (3): 538–567.

Fairlie, R. W. and Meyer, B. D. (1996) 'Ethnic and racial self-employment differences and possible explanations', *Journal of Human Resources*, 31 (4): 757–793.

Fairlie, R. W. (2004) 'Recent trends in ethnic and racial business ownership', *Small Business Economics*, 23 (3): 203–218.

Folster, S. (2002) 'Do lower taxes stimulate self-employment?' *Small Business Economics*, 19 (2): 135–145.

Foreman-Peck, J. (1985) 'Seedcorn or chaff? new firm formation and the performance of the interwar economy', *Economic History Review*, XXXVIII (3): 402–422.

Forum of Private Business (1996) 'Memorandum by the forum of private business', in Business Links, House of Commons Trade and Industry Select Committee, Fifth Report, HC302-II, London: HMSO.

Fothergill, S. and Guy, N. (1990) *Retreat from the Regions*, London: Jessica Kingsley.

Fotopoulos, G. and Louri, H. (2000) 'Location and survival of new entry', *Small Business Economics*, 14 (4): 311–321.

Fraser of Allander Institute (2001) *Promoting Business Start-ups: A New Strategic Formula; Stage 1: Progress Review; Final Report*. Fraser of Allander Institute for Research on the Scottish Economy, University of Strathclyde, Glasgow.

Fraser, S. (2005) *Finance for Small and Medium-Sized Enterprises A Report on the 2004 UK Survey of SME Finances*, CSME, University of Warwick: Coventry.

Fraser, S. and Greene, F. J. (2004) 'Are entrepreneurs eternal optimists or do they get real', *CSME Working Paper*, 85, University of Warwick.

Fraser, S. and Greene, F. J. (2006) 'Are entrepreneurs eternal optimists or do they "get real"', *Economica*, 73 (290): 169–192.

Fraser, S., Greene, F. J. and Mole, K. F. (2007) 'Sources of bias in the recall of self-generated data: The role of anchoring', *British Journal of Management* 18(2): 192–208.

Fritsch, M., Brixy, U. and Falck, O. (2006) 'The effect of industry, region, and time on new business survival – a multi-dimensional analysis', *Review of Industrial Organization*, 28 (3): 285–306.

Garofoli, G. (1994) 'New firm formation and regional development: the case of Italy', *Regional Studies*, 28: 381–393.

Gartner, W. B. (1988) '"Who is an entrepreneur?" is the wrong question', *American Journal of Small Business*, Spring, 12 (1): 11–32.

Gibb, A. A. (1987) 'Enterprise culture – its meaning and implications for education and training', *Journal of European Industrial Training*, 11 (2): 1–35.

Gimeno, J., Folta T. B., Cooper, A. C. and Woo C. C. (1997) 'Survival of the fittest? entrepreneurial human capital and the persistence of under-performing firms', *Administrative Science Quarterly*, 42: 750–783.

Girden, E. R. (2001) *Evaluating Research Articles*, London: Sage.

Goedhuys, M. and Sleuwaegen, L. (2000) 'Entrepreneurship and growth of entrepreneurial firms in Cote d'Ivoire', *Journal of Development Studies*, 36 (3): 123–145.

Graham, T. (2004) *Graham Review of the Small Firms Loan Guarantee: Interim Report*, London: HM Treasury.

Grant, R. M. (1991) 'The resource-based theory of competitive advantage: implications for strategy formulation', *California Management Review*, Spring, 114–135.

Greene, F. J. (2002) 'An investigation into enterprise support for younger people, 1975–2000, *International Small Business Journal*, 20 (3): 315–336.

Greene, F. J. and Saridakis, G. (2007) 'Understanding the Factors Influencing Graduate Entrepreneurship', *Research Report 001/2007*, Birmingham: National Council for Graduate Entrepreneurship.

Guesnier, B. (1994) 'Regional variations in new firm formation in France'. *Regional Studies*, 28 (4): 347–358.

Hamilton, B. H. (2000) 'Does entrepreneurship pay? an empirical analysis of the returns to self-employment', *Journal of Political Economy*, June, 108 (3): 604–631.

Hannah, L. (2004) 'A failed experiment: the state ownership of industry', in *The Cambridge Economic History of Modern Britain*, Floud, R. and Johnson, P. (eds) Cambridge: Cambridge University Press, 84–111.

Hannan, M.T. and Carroll, G.R. (1992) *Dynamics of Organizational Populations: Density, Legitimation, and Competition*. New York, NY: Oxford University Press.

Harada, N. and Honjo, Y. (2005) 'Does the creative business promotion law enhance SMEs' capital investments? evidence from a panel dataset of unlisted SMEs in Japan', *Japan and the World Economy*, 17 (4): 395–406.

Harhoff, D., Stahl, K. and Woywode, M. (1998) 'Legal form, growth and exit of west german firms – empirical results from manufacturing, construction, trade and service industries', *Journal of Industrial Economics*, 66 (4): 453–488.

Harrison, B. (1994) *Lean and Mean*, New York: Basic Books.

Hart, M. and Gudgin, G. (1994) 'Spatial variations in new firm formation in the Republic-of-Ireland, 1980–1990', *Regional Studies*, 28 (4): 367–380.

Hart, M. and McGuinness, S. (2003) 'Small firm growth in the UK regions 1994–1997: towards an explanatory framework', *Regional Studies*, 37 (2): 109–122.

Hart, M. and Hanvey, E. (1995) 'Job Generation and New and Small Firms: Some Evidence from the Late 1980s', *Small Business Economics*, 7:2, 97–109.

Headd, B. (2003) 'Redefining business success: distinguishing between closure and failure', *Small Business Economics*, 21: 51–61.

Henley, A. (2004) 'Self-employment status: the role of state dependence and initial circumstances', *Small Business Economics*, 22 (1): 67–82.

Henley, A. (2005) 'Job creation by the self-employed: The roles of entrepreneurial and financial capital', *Small Business Economics*, 25 (2): 175–196.

Hjalmarsson, D. and Johansson, A. W. (2003) 'Public advisory services; theory and practice', *Entrepreneurship and Regional Development*, 15: 83–98.

Hofer, C. (1975) 'Toward a contingency theory of business strategy', *Academy of Management Journal*, 18: 784–810.

Holtz-Eakin, D., Joulfaian, D. and Rosen, H. S. (1994a) 'Entrepreneurial decisions and liquidity constraints', *Journal of Political Economy*, 102: 53–75.

Holtz-Eakin, D., Joulfaian, D. and Rosen, H. S. (1994b) 'Sticking it out: entrepreneurial survival and liquidity constraints', *Rand Journal of Economics*, Summer, 25 (2): 334–347.

Honjo, Y. (2004) 'Growth of new start-up firms: evidence from the Japanese manufacturing industry', *Applied Economics*, 36 (4): 343–355.

Hoogstra, G. J. and van Dijk, J. (2004) 'Explaining firm employment growth: Does location matter?' *Small Business Economics*, 22 (3–4): 179–192.

House of Commons ODPM Select Committee (2003) *Reducing Regional Disparities in Prosperity*, HC 492-I, London: Stationery Office.

Hughes, A. (1997a) 'Small firms and employment', *CBR Working Paper*, 71.

Hughes, A. (1997b). 'Finance for SMEs: a UK perspective'. *Small Business Economics*, 9 (2): 151–166.

Hundley, G. (2000). 'Male/female earnings differences in self-employment: the effects of marriage, children, and the household division of labor', *Industrial & Labor Relations Review*, 54 (1): 95–114.

IDA (2001) *Industrial Development Act Annual Report*, London: HMSO.

IMD (2004) *World Competitiveness Yearbook*, http://www02.imd.ch/wcc/yearbook/ (accessed 22nd August, 2005).

Janssen, F. (2006) *The Conceptualization of Growth: Are Employment and Turnover Interchangeable Criteria?* Working paper 09/2006, Center for Research in Change, Innovation and Strategy.

Johnson, S. (2005) 'SME support policy: efficiency, equity, ideology or vote-seeking?' ISBE 28th National Small Firms Policy and Research Conference, University of Lancaster, Blackpool, November, 2005.

Joseph, K. (1976) *Stranded on the Middle Ground?: Reflections on Circumstances and Policies*, London: Centre for Policy Studies.

Jovanovic, B. (1982) 'Selection and the evolution of industry', *Econometrica*, 50 (3): 649–670.

Jovanovic, B. (2001) 'New Technology and the small firm', *Small Business Economics*, 16 (1): 53–55.

Kalantaridis, C. and Bika, Z. (2006) 'Local embeddedness and rural entrepreneurship: case-study evidence from Cumbria', *Environment and Planning A*, 38 (8): 1561–1579.

Kaplinsky, R. (1990) *The Economies of Small: Appropriate Technology in a Changing World*, London: Intermediate Technology Publications.

Katz, J. A. and Green, R. P. (2007) *Entrepreneurial Small Business*, London: McGraw-Hill.

Keat, R. (1990) 'Starship Britain or universal enterprise' in *Enterprise Culture*, Keat, R. and Abercrombie, N. (eds) London: Routledge, 1–17.

Keeble, D. and Wilkinson, F. (eds) (2000) *High Technology Clusters, Networking and Collective Learning in Europe*, Ashgate: Aldershot.

Keeble, D., Bryson, J. and Wood, P. (1992) 'The rise and role of small business service firms in the United Kingdom', *International Small Business Journal*, 11 (1): 11–22.

Keep, E. and Mayhew, K. (1999) 'The assessment: knowledge, skills and competitiveness', *Oxford Review of Economic Policy*, 15 (1): 1–15.

Keogh, W. and Mole, K. (2005) The changing role of the public sector business adviser, presented at the *28th ISBE National Small Businesses Policy and Research Conference*, Blackpool, 1–3rd November.

Kidd, M. P. (1993) 'Immigrant wage differentials and the role of self-employment in Australia', Australian Economic Papers, 32 (60): 92–115.

Kihlstrom, R. E. and Laffont, J. J. (1979) 'A general equilibrium entrepreneurial theory of firm formation based on risk aversion', *Journal of Political Economy*, 87, 719–749.

Kirchhoff, B. A. and Greene, P. G. (1998) 'Understanding the theoretical and empirical content of critiques of US job creation research', *Small Business Economics*, 10 (2): 153–169.

Kitson, M., Martin, R. and Tyler, P. (2004) 'Regional Competitiveness: An Elusive yet key concept?', *Regional Studies*, 38 (9): 991–999.

Knight, F. (1921) *Risk, Uncertainty and Profit*, Boston: Houghton Mifflin.

Kon, Y. and Storey, D.J. (2003) 'A theory of discouraged borrowers', *Small Business Economics*, 21 (1): 37–49.

Laferrere, A. and McEntee, P. (1995) 'Self-employment and intergenerational transfers of physical and human capital: an empirical analysis of French data', *Economic and Social Review*, 27 (1): 43–54.

Lambrecht, J. and Pirnay, F. (2005) 'An evaluation of public support measures for private external consultancies to SMEs in the Walloon Region of Belgium', *Entrepreneurship and Regional Development*, 17: 89–108.

Lazear, E. P. (2005) 'Entrepreneurship', *Journal of Labor Economics*, 23 (4): 649–680.

Le, A. T. (1999) 'Empirical studies of self-employment', *Journal of Economic Surveys*, 13, 381–416.

Levenson, A. R. and Willard, K. L. (2000) 'Do firms get the financing they want? measuring credit rationing experienced by small businesses in the US', *Small Business Economics*, 14 (2): 83–94.

Lewis, W. W., Palmade, V., Regout, B. and Webb, A. P. (2002) 'What's right with the US economy', *McKinsey Quarterly*, 1: 31–40.

Lin, Z. X., Picot, G. and Compton, J. (2000) 'The entry and exit dynamics of self-employment in Canada'. *Small Business Economics*, 15 (2): 105–125.

Lindh T. and Ohlsson, H. (1996) 'Self-employment and windfall gains: evidence from the Swedish lottery', *Economic Journal*, November, 106 (439): 1515–1526.

Littunen, H. (2000) 'Networks and local environmental characteristics in the survival of new firms'. *Small Business Economics*, 15 (1): 59–71.

Loebl, H. (1978) 'Government-financed factories and the establishment of industries by refugees in the special areas of the north of England, 1937-1961' *Unpublished M. Phil thesis*, Durham: University of Durham.

Love, J. H. (1996) 'Entry and exit: A county-level analysis', *Applied Economics* 28(4): 441–51.

Lucas, R. E. (1978) 'On the size distribution of business firms', *Bell Journal of Economics*, 9, 508–523.

Lundstrom, A. and Stevenson, L. (2005) *Entrepreneurship Policy: Theory and Practice*, Stockholm: Swedish Foundation for Small Business Research.

MacDonald, R. and Coffield, F. (1991) *Risky Business? Riders, Fallers and Plodders*, London: Falmer Press.

MacDougall, P. and Robinson, R.B (1990) 'New venture strategies: an empirical identification of eight 'archetypes' of competitive strategies for entry', *Strategic Management Journal*, 11 (6): 447–467.

Macmillan Committee (1931) *Report of the Committee on Finance and Industry*, London: HMSO.

Mahmood, T. (2000) 'Survival of newly founded businesses: A log-logistic model approach', *Small Business Economics*, 14 (3): 223–237.

Malecki, E. (1997) *Technology and Economic Development: The Dynamics of Local, Regional and National Competitiveness*, Harlow: Addison Wesley Longman.

Marlow, S. (2000) 'People and the small business', in *Enterprise and Small Business*, Carter S. and Jones-Evans D. (eds) Harlow: Prentice Hall, 300–322.

Marlow, S. (2006) 'Enterprising, futures or dead-end jobs? women, self employment and social exclusion', *International Journal of Manpower*, 27 (6): 588–600.

Martin, R. and Sunley, P. (2003) 'Deconstructing clusters: chaotic concept or policy panacea?, *Journal of Economic Geography*, 3: 5–35.

Mason, C. and Harrison, R. (2003) 'Closing the regional equity gap? A critique of the Department of Trade and Industry's regional venture capital funds initiative'. *Regional Studies*, 37 (8): 855–868.

Mason, C. M. and McNally, K. N. (1997) 'Market change, distribution, and new firm formation and growth: the case of real-ale breweries in the United Kingdom', *Environment and Planning A*, 29 (3): 405–417.

Masuda, T. (2006) 'The determinants of latent entrepreneurship in Japan', *Small Business Economics*, 26 (3): 227–240.

Mata, J. and Portugal, P. (1994) 'Life duration of new firms', *The Journal of Industrial Organisation*, XLII, 227–245.

Mata, J., Portugal, P., and Guimaraes, P. (1995) 'The survival of new plants: Start-up conditions and post-entry evolution', *The Journal of Industrial Organisation*, 13: 459–481

McCann, P. and Sheppard, S. (2003) 'The rise, fall and rise again of industrial location theory', *Regional Studies*, 37 (6&7): 649–663.

McClelland, D. C. (1971) 'The achievement motive in economic growth', in *Entrepreneurship and Economic Development*, Kilby, P. (ed.) New York: Free Press, 109–122.

Meager, N., Bates, P. and Cowling, M. (2003) 'An evaluation of business start-up support for young people', *National Institute Economic Review*, October, 186: 70–83.

Metzger, G. (2006) 'Once bitten, twice shy? the performance of entrepreneurial re-starts', *ZEW Discussion Paper*, 06–083, Mannheim.

Minniti, M. and Bygrave, W. (2001) 'A dynamic model of entrepreneurial learning', *Entrepreneurship Theory & Practice*, 25 (3): 5–16.

Mitchell, B. R. (1998) *British Historical Statistics*, Cambridge: CUP.

Mole, K. (1999) 'UK Support for Small Firms: An Examination of Business Advisors Heuristics', *Unpublished Ph.D Thesis*, University of Wolverhampton.

Mole, K. (2002) 'Business advisers impact on SMEs: an agency theory approach', *International Small Business Journal*, 20 (2): 137–157.

Mole, K. F. and Bramley, G. (2006) 'Making policy choices in non-financial business support: an international comparison', *Environment and Planning C: Government and Policy*, 24 (6): 885–908.

Mole, K. F., Hart, M., Roper, S. and Saal, D. (2007) *An Economic Evaluation of Business Link*, London: SBS.

Mueller, P., van Stel, A. and Storey, D. J. (2008) 'The effects of new firm formation on regional development over time: the case of Great Britain', *Small Business Economics* (forthcoming).

Murphy, G. B., Trailer, J. W. and Hill, R. C. (1996) 'Measuring performance in entrepreneurship', *Journal of Business Research*, 36: 15–23.

Myers, S. C. and Majluf, N. C. (1984) 'Corporate financing and investment decisions when firms have information that investors do not have', *Journal of Financial Economics*, 13: 187–221.

Nafziger, W. E. and Terrell, D. (1996) 'Entrepreneurial human capital and the long-run survival of firms in India', *World Development*, 24, 689–696.

National Audit Office (NAO) (2006) *Supporting Small Business*, Report by the Comptroller and Auditor General, HC 962 Session 2005–2006, 24 May.

Natwest/SBRT (2003) *Natwest Quarterly Survey of Small Business Customers*, Small Business Research Trust.

Nayak, A. and Greenfield, S. (1994) 'The use of management accounting information for managing micro-business', in *Finance and the Small Firm*, Storey, D. J. and Hughes A. (eds) London: Routledge, 182–231.

Nelson, P. (1970) 'Information and Consumer Behavior', *Journal of Political Economy*, 78:2, 311–329.

Nicholls-Nixon, C. L., Cooper, A. C. and Woo, C. Y. (2000) 'Strategic experimentation: understanding change and performance in new ventures', *Journal of Business Venturing*, 15: 493–521.

Nomis (2005) *Population and Neighbourhood Statistics*, http://www.nomisweb. co.uk/ (accessed 22nd August, 2005).

Nucci, A. R. (1999) 'The demography of business closings', *Small Business Economics*, 12 (1): 25–39.

Nziramasanga, M. and Lee, M. (2002) 'On the duration of self-employment: the impact of macroeconomic conditions', *Journal of Development Studies*, 39 (1): 46–73.

ODPM (2004) *The English Indices of Deprivation 2004 (revised)*, London: ODPM.

ONE North East (1999) *Unlocking our Potential*, Newcastle: ONE North East.

O'Gorman, C. (2000) 'Strategy and the small business', in *Enterprise and Small Business: Principles, Practice and Policy*, Carter, S. and Jones-Evans, D. (eds) Pearson Education: Harlow, 283–299.

PACEC (2003) *A Review of Business Support Organisations and Services*, Cambridge: PACEC.

PACEC (2005) *Small Business Service Mapping of Government Services for Small Business Final Report*, Cambridge: PACEC.

Parker, S. van Witteloostuijn, A. and Storey, D. J. (2005) 'What happens to gazelles? the importance of dynamic management strategy', *Centre for Entrepreneurship Discussion Paper No. 12*, Durham: University of Durham.

Parker, S. C. (2004) *The Economics of Self-employment and Entrepreneurship*, Cambridge: Cambridge University Press.

Parker, S. C. (2006) 'Learning about the unknown: How fast do entrepreneurs adjust their beliefs?' *Journal of Business Venturing* 21(1): 1–26.

Parker, S.C. and Robson, M.T. (2004) 'Explaining International Variations in Self-Employment: Evidence from a Panel of OECD Countries', *Southern Economic Journal*, 71(2): 287–301.

Parker, S. C. and Belghitar, Y. (2006) 'What happens to nascent entrepreneurs? an econometric analysis of the PSED', *Small Business Economics*, 27 (1): 81–101.

Parkinson, M., Hutchins, M., Simmie, J., Clark, G. and Verdonk, H. (2004) *European Cities: Where do the Core Cities Stand?*, London: ODPM.

Partington, J. and Mayell, C. (1998) 'Revision of annual employment survey results for 1995 and 1996', *Labour Market Trends*, July, 387–397.

Peli, G. and Nooteboom, B. (1999) 'Market partitioning and the geometry of resource space', *American Journal of Sociology*, 104: 1132–53.

Penrose, E. (1959) *The Theory of the Growth of the Firm*, Oxford: Oxford University Press.

Persson, H. (2004) 'The survival and growth of new establishments in Sweden, 1987–1995'. *Small Business Economics*, 23 (5): 423–440.

Pettigrew, A., Hendry, C. and Sparrow, P. (1989) *Training in Britain: Employers' Perspectives on Human Resources*, London: HMSO.

Pfeiffer, F. and Reize, F. (2000) 'Business start ups by the unemployed- an econometric analysis based on firm data', *Labour Economics*, 7 (5): 629–663.

Picot, G. and Dupuy, R. (1998) 'Job creation by company size class: the magnitude, concentration and persistence of job gains and losses in Canada', *Small Business Economics*, 10 (2): 117–139.

Podsakoff, P. M., Ahearne, M. and MacKenzie, S. B. (1997) 'Organizational citizenship behavior and the quantity and quality of work group performance', *Journal of Applied Psychology*, 82(2): 262–270.

Porter, M. E. (1980) *Competitive Strategy: Techniques for Analysing Industries and Competitors*, London: MacMillan.

Porter M. E. (1998) *On Competition*, Harvard Business Review Press: Cambridge MA.

Porter, M. E. (2003) 'The economic performance of regions', *Regional Studies*, 37 (6&7): 549–578.

Porter, M. E. and Ketels, C. H. M. (2003) UK Competitiveness: Moving to the next stage, *DTI Economics Paper No. 3*, DTI: London.

Ramachandran, V. and Shah, M.-K. (1999) 'Minority entrepreneurs and firm performance in Sub-Saharan Africa', *Journal of Development Studies*, 36 (2): 71–87.

Rees, H. and Shah, A. (1986) 'An empirical analysis of self-employment in the UK', *Journal of Applied Econometrics*, 1: 95–108.

Reid, G. C. (1999) 'Complex actions and simple outcomes: how new entrepreneurs stay in business', *Small Business Economics*, 13 (4): 303–315.

Reid, G. C., Jacobson, L. and Anderson, M. (1993) *Profiles in Small Business: A Competitive Strategy Approach*, London: Routledge.

Reid, G. C. and Smith, J. A. (2000). 'What makes a new business start-up successful?' *Small Business Economics*, 14 (3): 165–182.

Reynolds, P., Storey, D. J. and Westhead, P. (1994) 'Cross-national comparisons of the variation in new firm formation rates', *Regional Studies*, 28 (4): 443–456.

Reynolds, P. D., Carter, N. M., Gartner, W. B. and Greene, P. G. (2004) 'The prevalence of nascent entrepreneurs in the United States: evidence from the panel study of entrepreneurial dynamics', *Small Business Economics*, 23 (4): 263–284.

Richardson, R., Belt, V. and Marshall, N. (2000) 'Taking calls to Newcastle: the regional implications of the growth in call centres', *Regional Studies*, 34 (4): 357–369.

Ritchie, J. (1991) 'Enterprise cultures: a frame analysis', in *Deciphering the Enterprise Culture*, Burrows, R. (ed.) London: Routledge, 17-34.

Ritsila, J. and Tervo, H. (2002) 'Effects of unemployment on new firm formation: Micro-level panel data evidence from Finland', *Small Business Economics*, 19 (1): 31–40.

Roberts, M. (2004) 'The growth performances of the GB counties: some new empirical evidence for 1977–1993', *Regional Studies*, 38 (2): 149–165.

Robinson, P. (1988) *The Unbalanced Recovery*, Oxford: Phillip Allan.

Robinson, P. B. and Sexton, E. A. (1994) 'The Effect of Education and Experience on Self-Employment Success', *Journal of Business Venturing*, 9, 141–156.

Robson, M. T. (1996) 'Macroeconomic factors in the birth and death of UK firms: evidence from quarterly VAT registrations', *Manchester School of Economic and Social Studies*, LXIV (2): 170–188.

Robson, P. J. A. and Bennett, R. J. (2000a) 'SME growth: The relationship with business advice and external collaboration', *Small Business Economics*, 15 (3): 193–208.

Robson, P. J. A. and Bennett, R. J. (2000b) 'Central government support to SMEs compared to business link, business connect and business shop and the prospects for the small business service', *Regional Studies*, 33 (8): 779–787.

Romer, P. (1986) 'Increasing returns and long run growth', *Journal of Political Economy*, 94 (5): 1002–1037.

Romer, P. (1990) 'Endogenous technological change', *Journal of Political Economy*, 98 (5): S71–S102.

Roper, S. and Hewitt-Dundas, N. (2001) 'Grant assistance and small firm development in Northern Ireland and the Republic of Ireland', *Scottish Journal of Political Economy*, 48 (1): 99–117.

Rosa, P (2003) '"Hardly likely to make the Japanese tremble" – the businesses of recently graduated university and college "entrepreneurs"', *International Small Business Journal*, 21 (4): 435–459.

Rosa, P., Kodithuwakku, S. and Balunywa, W. (2006) 'Reassessing necessity entrepreneurship in developing countries', Paper presented at the ISBE Conference, Cardiff, November.

Rotefoss, B. and Kolvereid, L. (2005) 'Aspiring, nascent and fledgling entrepreneurs: an investigation of the business start-up process', *Entrepreneurship and Regional Development*, 17 (2): 109–127.

Rotter, J. B. (1966) 'Generalised Expectancies for Internal Versus External Control of Reinforcement', *Psychological Monographs*, Whole No. 609, 80, 1.

Rumelt, R. (1991) 'How much does industry matter?' *Strategic Management Journal*, 12, 167–185.

Saemundsson, R. and Dahlstrand, A. L. (2005) 'How business opportunities constrain young technology-based firms from growing into medium-sized firms', *Small Business Economics*, 24 (2): 113–129.

Sahlman, W. A. and Stevenson, H. H. (1989) 'The entrepreneurial process' in *Small Business and Entrepreneurship*, Paul Burns, P. and Dewhurst, J. (eds) London: MacMillan, 94–157.

Sapienza, H. J., Smith, K. G. and Gannon, M. J. (1988) 'Using subjective evaluations of organizational performance in small business research', *American Journal of Small Business*, 12 (2): 45–53.

Saradakis, G. Mole, K, and Storey, D.J. (2008) 'New Firm Survival in England', Empirica (forthcoming).

Saxenian, A. (1999) 'Silicon Valley's New Immigrant Entrepreneurs', San Fransisco: Public Policy Institute of California.

SBS (2001/2002) *Small Business Omnibus Survey*, Small Business Service: London

SBS (2006) *Grant and Support Directory*, http://www.businesslink.gov.uk/bdotg/action/gsdChoosePurposeCommit (accessed 25th August 2006).

SBS (2004) *A Government Action Plan for Small Business*, London: DTI.

Scarpetta, S., Hemmings, P., Tressel, T. and Woo, J. (2002) 'The role of policy and Institutions for Productivity and Firm Dynamics: evidence from Micro and Industry data', *Economics Dept Working Paper, No. 329*, OECD, Paris.

Schultz, T. W. (1980) 'Investment in entrepreneurial ability', *Scandinavian Journal of Economics*, 82: 437–448.

Schutjens, V. A. J. M. and Wever, E. (2002) 'Determinants of new firm success', *Papers in Regional Science*, 79: 135–159.

Scott, P. (2000) 'The audit of regional policy: 1934–1939', *Regional Studies*, 34 (1): 55–65.

Scottish Enterprise (1993) *Improving the Business Birth Rate: A Strategy for Scotland*, Glasgow: Scottish Enterprise.

Sear, L. and Agar, J. (1996) 'Business links and personal business advisers: selling services irrespective of client's needs?' Paper presented at the 19th ISBA Conference, Birmingham.

Shaffer, R., and Pulver, G. (1985) 'Regional variation in capital structure of new small businesses: the Wisconsin case', in *Small Firms in Regional Economic Development*, Storey, D. J. (ed.) Cambridge: Cambridge University Press, 166–192.

Shaw. E., Carter, S. and Brierton, J. (2001) *Unequal Entrepreneurs: Why Female Enterprise Is An Uphill Business*, London: Industrial Society.

Shutt, J. and R. Whittington (1987) 'Fragmentation strategies and the rise of small units: cases from the North West', *Regional Studies*, 21: 13–23.

Sleuwaegen, L. and Goedhuys, M. (2002) 'Growth of firms in developing countries, evidence from Cote d'Ivoire', *Journal of Development Economics*, 68 (1): 117–135.

Spicer and Pegler (1983) *Financing your Business in the North East*, London: Spicer and Pegler.

Stanworth, M. J. K. and Curran, J. (1973) *Management Motivation in the Smaller Business*, Aldershot: Gower.

Stearns, T., Carter, N., Reynolds, P. and Williams, M. (1995) 'New business survival: industry, strategy and location', *Journal of Business Venturing*, 10: 23–42.

Stewart, W. H., Watson, W. E., Carland, J. C. and Carland, J. W. (1999) 'A proclivity for entrepreneurship: a comparison of entrepreneurs, small business owners, and corporate managers'. *Journal of Business Venturing*, 14 (2): 189–214.

Stiglitz, J. E. and Weiss, A. (1981) 'Credit rationing markets with imperfect information', *American Economic Review*, 71 (3): 393–410.

Stiglitz, J. E. (2000) 'The contributions of the economics of information to twentieth century economics', *Quarterly Journal of Economics*, 115: 1441–1478.

Stinchcombe, A. L. (1965) 'Social structure and organizations' in *Handbook of Organizations*, J. G. March (ed.) Chicago: Rand McNally Publishers, 142–193.

Stinchcombe, A. L. (1990) *Information and Organizations*, Berkeley CA.: University of California Press.

Storey, D. J. (1980) 'Guide to Regional Aid', *Bankers Magazine*, October.

Storey, D. J. (1982) *Entrepreneurship and the New Firm*, London: Croom Helm.

Storey, D. J. (1994a) *Understanding the Small Business Sector*, London: Routledge.

Storey, D. J. (1994b) 'New firm growth and bank financing', *Small Business Economics*, 6 (2): 139–150.

Storey, D. J. (2003) 'Entrepreneurship, small and medium sized enterprises and public policies', in *The Handbook of Entrepreneurship*, Audretsch, D. and Acs, Z. (eds) London: Kluwer, 473–511.

Storey D.J. (2004) 'Exploring the link, among small firms, between management training and firm performance: a comparison between the UK and other OECD countries, *International Journal of Human Resource Management*, 15(1): 112–130.

Storey, D. J. and Johnson, S. (1986) 'Job generation in Britain: a review of recent studies', *International Small Business Journal*, 4 (4): 29–46.

Storey, D. J. and Johnson, S. (1987) *Job Generation and Labour Market Change*, London: Macmillan.

Storey, D. J. and Strange, A. (1992) *Entrepreneurship in Cleveland 1979–1989: A Study of The Effects of The Enterprise Culture*, Department of Employment, Research Series No. 3, London: HMSO.

Storey D. J. Keasey, K., Watson, R. and Wynarczyk, P. (1987) *The Performance of Small Firms*, London: Croom Helm.

Storey, D. J. and Wynarczyk, P. (1996) 'The survival and non-survival of micro firms in the UK', *Review of Industrial Organization*, 11 (2): 211–229.

Storey, D. J., Keasey, K. and Wynarczyk, P. (1989) 'Fast growth small businesses: case studies of 40 small firms in North East England', *Department of Employment, Research Paper 67*, London: Department of Employment.

Sutton, J. (1991) *Sunk costs and market structure: Price competition, advertising and the evolution of concentration*, London: Cambridge Mass.: MIT Press.

Taylor, M. P. (1999) 'Survival of the fittest? an analysis of self-employment duration in Britain', *Economic Journal*, 109 (454): C140–C155.

Taylor, M. P. (2001) 'Self-employment and windfall gains in Britain: evidence from panel data'. *Economica*, 68 (272): 539–565.

Thatcher, M. (1982) *TV Interview for Thames TV TV Eye*, 18th February.

Thatcher, M. (1984) 'Speech to the small business bureau conference', in *Small Today, Bigger Tomorrow: Three Speeches from the 1984 Small Business Bureau Conference*, London: Conservative Political Centre.

Tomlinson, J. (2004) 'Economic policy' in *The Cambridge Economic History of Modern Britain*, Floud, R. and Johnson, P. (eds) Cambridge: CUP, 189–212.

Trade and Industry Select Committee (1996) *Business Links*, Fifth Report, HC302-I, London: HMSO.

Treasury H. M. (2001) *Productivity in the UK: 3 – The Regional Dimension*, London: H. M. Treasury.

Tregaskis, O. and Brewster, C. (1998) 'Training and development in the UK context: an emerging polarisation?', *Journal of European Industrial Training*, 22: 4, 180–189.

Tsionas, E. G. and Papadogonas, T. A. (2006) 'Firm exit and technical inefficiency', *Empirical Economics*, 31 (2): 535–548

Turok, I. and Raco, M. (2000) 'Developing expertise in small and medium-sized enterprises: an evaluation of consultancy support', *Environment and Planning C: Government and Policy*, 18, 409–427.

TVJSU (2005) *Population And Household Projections For The Tees Valley 2003–2021*, http://www.teesvalley-jsu.gov.uk/reports/i&f/JSU0504.pdf (accessed 22nd August, 2005).

US Census Bureau (2007) *Sector 00: Survey of Business Owners (SBO): Company Statistics Series: Statistics for Respondent Firms by Sources of Capital Needed to Start or Acquire the Business by Kind of Business, Hispanic or Latino Origin, Race, and Gender: 2002*, http://factfinder.census.gov/servlet/IBQTable?_bm=y&-geo_id=&-ds_name=SB0200CSCB07&-_lang=en (accessed 28th February, 2007).

van Auken, H. E. and Carter, R. B. (1989) 'Acquisition of capital by small business', *Journal of Small Business Management*, 27 (2): 1–9.

van Oort, F. G. and Atzema, O. (2004) 'On the conceptualization of agglomeration economies: The case of new firm formation in the Dutch ICT sector', *Annals of Regional Science*, 38 (2): 263–290.

van Praag, M. (2003) 'Business survival and success of young small business owners', *Small Business Economics*, 21: 1–17.

van Stel, A. J. (2005) 'Entrepreneurship and Economic Growth: Some Empirical Studies', *Tinbergen Institute Research Series*, Erasmus University.

van Stel, A. J. and Storey, D. J. (2004) 'The link between firm births and job creation: Is there a Upas tree effect?' *Regional Studies*, 38 (8): 893–909.

Verheul, I., Van Stel, A. and Thurik, R. (2006) 'Explaining female and male entrepreneurship at the country level', *Entrepreneurship and Regional Development*, 18 (2): 151–183.

Vesper, K. (1996) *New Venture Experience*, Seattle: Vector Books.

Vickerstaff, S. and Parker, K. T. (1995) 'Helping small firms: the contribution of TECs and LECs, *International Small Business Journal*, 13 (4): 56–72.

Wagner, J. (1995) 'Firm size and job creation in Germany', *Small Business Economics*, 7 (6): 469–474.

Wagner, J. (1999) 'The life history of cohorts of exits from German manufacturing'. *Small Business Economics*, 13 (1): 71–79.

Weinzimmer, L. G., Nystrom, P. C. and Freeman S. J. (1998) 'Measuring organizational growth: issues, consequences and guidelines', *Journal of Management*, 24 (2): 235–262.

Westhead, P. (1995) 'Survival and employment growth contrasts between types of owner managed high technology firms', *Entrepreneurship Theory and Practice*, 20 (1): 5–28.

Westhead, P. (2003) 'Comparing the performance of male- and female-controlled businesses: Relating outputs to inputs', *International Small Business Journal*, 21 (2): 244–247.

Westhead, P. and Storey, D. (1999) 'Training provision and the development of small- and medium-sized enterprises: A critical review', *Scottish Journal of Adult and Continuing Education*, 5: 1, 35–41.

Westhead, P. and Wright, M. (1998), 'Novice, portfolio and serial founders in rural and urban areas', *Entrepreneurship Theory and Practice*, 20 (4): 63–100.

Westhead, P., Wright, M. and Ucbasaran, D. (2001) 'The internationalization of new and small firms: A resource-based view', *Journal of Business Venturing*, 16(4): 333–58.

Whyley, C. (1998) *Risky Business: The Personal and Financial Costs of Small Business Failure*, London: Policy Studies Institute.

Wiklund, J. (1998). *Small Firm Growth and Performance: Entrepreneurship and Beyond*. Doctoral dissertation. Jönköping: Jönköping International Business School.

Wiklund, J. and Shepherd, D. (2005) 'Entrepreneurial orientation and small business performance: a configurational approach', *Journal of Business Venturing*, 20(1): 71–91.

Williams, D. R. (2004) 'Youth self-employment: its nature and consequences', *Small Business Economics*, 23, 323–336.

Wilson Committee (1979) *Interim Report on the Financing of Small Firms*, Cmnd 7503, London: HMSO.

Wilson, R. (2004) *Business Finance 2004*, London: Institute of Directors.

Woods, A., Blackburn, R. and J. Curran (1993) *A Longitudinal Study of Small Enterprises in the Service Sector*, Brunel University: Small Business Research Centre and Department of Management Studies.

Wren, C. (1989) 'The revised regional development grant scheme: a case study in cleveland county of a marginal employment subsidy' *Regional Studies*, 23 (2): 127–137.

Wren, C. (1996) *Industrial Subsidies: The UK experience*, Basingstoke: Macmillan.

Wren, C. (2003) 'UK regional policy: does it measure up?' paper presented at. the ESRC Urban and Regional Economics Seminar Group, Regional Policy, October.

Wren, C. and Storey D. J. (2002) 'Evaluating the effect of "soft" business support upon small firm performance', *Oxford Economic Papers*, 54: 334–365.

Yasuda, T. (2005) 'Firm growth, size, age and behavior in Japanese manufacturing', *Small Business Economics*, 24 (1): 1–15.

# Index

## Introductory Note

References such as '178–9' indicate (not necessarily continuous) discussion of a topic across a range of pages, whilst '123t10.4' indicates a reference to Table 10.4 on page 123 and '123f10.1' a reference to figure 10.1 on page 123. Wherever possible in the case of topics with many references, these have either been divided into sub-topics (indented below the main heading) or the most significant discussion of the topic is indicated by page numbers in bold.